THE 2004 TOUR DE FRANCE

ARMSTRONG REWRITES HISTORY

by Andrew Hood

with rider diaries from Tyler Hamilton, Magnus Bäckstedt, and Christian Vande Velde

BOULDER, COLORADO

The 2004 Tour de France

Printed in the United States of America.

10 9 8 7 6 5 4 3 2 1

Distributed in the United States and Canada by Publishers Group West.

International Standard Book Number: 1-931382-47-6

Library of Congress Cataloging-in-Publication Data

Hood, Andrew 1964–
2004 Tour de France / Andrew Hood.
p. cm.
ISBN 1-931382-47-6 (pbk. : alk. paper)
1. Tour de France (Bicycle race) (2004) I. Title.
GV1049.2.T68H66 2004
796.6'2'0944—dc22

2004018609

VeloPress®
1830 North 55th Street
Boulder, Colorado 80301–2700 USA
303/440-0601 • Fax 303/444-6788 • E-mail velopress@insideinc.com

To purchase additional copies of this book or other VeloPress® books, call 800/234-8356 or visit us on the Web at velopress.com.

Cover and interior design by Erin Johnson Design

FRONT COVER PHOTOS: Lance Armstong in stage 15 victory, GRAHAM WATSON; Floyd Landis and U.S. Postal at the front of the peloton, stage 20, CASEY B. GIBSON

BACK COVER PHOTOS: Armstrong and Ivan Basso, stage 16, CASEY B. GIBSON; Robbie McEwen, Armstrong, Richard Virenque, and Vladimir Karpets on the podium, ROBERT LABERGE/Getty Images

Contents

To "Momma" Hood, for allowing me to chase my dreams,
and to MJ, for making my dreams come true

Acknowledgments

A first book for any author is a daunting, almost paralyzing prospect. Heartfelt thanks go out to Amy Rinehart and Ted Costantino for believing in this project and everyone at VeloPress who helped edit and refine the text and produced the fine quality design, maps, and illustrations. Special thanks, too, to my colleagues at *VeloNews*, particularly John Wilcockson, who's been both a mentor and a friend.

Living in Planet Tour is an often surreal adventure enhanced by the camaraderie among the many journalists who liven up the race. They are far too numerous to name, but special thanks go to Rupert Guinness, Jeremy Whittle, James Raia, Sal Ruibal, James Startt, Sam Abt, Graham Watson, Casey Gibson, Kip Mikler, Charles Pelkey, Tim Maloney, Stephen Farrand, the Fotheringham brothers, Bonnie DeSimone, and John Henderson.

Hats off to Tyler Hamilton, Magnus Bäckstedt, and Christian Vande Velde for providing insightful, captivating diaries filed diligently in the heat of the battle. Thanks, too, to the many professional racers who've shared their experiences through both highs and lows, especially the Americans whose names read off like the Beatles: Tyler, George, Bobby, Levi, Lance, Christian, and Floyd.

Final thanks to my mother, who's supported me no matter what, and my beloved wife, Maria Jesus, who endured months of exasperation induced by writer's block and looming deadlines.

Andrew Hood
León, Spain
August 2004

Preface

Armstrong Storms into History

There were a lot of questions before the start of the 91st Tour de France. The first, and most obvious, was whether Lance Armstrong could win again. The five-time Tour champion had struggled in the 2003 Tour, eventually squeaking out a slim, 61-second margin of victory. Now 32 years old, was Armstrong capable of returning to his top level?

And what of Armstrong's top rivals? Could Jan Ullrich, Tyler Hamilton, Iban Mayo, and a long list of contenders finally topple the unstoppable Texan? Or could Armstrong achieve what cycling legends Jacques Anquetil, Eddy Merckx, Bernard Hinault, and Miguel Induráin could not, and break the Tour's venerated five-win barrier?

By the time the three-week, twenty-stage Tour assembled for the start in Liège, Belgium, on July 3, Ullrich, Hamilton, and Mayo were brimming with confidence. Each had recorded impressive pre-Tour victories that seemed to bolster their chances. Ullrich brushed off doubts about his form with a one-second victory at the Tour de Suisse in June. Hamilton successfully defended his title at the Tour of Romandie in May and looked robust at the Dauphiné Libéré race in June, finishing ahead of Armstrong in a grueling climbing time trial up Mont Ventoux. And in that same Dauphiné race, Mayo, the most explosive climber since the arrival of Marco Pantani a decade ago, took nearly two minutes out of Armstrong while breaking the record time for climbing Ventoux, a mountain known for its ominous steepness.

Yet the Tour's pressing questions would have to wait for a tense twelve days to be answered. Cold, wind, rain, and crashes marred the opening week. Anxious not to waste energy with the looming two-stage battle in the Pyrénées, the favorites neutralized three potentially explosive stages in the Massif Central at the end of the second week. Nothing would be known until the peloton approached the race's first real test in the Pyrénées.

Indeed, the Tour organizers had created a course that, if their plans bore fruit, would result in another down-to-the-wire battle, evoking the excitement of the Tour's much-celebrated centenary edition in 2003. The unconventional 2004 course packed all the decisive stages into the final nine days of racing.

That plan worked, at least until the Tour reached the first mountain stage to La Mongie. Hamilton and Ullrich both started the 197.5-kilometer stage 12 within one minute of the Texan. But by the end of the final 12.8-kilometer climb to the finish line, Armstrong had erased any doubts about how the 91st Tour de France would end. Italian sensation Ivan Basso was the only rider strong enough to follow Armstrong's trademark accelerations, while the rest of the peloton was devastated in his wake.

By the time Armstrong sprang to victory the next day at Plateau de Beille, it was obvious nothing was going to stop him. Intent on leaving his mark on the Tour, Armstrong stormed to five stage victories to create a club of his own. Not content just to win the record sixth maillot jaune, Armstrong set out to stamp his authority on the Tour. He won four successive mountain stages—a first in Tour history—including a dominant time trial victory while wearing the yellow jersey up the 21 hairpin turns at cycling's most famous climb at l'Alpe d'Huez. His challengers folded in the face of his superior preparation and the strength of the U.S. Postal Service team. Angry fans who booed and spit on him, and accusations of doping set forth in a controversial book published in France in the weeks before the Tour, only fueled Armstrong's desire to silence the critics with the most resounding victory since Bernard Hinault won five stages in 1981.

This fifth annual Tour de France recap from *VeloNews* examines the drama inside Armstrong's run for history. Part I reviews Armstrong's unlikely rise as Tour dominator and his determination to erase the bad memories of the 2003 Tour that saw him under attack as never before. There's also an assessment of Armstrong's challengers and a look at the other Americans racing in the Tour. We also look back at the original members of the Tour's five-win club and recount their attempts to win a sixth Tour.

Part II provides detailed reports from each stage of the 91st Tour de France, complemented by stage maps and elevation profiles, and incomparable photos of the race by top Tour shooter Graham Watson. Also included are behind-the-scenes race diaries by Tyler Hamilton, the gritty New Englander who once again saw his Tour hopes derailed by a costly crash; Magnus Bäckstedt, the Paris-Roubaix winner who searched in vain for a stage victory; and Christian Vande Velde, Armstrong's former teammate who followed Roberto Heras to Liberty Seguros to get a ticket back to the Tour.

The Epilogue provides an analysis of how Armstrong barnstormed to history and a look at whether he will be back for another Tour. For after the dust settled on the Champs-Élysées, that was the only real question remaining. One thing seemed sure: After six straight Tour victories, it was obvious there was nothing stopping Armstrong except his own desire to make the sacrifices necessary to win cycling's hardest race.

PART I

The Road to the Tour

Chapter 1

Against the Odds: Lance Armstrong Aims for Six

Lance Armstrong entered the 2004 season on the cusp of history. After joining the exclusive club of five-time Tour de France winners in 2003, he was now gearing up to chase an unprecedented sixth Tour victory. A sixth win would not only set a new record for the event; it would also add legitimacy, if any were needed, to Armstrong's unconventional approach to winning the most important bicycle race in the world.

Lance Armstrong is nothing if not a maverick. In a deeply conservative sport, he is an innovator, a master tactician, and a ceaseless questioner of all that is enshrined as convention. From the beginning, Armstrong's methods have been belittled by the old guard in cycling. The way Armstrong builds his team each year, selecting riders for their potential to serve only his interests in the Tour, is seen as narrow. His season schedule, where he picks and chooses his races only with an eye toward their utility in preparing for the Tour, is seen as opportunistic. His training methods, his habit of riding the Tour's key stages over and over until he knows each pebble on the road, his unconventional climbing rhythm, even his insistence on installing his own chef in the various hotel kitchens each night—all these and more are disliked, derided, dismissed by cycling's traditionalists. And Armstrong's single-minded focus on the Tour de France, only the Tour de France, always the Tour de France, at the expense of the rich calendar of races that the sport presents each season, is the biggest insult of all.

What's hard to remember today, after all these years of Armstrong's success, is that the 32-year-old Texan wasn't supposed to win one Tour de France, let alone five straight.

In October 1996, when the then 25-year-old was diagnosed with advanced testicular cancer, bike racing seemed very far away. With malignancies in his lungs and brain, Armstrong's future was filled edge to edge with the horrors of surgery and chemotherapy. He had, it seemed, only the uncertainty of recovery to look forward to.

But his well-documented battle against the disease transformed Armstrong into a leaner, more inspired racing machine. Before he was stricken with cancer, Armstrong finished just one Tour in four starts between 1993 and 1996, with 36th in 1995 as his best result.

In 1999, his resurrection to become just the second American to win the Tour was the stuff of Hollywood. Armstrong's gutsy performance in that first Tour victory inspired millions and turned Armstrong into a sports superstar and cultural icon.

In 1999, his resurrection to become just the second American to win the Tour was the stuff of Hollywood.

The following year, Armstrong erased any doubts about his staying power, squashing the likes of Jan Ullrich and Marco Pantani en route to a second successive crown. By 2001, Armstrong was a household name with high-profile endorsements from Coca-Cola, Nike, and Bristol-Myers Squibb, the star of television ads, and the celebrated visitor of fellow Texan George Bush in the White House. His well-oiled "Blue Train," the nickname of his U.S. Postal Service team, swept him to his third straight win.

In 2002—with archrival Ullrich suffering in the aftermath of an arrest for drunken driving, a season missed due to injury, departure from his longtime Telekom team, and a racing ban after testing positive for amphetamines—Armstrong was untouchable. "The first year was about cancer, the second about confirmation, the third year was about the team. This year was just fun," Armstrong gushed after that win.

"Big Tex" was on top of the world, seemingly in complete control of his universe. By the start of the 2003 race, he was looking confidently toward joining the Tour's five-win club. But then things started to fall apart.

Against the backdrop of the Tour's centenary celebration, Armstrong endured his most harried and difficult Tour yet. Fans worldwide saw the most exciting Tour in a generation as Armstrong battled multiple crashes, a devastating case of dehydration in the first time trial, an infection picked up from his son, backaches and muscle soreness from untested equipment, and a fall at the foot of Luz-Ardiden, among other woes.

That 2003 Tour saw Armstrong at his worst, but also at his best. Against the ropes, he came out swinging. His decisive winning attack on Luz-Ardiden in the Tour's third week saw Armstrong unplugged. This was no rope-a-dope; there was no "look." Instead, this Armstrong was gaunt, his eyes bloodshot, skin ashen, and his body pushed to extreme lengths. Super Lance looked human after all.

Armstrong managed to win, of course, but his margin was an uncharacteristically small 61 seconds. Discussing his perseverance against the countless obstacles he faced on the way to victory, Armstrong said, "It made it sweet, but if I had to choose between the two, I would prefer a 5-minute lead versus a 15-second cushion." It was, as he said, "Too stressful."

After the close call, Armstrong retreated to his Austin ranch to determine what went wrong and why. Dissecting each segment of his performance, Armstrong was intent on recapturing the dominance he held in his first four Tour wins. Nothing was beyond question as he took a hard look at his team, his equipment, and himself. "Change is always a little risky, but some changes are absolutely necessary," he decided.

First for retooling was Armstrong's training and preparation. For a rider who focuses entirely on the Tour, Armstrong admitted he put too much effort in 2003 into trying to win races that were normally tune-ups for him, events such as Liège-Bastogne-Liège in April and the Dauphiné Libéré in June.

"I went too deep at those races," Armstrong recounted. "There's only one bike race to win. I really hurt myself at the Dauphiné last year. I won't risk that again."

And indeed, in 2004 he skipped Liège and the other spring classics for the first time since his 1999 cancer comeback. Instead, he raced—in a measured, careful performance, rather than an all-out assault—and won the Tour de Georgia in the United States in April. In June, he was content to let his Spanish rival and Tour favorite Iban Mayo take victory at Dauphiné. Even the Olympics, where Armstrong had failed to win a gold medal in three previous games, were given a backseat. Everything was focused on the sixth Tour.

The 2004 Tour route created new challenges as well. With the decisive stages coming in the final half of the Tour, Armstrong worked closely with longtime coach Chris Carmichael and controversial Italian doctor Michele Ferrari—the sports physician who had once defended the use of the blood-booster EPO by declaring it no more harmful than orange juice—to time his fitness for a mid-July peak. "The last week looks really tough, the toughest we have ever done," said

Armstrong, who would be starting his tenth career Tour. "It will be much better to have a stronger second half than a strong first half."

Known for his meticulous attention to equipment, Armstrong also insisted on a complete technology upgrade, making changes to both his road bike and time trial bike. He brought all of his sponsors and suppliers together and charged them with creating significant improvements in all areas—lighter weight, better aerodynamics, greater efficiency. "We started this project in September, maybe even in late August," Armstrong later revealed. "It was an amazing undertaking, getting everybody aligned and working together—truly a Formula 1-esque effort. Nike, Trek, Giro, Shimano, everyone involved in the time trial bike; the handlebars, the bike, the apparel, the shoes, the components, the helmet—everything."

ARMSTRONG

Armstrong also underwent wind-tunnel testing for the first time since 2002 in an effort to create a more efficient position, ultimately moving his elbows lower and closer together on newly configured aerodynamic handlebars. "We had a projector that projected in front of me a huge line graph with real-time data. It's amazing that you can see the drag coefficient. When I do the things I do, reach back to adjust my shorts, move my head, even take a deep breath, you can see it change. It was great to see."

Armstrong made his first test of the changes during the Tour of the Algarve, a minor stage race in February in southern Portugal. He promptly won the 24-kilometer individual time trial, sufficient proof that the alterations were bearing fruit.

Armstrong subjected his U.S. Postal Service team selections to closer scrutiny too. In choosing the eight riders who would support him in 2004, he left off strong worker Victor Hugo Peña, who helped Armstrong win three Tour victories in 2001–2003 and became the first Colombian to wear the yellow jersey in the 2003 Tour. Instead, Armstrong picked Spanish rider Benjamin Noval, a Tour rookie who had impressed him during training camps and early season races.

"With Noval, we don't know him real well at this level; he's new to the team and he's never been to the Tour," Armstrong admitted. "But he was too strong at the racing and at the training. We felt it was time [for him] to come to the Tour de France and come onto the team."

Why so many changes? For Armstrong, it was all about refining the process and actively increasing his chances for victory. "I always come back to the fact that I'm not a retired racer sitting at the bar telling stories about my glory days. I'm still here, I'm still competitive, and I think I can win another one," he said. "That's where I choose to focus."

Armstrong was hard at work behind the scenes, but you wouldn't have known that by reading the newspapers over the winter. Following a painful separation from his wife, Armstrong's private life had become fodder for the gossip magazines. First he was linked to actress Sandra Bullock, then to rock singer Sheryl Crow. There was no denying that story when the pair was "outed" during a Los Angeles Lakers basketball game. More tabloid fodder followed when Crow joined Armstrong in January on his return to his European base in Girona, Spain. Soon the papers were full of speculation that Armstrong was going soft, that he was ignoring his normally relentless winter training schedule, a misconception reinforced by an offhand joke by Crow that she and Lance were getting out occasionally for doughnuts. Doughnuts?!? That hardly sounded like Armstrong's usual Spartan fare.

Armstrong shrugged it off. "Sheryl is a great girl. It's nice to have her over here," Armstrong said. "She's made a big commitment to be with me, to come to this world of cycling. She has a big life also—she's not just a bike fan, she's a big rock star. It's a big commitment on her part to come live the life of a cycling girlfriend, do laundry, cook food, do all the things that all wives or girlfriends do."

For Crow—a Grammy winner and multiplatinum singer/songwriter best known for her single "All I Wanna Do"—it was all a labor of love. "I've had so many incredible things happen to me, and I'd say meeting Lance has been the most incredible," she said. "It's changed my life, and I'm happier than I've ever been. I'm with someone I admire greatly and enjoy being with, so it works out great."

Crow is a keen runner and cyclist who often joined Armstrong on his training forays up Europe's steepest mountains. Before the Tour, when Armstrong and key teammates were training on l'Alpe d'Huez, Crow rode up the difficult climb on a mountain bike.

"I don't know how he does it, but I will say that he's an amazing example of the incredible will of the human spirit to defy what the body is saying," Crow said. "He's mind over matter all the way. More than that, he loves it and enjoys it. It's all wrapped up in one."

By early spring, the gossip columns were forgotten, and Armstrong was back where he's happiest—racing his bike. Things started well with that season debut at the Tour of Algarve, with Armstrong taking the time trial win and his teammate Floyd Landis taking the final stage and overall victory. "Not bad for someone who's been eating doughnuts all winter," team director Johan Bruyneel smirked after Armstrong came through the winner.

Armstrong was feeling good. "I still love what I do," he said the night before winning the time trial. "To get a result, there's a process. To do the process, you have to have the passion. That's what I still have, fortunately."

Joining Armstrong in Algarve was Postal newcomer José Azevedo, who finished sixth in the 2002 Tour while riding for ONCE. Azevedo had been brought onboard to replace two-time Vuelta a España champion Roberto Heras, who had left the Postal team to lead the new Liberty Seguros squad.

"If you look at the two riders in the Tour de France, I think José is as strong if not stronger than Roberto," Armstrong said. "It's not a question of who wins the Vuelta a España, but it is a question of who wins the Tour de France."

The remainder of the spring went smoothly for Armstrong. He faced longtime rival Ullrich in the Tour of Murcia in early March, but neither man was riding for the win. Armstrong then skipped the spring classics and instead returned to the United States to race in the Tour de Georgia, winning two stages and taking the overall title.

Back in Europe, Armstrong contested both the Tour du Languedoc-Roussillon (formerly the Midi Libre) and the Dauphiné Libéré. He raced both events without expectations for the overall, but couldn't help himself at Languedoc-Roussillon in late May, taking the final stage. At the Dauphiné Libéré in early June, Iban Mayo fired a pre-Tour warning shot by blazing to a dramatic overall victory. Most impressive was his record ascent of the 21.6-kilometer climb to the top of Mont Ventoux in a demanding time trial. The superambitious Basque squashed the previous record set by American Jonathan Vaughters in 1999 of 56:50, setting a new mark of 55:51 with an average speed of 23.202kph. Armstrong lagged up the climb 5th at 1:57 back and finished 4th overall.

ARMSTRONG LIKES A GOOD FIGHT, but in the days immediately before the Tour start he faced a more elusive enemy when doping allegations were leveled against him in a book published in France. Armstrong, who has never tested positive for banned substances, energetically denied the accusations in a packed press conference just two days before he started his run for a record sixth Tour crown.

"Extraordinary accusations must be followed up with extraordinary proof," Armstrong said. "They have not come up with extraordinary proof."

In this case "they" referred to French journalist Pierre Ballester and London *Times* reporter David Walsh who had coauthored a 375-page book entitled *L.A. Confidentiel: Les Secrets de Lance Armstrong.* Among Armstrong's alleged secrets, said ex-Postal team assistant Emma O'Reilly in the book, was that Armstrong had asked her to dispose of used syringes and that she had used makeup to hide needle marks on his arms. The book also quoted Armstrong's former Motorola teammate Stephen Swart, who said Armstrong and others on the team in the mid-1990s were using EPO, the banned blood-booster.

"I can absolutely confirm that we do not use doping products," Armstrong said during a press conference in June when it was announced that cable giant Discovery Channel was taking over title sponsorship of the team for 2005. "I can also remind everyone here and everybody listening that this is not the first time this has happened," Armstrong continued. "I heard it in 1999. I heard it in 2001, and again in 2003. And every time, we've chosen to sit back and let it pass. But we've sort of reached a point where we really can't tolerate it anymore, and we're sick and tired of these allegations, and we're going to do everything we can do to fight them."

The authors, who had spent more than three years compiling their charges, admitted that their book offered only circumstantial evidence of doping within the Postal camp. But Walsh, who in 2001 had revealed Armstrong's close relationship with Dr. Michele Ferrari, said, "People tend to denigrate circumstantial evidence, but in the U.K. and America people are convicted on circumstantial evidence all the time. We want people to read the book with an open mind, and then form their own conclusion. We wanted to put it out there when it would get the most attention."

Despite the unsettling timing, Armstrong professed to be unfazed. "I am not worried at all. In fact, it motivates me even more," he said. "They interviewed hundreds of people, maybe thousands, and they found only two who said these absolute lies. They didn't quote the others at all."

Armstrong promised legal action, but early efforts to force the inclusion of an Armstrong-written denial into the book were shot down by French courts. "The case is now incredibly complicated and it will be a long one, but I have engaged lawyers in both England and France," he said. "I will spend whatever it takes and do whatever it takes to bring justice to the case."

Those close to Armstrong said he was deeply angered over the book's contents and had promised to wreak his revenge by winning a record sixth Tour. Anger has always fueled Armstrong's best performances, and as the Tour approached, the book's charges seemed to have given him an extra gear.

"He's been dealing with Walsh for four years now, so he doesn't let it bother him that much," said former teammate Christian Vande Velde, now racing on rival Liberty Seguros. "Lance almost likes a little conflict; it keeps him sharp, keeps him motivated."

Was he really extra motivated? Would that motivation push him to an easy win? Like most cyclists, Armstrong is a little superstitious, unwilling to tempt the cycling gods with brash predictions. Sure, after all his preparation, he liked his chances. But he wasn't going to declare victory prematurely. In the end, all he would say was "I'm still here, I'm still competitive, and I think I can win another one." And as the minutes ticked down to the start in Liège, that seemed like a safe bet.

Chapter 2
Hamilton Eyes the Prize

Tyler Hamilton might not seem like the betting kind, but the gritty, hard-working New Englander entered the 2004 season taking the biggest gamble of his career. After riding with extraordinary success under the tutelage of 1996 Tour winner Bjarne Riis—a two-year run that included a stage victory and 2nd place in the 2002 Giro d'Italia, followed by a stage victory and 4th place overall at the 2003 Tour de France despite cycling's most famous broken collarbone—Hamilton left the comfort of Team CSC for the unproven Phonak squad.

Although his two-year contract was up at the end of the 2003 season, Hamilton wasn't seriously considering leaving Team CSC. Earlier that spring, he went so far as to publicly declare he wanted to end his career with Riis, but that was before Phonak, a Swiss team with deep pockets and big ambitions, came to the table with an offer he eventually found he couldn't refuse.

Talks with the Swiss outfit began quietly before the 2003 Tour started. Former 7-Eleven/Motorola manager Jim Ochowicz, who works with Phonak as an advisor, helped steer negotiations. Hamilton, who is also represented by Lance Armstrong's agent, Bill Stapleton, finally made the difficult decision to leave Team CSC after being convinced Phonak would give him unprecedented support.

"The team is focused on me, the way U.S. Postal Service has been focused on Lance," Hamilton explained. "If you have the strength to win the Tour, that's the way to win. You need to focus on one objective and that's to win the Tour de France."

Hamilton admitted it was difficult to leave the Danish team, which plucked him from Armstrong's shadows at the end of the 2001 season and gave him the chance to flower into a team leader. Behind the scenes though, Hamilton was slowly becoming frustrated with Riis's top-heavy, military-like organization and the insistence on teamwork in a frenetic search for UCI points and stage victories over individual results.

It was during the 2003 Tour that Hamilton finally realized his goals no longer meshed with those of the balding Dane. His courageous ride with a broken collarbone earned him nearly as much ink as Armstrong's record-tying fifth victory, but Hamilton thought that perhaps he could have finished even better. With Riis sending his CSC riders into breakaways in pursuit of stage victories—something Postal Service almost never does unless it serves the larger goal of overall victory—Hamilton was feeling isolated in key moments of the race.

Things came to a head in stage 13, when Carlos Sastre stayed away to win atop Ax-3 Domaines. Earlier in the stage, Riis drove the team's front support vehicle away from his position near Hamilton to follow Sastre and the second team car couldn't push past on the narrow climb at Port de Pailhères to reach Hamilton. Hamilton, left without team support, ran out of water on the blistering hot day and conceded more than a minute to Ullrich and Armstrong.

As Hamilton considered his options in August, he decided that having the full support of an entire squad was his only real hope of challenging Armstrong and made the decision to join Phonak. It was a calculated move with one goal in mind: winning the Tour de France. And it was a huge boost for Phonak, a good but not spectacular team that had been snubbed by Tour officials until they wooed the 33-year-old from Marblehead, Massachusetts.

"I have to think that I can win," Hamilton said. "I know it's a tough task, but I have to train and be mentally and physically prepared for that. On the start line, if you're already thinking about the podium, you're already behind."

FROM WATERBOY TO TOUR CONTENDER

Declarations like that reveal just how far Hamilton has evolved as a rider since his first uncertain days as a pro back in 1995 after capturing the NCAA road cycling title the previous year. A deft climber who can defend in the individual time trials, Hamilton's evolution from unknown pack fodder, to *super-domestique,* to team captain has been on a steady, upward projection.

The first glimpse of Hamilton's Tour potential came in the scandal-marred 1998 Tour. While the cycling world was overwhelmed with the Festina doping scandal and the battle between Jan Ullrich and eventual winner Marco Pantani for the spoils, U.S. Postal Service, with Hamilton aboard, was struggling to get through its second Tour. In those days, before Armstrong transformed the team into a Tour winner, just getting to Paris with all nine riders was deemed a success for the Americans.

In the first individual time trial—a hilly, 58-kilometer course to Corrèze—Hamilton finished a surprisingly strong 2nd to Ullrich. While some shrugged off the performance as a fluke, for Hamilton and Postal it was a confirmation of his potential.

Just two days later, Hamilton revealed another characteristic that would set him apart as a racer—his unbending willpower to overcome pain. Overcooked from his effort in the time trial, bothered by a stomach bug, and wilting under intense heat, Hamilton lost contact with the peloton in the 210-kilometer stage from Montauban to Pau. Hamilton rode alone over the next 40 kilometers, doggedly refusing to quit despite pleadings from then team manager Mark Gorski. Hamilton waved off teammates Marty Jemison and Frankie Andreu so they wouldn't risk getting eliminated by the time cut. Hamilton wobbled across the line, but he went on to finish the Tour.

With Armstrong's arrival in 1998, Hamilton quickly found a keen training partner and role model in his new teammate. Hamilton and his wife, Haven, even bought an apartment in the same refurbished building in downtown Girona, Spain, where Armstrong purchased a home.

Hamilton helped the Texan win his first Tour in 1999 and played an even more important role in the following two Tours, supporting Armstrong ably in the mountain stages. But after the 2001 season, Hamilton was feeling stymied in his role and jumped at the chance to join Team CSC. Riis, a canny judge of talent and a peerless coach, saw Hamilton's promise and signed the man from Marblehead to a two-year deal.

Working closely with Riis and Italian coach Luigi Cecchini, Hamilton lost weight, increased his strength and durability, and developed Armstrong-esque pedal speed on the steep climbs. "It's a huge difference from three years ago," Hamilton said. "I owe a lot of credit to Bjarne Riis, who helped me grow from a *domestique* to team leader. I learned a lot from Lance as well, how he can stay focused on the important things, stay calm in difficult situations."

Hamilton was ready to put the hard work on the line. His first test came in the 2002 Giro. After he crashed into the barriers at the prologue in Holland, Hamilton suffered a spectacular fall on the descent of the Colletto del Moro when the freewheel in his rear wheel broke, releasing all pressure in the pedals and catapulting him over the handlebars.

Luckily, Hamilton was able to remount his bike and finish the stage, but he crashed again on the next stage. Hamilton could barely move his shoulder, and team staff was so nervous that their star was KO'd that no one wanted to see an X-ray until after the Giro.

Indeed, Hamilton had cracked his left shoulder in the crash in stage 5. But he battled on to the finish, with pain so searing that he ground his teeth to get through the stages—so much so he had to have 11 teeth recapped in the off-season. He shot into contention with his time trial victory in stage 14 to become the fourth American to win a Giro stage, joining Andy Hampsten, Greg LeMond, and Ron Keifel. (Sprinter Fred Rodriguez joined the list in 2004.)

He might have won the Giro outright had he not bonked on the final ramps of the Giro's last climb to Passo Coe. In a dramatic day that saw Cadel Evans, Dario Frigo, and Aitor González all suffer meltdowns, Hamilton couldn't respond when eventual winner Paolo Savoldelli shot away. Hamilton rebounded in the final time trial to secure 2nd place overall—the second best ever by an American.

A month later, Hamilton raced much of the 2002 Tour sick but still quietly finished 15th overall. His season ended with yet another crash when he was "doored" while warming up for the GP Eddy Merckx in August and broke his shoulder again.

HAMILTON

A RUN FOR THE PODIUM

After the Giro success, Hamilton and Riis were even more confident and entered the 2003 season with their eyes cast toward the Tour podium. First came a spring campaign that would carve Hamilton's name in the history books.

After finishing second to Basque climber Iban Mayo at the rainy Tour of the Basque Country in early April, Hamilton entered Liège-Bastogne-Liège in the shadow of Armstrong, who was putting in a full effort at trying to win the Ardennes one-day classic. Hamilton said he thought he missed the winning move when Armstrong chugged away on the Côte du Sart-Tilman with 16 kilometers to go, but Team CSC did most of the work to bring back the Texan. Hamilton saw his opening on the descent of the Côte de St. Nicolas, with 3 kilometers to go before the climbing finish to Ans, and slipped away just as the lead pack hesitated.

"When the group with Armstrong went away I thought, 'That's the move and I think I missed it,'" Hamilton recounted after becoming the first American to win the legendary classic. "To be the first American to win is really incredible. Not just that, but to win this race . . . in my opinion it's the most difficult World Cup. Ever since I did the race in 1997 I wanted to come back here and do a strong race. I can't tell you how special it is to have this victory."

Hamilton carried that sensational form into early May and the challenging Tour de Romandie in Switzerland, winning the final time trial en route to the overall title.

After a quiet Dauphiné Libéré in June, Hamilton was finally ready to take on his boss. While mild-mannered in public, Hamilton has fierce determination to complement his work ethic and arrived in Paris in the best form of his career. Also in tow was a crew of filmmakers from the large-screen IMAX film company, which was using Hamilton and the Tour de France as a backdrop for a film about the human brain.

"It hurt all day, a dull ache in my shoulder, but the important thing was that I made it to the finish . . . . This morning I didn't think I'd make it the first 10 miles."

Hamilton and the IMAX crew got more than they bargained for when he got tangled in the finish-line pileup coming into Meaux. Hamilton landed hard on his right shoulder, breaking his collarbone, and limped across the finish line with his left hand on the wound. The team held an emotional press conference that evening, where Hamilton, who was not expected to start the next stage, admitted he had begun the Tour expecting to land on the final podium.

Defying all expectations, and after sleeping only four hours overnight, Hamilton decided to push on. His right clavicle was thoroughly bandaged, and mechanics added layers of padded tape to his handlebars and deflated the pressure on his tires to ease the ride.

"It hurt all day, a dull ache in my shoulder, but the important thing was that I made it to the finish," said Hamilton after making it through stage 2 to Sedan. "This morning I didn't think I'd make it the first 10 miles."

Hamilton made it more than 10 miles. He made it all the way to Paris in a performance that captured the hearts of fans worldwide. His Tour quest became one of the top story lines of the centennial Tour.

Hamilton vowed to pull out if he lost more than 15 minutes in a stage, but he arrived at the decisive stage 8 at l'Alpe d'Huez vowing to continue the fight. On the twisting, steep switchbacks, surrounded by nearly 500,000 fans, Hamilton surprised even himself to finish alongside Armstrong and five other riders in a group 2:12 behind stage-winner Iban Mayo.

Hamilton made it through the Alps by finishing with the Armstrong group into Gap, but he didn't dare believe that the worst was behind him. While Hamilton's bone slowly improved with each day, his frail body took a beating from the intensity of the racing and the pounding of the roads. He contorted himself to compensate for the pain in his shoulder, causing a pinched nerve that was even more painful than the broken bone.

Team CSC physical therapist Ole Kaere Føli continued to work Hamilton nightly, but sleep was still scarce. The injury caught up to him in the Pyrénées, and by the end of stage 15 his hopes of a podium miracle faded as he slipped to 7th overall at more than 9 minutes back.

But Hamilton "the Warrior" had one surprise left in him. After a scouting trip in May, Hamilton knew that stage 16, with two Category 1 climbs midway through the stage and a rolling, 60-kilometer run into Bayonne, would be decisive.

The climb soon became part of the Hamilton legend. After nearly getting dropped by the bunch on an unmemorable Cat. 4 climb at 10 kilometers, Hamilton shot off the front of the main bunch on the 1,540-meter Col du Soudet. He quickly reeled in an early move that featured CSC teammate Nicki Sörensen and six others and drove the group toward the jagged summit.

Hamilton dropped the remainders of the break on the foggy, twisting climb up the 1,327-meter Col Bagarguy, where tens of thousands of Basque fans lining the course cheered him on as he disappeared into the mist. Hamilton pushed hard on the roller-coaster run into Bayonne and held a winning margin at the end of the stage of nearly 2 minutes despite strong crosswinds.

"Today has made up for everything. It's beyond my wildest dreams," Hamilton said after his victory. "Up until now the Tour has been a little disappointing. Under the circumstances of my injury, I've done a respectable Tour. Without the injury, I could have done more. But now I am going to forget about the disappointment. I am extremely happy."

Hamilton's win put him into elite company, joining Armstrong, Greg LeMond, Jeff Pierce, Davis Phinney, and Andy Hampsten as the only Americans to win a Tour stage.

Incredibly, Hamilton had one more trick up his sleeve. On a miserable, rainy, windy ride to Nantes on the Tour's decisive final time trial, Hamilton finished just

8 seconds slower than winner David Millar. But more importantly, Hamilton clawed his way back to 4th overall.

How did he endure the pain? He said part of his determination came from skiing on the cold, bleak mountains of his native New Hampshire. "I don't think I'm a hero," Hamilton said. "I'm just doing my job."

Unfortunately, Hamilton's season ended on a familiar note. His last race in Team CSC colors was marked by a bloody spill in the Tour of Holland on August 20. He crossed the line gushing blood from cuts, and an MRI later revealed a hairline fracture in his right femur.

STARTING 2004 ON THE RIGHT FOOT

Phonak has invested heavily in Hamilton, signing him to a lucrative two-year deal that made him one of the best paid riders. Since his arrival, Hamilton has worked closely with sport director Alvaro Pino and team manager Urs Freuler to bring in key riders such as Santos Gonzalez, Oscar Sevilla, and others who would be his helpers in the Tour.

By early April, Hamilton was starting to ramp up his fitness for some pre-Tour goals that included defending his Romandie title in a confidence-boosting performance for his Phonak team. He then finished 2nd overall at the Dauphiné Libéré, despite a scary fall, and he finished 2nd to Mayo on the Dauphiné's fearsome stage 4 time trial up Mont Ventoux, besting Armstrong by 1:23.

Hamilton had reached a new level. He was the clear, uncontested team leader, and throughout the spring he projected new self-confidence and determination. At the dawn of the 2004 Tour, Hamilton reflected on his new position as top rival to his former boss. "In my selfish sort of way, I never want to look back and wish I'd done more. To achieve the ultimate goal, it's all about taking educated risks," Hamilton explained. "I'm not afraid to fail. I've showed that in my whole career I'm not afraid to take a risk. I always want to get better, to improve. I call it positive dissatisfaction. I'm never 100-percent satisfied."

It seems now Hamilton will only be satisfied when he wins the Tour de France.

PREVIOUS TOURS: 2003 4th + stage win; **2002** 15th; **2001** 94th; **2000** 25th; **1999** 13th; **1998** 51st; **1997** 69th

Chapter 3

Other Americans at the Tour

LEVI LEIPHEIMER (RABOBANK)

Levi Leipheimer was a very happy man last October when Tour officials unveiled the course for 2004. With the most challenging stages packed in over the final week, Leipheimer knew this was a Tour he could like. The harder the race, the better it is for the tough, Montana-born all-rounder.

"Each grand tour I've done, I've always been better in third week," Leipheimer explained. "It's a strong point for me, and I like it if the final week of the Tour is the most difficult. It favors me."

The 30-year-old is almost Ullrich-esque in his riding style—a steady American motor that admittedly takes awhile to get warmed up. With the first serious mountains not coming until the climbing finish to La Mongie in stage 12, Leipheimer figured he'd be firing with all cylinders just in time for the Tour's decisive moments.

"You have to come in fit because the Tour is always difficult, but you want to make sure you have the reserves to go into that third week fresh," he said. "You still have to have something in the gas tank."

Leipheimer established his reputation for being strong in the final week of grand tours back in 2001, when he went from faceless pack-fill to Tour contender in the Vuelta a España. In the final day's time trial, he bounced into 3rd place overall to become the first American to finish on the Spanish tour's podium.

In his Tour de France debut in 2002, Leipheimer rebounded nicely in the final week with a strong ride to La Plagne (won by teammate Michael Boogerd) and finished 8th overall for the third-best Tour debut by an American. (Greg LeMond was 3rd in 1984 and Andy Hampsten was 4th in 1986.)

His 2002 season was cut short when, two weeks after the Tour while racing at the Tour of Holland, Leipheimer felt sharp stomach pain late one night after a stage. A long-forgotten childhood surgery had left scar tissue that had blocked his intestines and twisted his stomach into an unnatural position against his diaphragm. Doctors needed three hours in the operating room, and Leipheimer endured two weeks on his back in a Dutch hospital. When he finally returned to his home base in California in September, he had lost nearly 20 pounds—most of it muscle.

Once he was able to train normally, Leipheimer quickly recovered the muscle mass and entered the 2003 Tour with high hopes. Those came crashing down in the costly stage 1 pileup that also took out Rabobank teammate Marc Lotz and left Tyler Hamilton with a broken collarbone.

Leipheimer went down hard on the back of his hip, fracturing his tailbone and compressing muscles and tendons in his legs. He was unable to walk, let alone race three weeks in the Tour. "It happened so fast. All I remember is seeing riders on the ground and falling to my left side," Leipheimer recounted. "I went to stand up and to get back on the bike and remember not being able to stand up. I just couldn't get up."

Leipheimer once again faced a painful recovery, but by August his Rabobank team officials were urging him to race September's three-week Vuelta a España. Unable to fully recover, Leipheimer struggled to finish 58th, more than two hours back.

"Last year was a bit of a throwaway year," Leipheimer said at the start of the 2004 season. "I'd like to just have a good year and put that behind me."

Rather than gamble everything on the Tour as he did in 2003, Leipheimer set some early season goals. In March, he won the "queen's stage" up the Category 1 summit to Port del Comte high in the Catalan Pyrénées during Setmana Catalana to score his first victory since the 2002 Route du Sud.

Unlike many of the Tour's top contenders, Leipheimer skipped attending any extensive pre-Tour training camps to scout out the key Tour stages—"Sometimes it's just not worth it," he said—and instead made a quick trip home to California to sharpen his skills for the Tour.

"I missed not doing it last year, so I'm excited to get back to the Tour," Leipheimer explained. "The best hope is to finish on the podium. My main goal is improving on 2002. That's all I can imagine right now and hope for the best possible result."

PREVIOUS TOURS: 2003 DNF; **2002** 8th

BOBBY JULICH (TEAM CSC)

What ever happened to Bobby J? That's a question many fans have asked since Bobby Julich's 3rd-place podium at the 1998 Tour de France. Before Lance Armstrong's cancer recovery, it was Julich who was America's great Tour hope.

But overshadowed by Armstrong's legendary comeback, and struggling with his own demons, Julich was soon eclipsed by Armstrong's five-year Tour dominance. "It just happened so fast you just kind of take it for granted and then it was gone so fast before you could even pull up the parking brake," Julich remembered. "It was over so fast, and it's so hard to get—it's like the Holy Grail."

Julich grew up in the Rocky Mountains, near the ski runs of Aspen and Vail, and dreamed of racing in the Tour like his hero Greg LeMond. A junior prodigy, Julich bounced between teams before landing a spot in the European peloton after a top ten finish in the 1996 Vuelta a España.

During the 1997 Tour, while Armstrong was struggling with the aftereffects of chemotherapy and facing an uncertain future, Julich turned some heads with his breakthrough 17th-place debut. But bigger things awaited Julich in the 1998 Tour.

His fate in that race changed dramatically when his Cofidis team captain, Francesco Casagrande, crashed out early, opening the door for Julich. While the scandal-plagued 1998 Tour teetered on self-destruction, Julich rode with surprising strength and tenacity to finish 3rd behind winner Marco Pantani and runner-up Jan Ullrich.

From that magical Tour, things quickly soured. With Pantani and Ullrich both missing the start, Julich started the 1999 Tour with the No. 1 bib, and there was much talk that he could win. But in the eighth stage—a time trial in Metz that marked the dawning of Armstrong's Tour reign—a struggling Julich fell hard on a corner and abandoned the Tour with a fractured elbow and ribs.

Despite crashing out again at the Vuelta later that year, Julich was one of cycling's hottest properties and penned a lucrative, two-year deal to lead Crédit Agricole in 2000–2001. He quickly discovered, though, that the French team wasn't what he had expected. Julich clashed with team manager Roger Legeay over Julich's wishes for lightweight bikes for mountain stages, demands for a team chef to accompany the team, and the confidence that he was the team captain.

After two frustrating years at Crédit Agricole—brightened by a team time trial victory in the 2001 Tour—Julich joined the German Telekom powerhouse, where he was reunited with former teammate Kevin Livingston. Instead of riding as team leader, however, Julich quickly discovered he was just "pack-fill," racing 88 days in 2002 and 102 in 2003. To add insult to injury, he was left off Telekom's 2003 Tour team.

"One thing I realized about Telekom is that I never had a peak," he said. "It was always pretty much the same, with a little peak here and there—basically a flat line. That was pretty much my motivation, too."

Julich was on the verge of retirement late in 2003 when Team CSC manager Bjarne Riis came calling. Riis had earned his reputation as cycling's Svengali, capable of reviving stalled careers. Laurent Jalabert won the King of the Mountains (KOM) jersey in 2002 for Riis, while Tyler Hamilton flowered into a grand-tour contender, finishing 2nd in the 2002 Giro and 4th in the 2003 Tour. Julich was intrigued and quickly fell under Riis's spell.

"I was very close to retirement and I'm very happy to get this chance to ride with Bjarne," Julich said early in the 2004 season. "I feel like I've gotten my last chance. It's time for me to stop looking in the past and stop regretting things I should have done or could have done and look forward to what I can change and can do."

Newly inspired, Julich finished a strong 3rd at Paris-Nice behind teammate Jörg Jaksche, and he won his first European race since 1997 when he beat Hamilton by less than a second to win a time trial at the Tour of the Basque Country in April. The 32-year-old struggled in the Tour de Suisse, where he started as team captain, but his place in CSC's starting lineup for the Tour was secure. Bobby J was back.

FORMER TOURS: 2002 37th; **2001** 18th + team time trial victory; **2000** 48th; **1999** DNF; **1998** 3rd; **1997** 17th

CHRISTIAN VANDE VELDE (LIBERTY SEGUROS)

Christian Vande Velde wanted so badly to return to the Tour de France he left U.S. Postal Service to get the chance. Since his promising Tour debut in 1999, when he was a key member of Armstrong's first Tour win, Vande Velde has had a rocky Tour road. He was sidelined by an infected spider bite just before the start of the 2000 Tour. In 2001, he crashed in the team time trial, also bringing down teammate Roberto Heras, and three days later he crashed into a light post and broke his arm.

Overlooked for the 2002 Tour team, Vande Velde shined at that year's Vuelta a España in service of Roberto Heras. The result could have returned him to the team's good graces, but he struggled with back injuries throughout much of 2003 and once again was left out of the Tour.

Realizing that he wasn't likely to get back to the big ring with Postal Service, Vande Velde walked away from the only team he'd ever raced for since turning pro in 1998. "Last year was just so frustrating with the injuries I had," the 28-year-old said before the start of this year's Tour. "It was just demoralizing. I could never get myself out of the hole and they didn't give me all the proper chances to get out of the hole. I was ready for something new."

He certainly got that at the Spanish-run Liberty Seguros, which, not coincidentally, was the new home of his former Postal teammate, Roberto Heras. Looking for a new start, Vande Velde called his old friend and offered his services. Heras did not need to be reminded of Vande Velde's selfless work in the mountains, and he quickly convinced the team management to bring Vande Velde aboard.

But the move was not without its challenges. After growing up within the ranks of the U.S. Postal Service team, Vande Velde was hit with a bit of culture shock. "The first night I came there I thought, 'Oh my God, what have I got myself into?' Most have been teammates before on ONCE—they were all close," Vande Velde said. "This is a full-blown Spanish team. The mentality is different. They're always going for stage wins, any kind of win every day. That's different from Postal where you're working for one person. If Armstrong wasn't going for the stage, you weren't either."

While Liberty Seguros team management told Vande Velde he was all but assured of a Tour spot, bureaucratic hassles with European working papers almost foiled his chances. In February, the team told him he needed an official work permit to race as an American on a European team. He wasn't allowed to race again until a month-long paper chase culminated in a trip to Los Angeles in early May to secure his residency visa.

Papers in hand, Vande Velde returned to racing at the hilly Vuelta a Asturias in mid-May and raced through the Volta a Catalunya in mid-June to hone his form with his eyes on the Tour. "That's one of the reasons I came to the team, to race the Tour," he said in May. "I can't wait for it. In some ways, the cards are stacked against me starting the season in the middle of May, but I think I can still pull it off." He did, learning in late June that his Tour start was secure.

FORMER TOURS: 2001 DNF; **1999** 85th

FLOYD LANDIS (U.S. POSTAL SERVICE)

A former mountain biker, Floyd Landis made a splash in his 2002 debut with U.S. Postal Service, finishing 2nd to Lance Armstrong at the Dauphiné Libéré and helping the Texan dominate the Tour. It was an impressive grand tour debut, but Landis almost missed the 2003 Tour after breaking his hip in a training crash in January. Remarkably, he recovered in time to make the nine-man squad, and once again showed his selfless dedication by driving the team in the flats and providing yeoman service in the early mountain stages.

Based in Girona, Spain, with most of the other Americans racing in Europe, Landis came into the 2004 season with even better form. In February, he won the final stage and the overall title at the Tour of Algarve, a small warm-up race where

Armstrong made his season debut with victory in the time trial. The wins were Landis's first since coming to Europe in 2002.

"When the team gives me a chance like that, I have to take advantage of it," Landis said. "Last year was a bit of a disaster. I wanted to have this kind of start last year. I've been real happy the past couple of days."

Landis was hoping for better luck at Paris-Nice, but missed a key break driven by Team CSC. By the Dauphiné Libéré, Landis and Co. were strictly in Tour mode and rode to prepare for July's big dance.

FORMER TOURS: 2003 77th; **2002** 61st

GEORGE HINCAPIE (U.S. POSTAL SERVICE)

George Hincapie has had a front-row seat to history. The 31-year-old native New Yorker is the only rider who's been on all of the U.S. Postal Service teams that have delivered Lance Armstrong to his Tour victories. "Being with Lance the last five years has meant a lot to me," Hincapie said. "Knowing how hard the Tour is, how hard Lance works—being a part of that is a big honor."

Hincapie almost missed last year's Tour when he was sidelined with a combination of a virus and parasites that zapped his strength. He had to forfeit his beloved classics while undergoing lengthy treatments involving nontraditional medicine, which helped revive the easygoing Hincapie in time for the Tour.

Hincapie, always a horse on the flats, was stronger than ever in the 2003 Tour, often riding at the front up the steep climbs in the Pyrénées. That strength has many wondering if Hincapie's priorities are misdirected. Although he's come close, Hincapie has never been able to win one of cycling's one-day classics. In March 2004, he did win the Three Days of De Panne, but that was his first European victory since Gent-Wevelgem in 2001.

Retired star Johan Museeuw, a legendary winner of 11 classics in his 17-year career, said Hincapie has the qualities to win a race like Paris-Roubaix but insisted the American isn't sufficiently focused on the spring season. "George was amazing in the Tour last year," said Museeuw, who is now a sport director at Quick Step. "If he had that same fitness in the classics, then he can win Flanders, he can win Roubaix. It's difficult to be the man for the team in the classics if he's focused so much on the Tour."

But it is the Tour that has allowed Hincapie to witness cycling history. He's one of Armstrong's closest friends, and for now he seems content with his place as the Texan's right-hand man.

PREVIOUS TOURS: 2003 47th; **2002** 59th; **2001** 71st; **2000** 65th; **1999** 78th; **1998** 53rd; **1997** 104th; **1996** DNF

Chapter 4

Lots of Chiefs, Not Many Indians

It seemed that after the nail-biter in 2003, everyone wanted to be a contender in the 2004 Tour de France. Indeed, the centenary Tour saw the most competitive race in a generation and raised the hopes of many that Lance Armstrong would be vulnerable after barely escaping Paris with his fifth title in the bag. But even before the peloton arrived in Belgium there were some noteworthy absentees.

Last year's 3rd-place finisher, Alexandre Vinokourov crashed coming around a traffic circle in the second stage of June's Tour de Suisse. T-Mobile's worst fears were realized when doctors confirmed the Kazakh had torn ligaments in his right shoulder, requiring surgery and a three-week rehab.

An inspired "Vino" had pumped excitement into the 2003 Tour with relentless attacks that started on the Col de la Ramaz in stage 7 and didn't stop until he finally ran out of gas in the Pyrénées. Vinokourov unleashed attacks every time the road went vertical, and his efforts paid off with a well-deserved victory into Gap.

The 30-year-old Vino's best-ever season in 2003 was also his saddest, however. In early March, his close friend Andreï Kivilev (Cofidis) died of head injuries after crashing in the second stage of Paris-Nice. Kivilev's death prompted UCI officials to require hard-shell helmets in all pro races except on summit finishes.

While Jan Ullrich has the distinction of never finishing worse than 2nd in the Tour, Spain's Joseba Beloki had never finished worse than 3rd until last year, when he suffered one of the most spectacular crashes in recent Tour history during stage 9 on Bastille Day. Beloki and Lance Armstrong were on the attack, chasing Vinokourov toward the finish in Gap. With about 6 kilometers remaining, on the descent of the Côte de la Rochette, Beloki's tire slipped on the road tar that had melted in the day's searing temperatures and the Spaniard high-sided over his bike, slamming into the pavement. Beloki broke his femur, elbow, and wrist, and he did not race again that season. Even before the 2003 Tour began, Beloki knew that ONCE was ending its sponsorship of his team. Many expected him to sign with a Spanish team for 2004, but in a surprising move, he instead inked a lucrative two-year deal with La Boulangère.

Unfortunately, Beloki hadn't recovered from last year's broken bones. Overtraining led to tendinitis in his ankle early on, and Beloki's spring of misfortune was littered with DNFs as he struggled to recover from his injuries. By the Bicicleta Vasca race in early June, the 30-year-old had had a falling out with the Boulangère brass over his preferred allergy medicine; the French team refused to let him use it for fear he would fail a doping test. News that the title sponsor was pulling out due to the extra costs incurred as part of next year's Pro Tour format only eased Beloki's early exit. Beloki decided to pull the plug on the Tour, look for a new team, and regroup for the Vuelta a España.

Both Vinokourov and Beloki would be sorely missed in the 2004 Tour, but despite their notable absence, there were still plenty of strong cyclists chasing after Armstrong's crown. As the Tour start loomed, these were the riders who topped the list of Tour contenders:

ULLRICH

JAN ULLRICH (T-MOBILE)

Germany's perennial favorite lined up alongside Armstrong in Liège as the only other starting Tour de France winner. In the pre-race interviews, Armstrong, as usual, singled out the 30-year-old as his top rival and, living up to his billing, Jan Ullrich overcame his typical early season lack of fitness just in time for the Tour, with a victory at the Tour de Suisse in June. He arrived for the Tour looking fit and ready.

Long before Armstrong's miracle cancer comeback, it was Ullrich who pundits predicted would be the first to win six Tours. As a former junior world champion and a 23-year-old Tour winner in 1997, Ullrich seemed unbeatable—that is, until Armstrong's resurgence in 1999.

Seven years on, Ullrich was still looking for his second Tour victory and desperately longing to beat the Texan. Last year, Ullrich endured a stomach bug on the Alpe d'Huez to come within 61 seconds of toppling Armstrong, and he might have won if his Bianchi team had had a stronger squad to support him.

Ullrich had some other strong moments in the centennial Tour as well. He shocked a dehydrated Armstrong with a time trial victory in stage 12 when he took 1:36 out of the Texan and pulled into 2nd place within 34 seconds heading into the Pyrénées. But a crash in the final time trial put Ullrich out of contention, and he rode into Paris in 2nd place once again.

After his *annis horribilis* in 2002—knee injury prevented him from starting the Tour, then he got a DUI and failed a doping test for the party drug Ecstasy before parting acrimoniously from Telekom—Ullrich's comeback with the cobbled-together Bianchi team won him 2003 German sportsman of the year honors ahead of world champion Formula 1 driver Michael Schumacher.

In 2004, Ullrich was back home at T-Mobile (formerly Telekom), but he started the year seemingly determined to repeat his mistakes of the past. While not as portly as in previous years, Ullrich was once again looking cherubic at the T-Mobile presentation in February. By April, poor form forced the five-time Tour runner-up to abandon Flèche Wallone and retreat from Liège-Bastogne-Liège.

Long before Armstrong's miracle cancer comeback, it was Ullrich who pundits predicted would be the first to win six Tours.

Asked about his rival, Armstrong openly questioned T-Mobile's apparent "democratic" style of racing, where Ullrich would share leadership duties with Alexandre Vinokourov and have *super-domestiques* Cadel Evans, Santiago Botero, and Paolo Savoldelli at his beck and call.

"There are too many chiefs, not enough Indians," Armstrong surmised early on.

But the loss of Vinokourov clearly left Ullrich in charge at T-Mobile, and his Tour de Suisse victory relieved any worries that he was not ready for the big show. And though many criticize him for failing to live up to his potential, Ullrich's view is quite different. "I still have one more victory than [Raymond] Poulidor," he said in reference to the Tour's eternal 2nd-place finisher. Fair enough, but that's not why he showed up for the 2004 Tour. And Ullrich knew that better than anyone.

PREVIOUS TOURS: 2003 2nd + stage win; **2001** 2nd; **2000** 2nd; **1998** 2nd + three stage wins; **1997** 1st + two stage wins; **1996** 2nd + stage win

IBAN MAYO (EUSKALTEL-EUSKADI)

Many forget there were *two* riders who fell in the famous *musette* incident last year on Luz-Ardiden. Iban Mayo, the 26-year-old Basque, was hot on Armstrong's wheel when the Texan's handlebars got tangled in the straps of a fan's feedbag, sending both riders tumbling to the tarmac.

"It all happened so fast," Mayo recounted. "I could see Armstrong was riding close to the fans, then suddenly he went down and my tire was just too close to react in time. Before I knew it, we were both on the ground."

With a touch of rock 'n' roll and a hint of long hair out the back of his helmet, Mayo was expected to be the breakout star of the 2004 Tour. In just his second Tour start in 2003, Mayo electrified the Tour with an explosive victory at l'Alpe d'Huez and finished 6th overall at 7:06 back.

MAYO

Mayo defended his Euskaltel-Euskadi team against criticism that he and teammate Haimar Zubeldia didn't race aggressively enough in 2003, when both lost ground against Vinokourov and Tyler Hamilton in the fight for the podium.

"We weren't conservative, it's just that we didn't have the experience and confidence in ourselves," Mayo admitted. "We arrived so fast that we didn't know how to react."

Mayo has an explosive acceleration in the mountains and confidence to match, but time trialing remains his Achilles' heel. For 2004, Mayo took advantage of having Euskaltel-Euskadi's Tour invitation in the bag and quietly worked on improving his strength in the race against the clock.

But Mayo's real strength lies in his attacking style. Mayo figures if he has enough of a lead after the climbs, he will only have to defend in the time trials. Of course, having one of this year's two individual time trials in his preferred hunting ground at l'Alpe d'Huez wouldn't hurt, either.

"I am improving in the time trial," Mayo insisted. "And this year's course helps climbers like me, there's no doubt."

After finishing second at the Tour of the Basque Country in April, May was a Mayo kind of month as he won five races in a nine-day run. He swept to overall victory after winning two of the three stages at Alcobendas, then he set a new record up the final climb of the midweek one-day race at Subida al Naranco. Later that week, he won the five-day Tour of Asturias after erasing a 46-second gap to Félix Cárdenas in a bold, final-day attack over rolling hills.

June saw an even stronger Mayo at the Dauphiné Libéré, where he won the opening prologue and took a jaw-dropping 1:57 out of Armstrong in the individual time trial up fearsome Mont Ventoux. Mayo also smashed Jonathan Vaughters's time trial record on the mountain by nearly a minute to claim the overall title.

Everyone—especially those inside the blue and red bus of U.S. Postal Service—was asking the same question: Had Mayo peaked too early?

"I've been asked 100 times and I'll say the same thing: No," Mayo replied. "The preparation has gone wonderfully, but I am at ease because I still have room to improve."

PREVIOUS TOURS: 2003 6th + stage win; **2002** 88th

HAIMAR ZUBELDIA (EUSKALTEL-EUSKADI)

ZUBELDIA

Quieter and less flashy than his teammate, Haimar Zubeldia has shown steady progress in his three Tour appearances and entered the 2004 Tour wanting nothing less than the podium. The 27-year-old Basque rider first made his presence felt in the 2000 Dauphiné Libéré, which he led in its early stages before giving way to Tyler Hamilton. The mild-mannered Zubeldia endured two injury-filled seasons in 2001 and 2002, but he survived his Tour debut in 2001, finishing 73rd. In 2002, he cracked into the top 40 and rolled into the centenary Tour healthy and determined.

"The first year was just to finish, the second year was to learn, and last year I went with ambitions," Zubeldia explained. "This year the goal is to improve again, with hopes for the podium," he said shortly before the Tour began.

Like most on the Euskaltel-Euskadi team, Zubeldia calls Spain's hilly Basque Country home and can hold his own in the mountains. Like Mayo, Zubeldia took advantage of Euskaltel's automatic bid to start the Tour, and instead of thrashing himself for results early in the spring, he prepared for the Tour in a more organized manner.

In early 2004 Zubeldia suffered knee pain caused by overtraining, but by early June he seemed to have overcome the setback by finishing 5th at the hilly

Bicicleta Vasca. As a strong time trialist and an excellent climber, he was not only gunning to support Mayo in his bid for the podium but was thinking that he might find a place there for himself as well.

PREVIOUS TOURS: 2003 5th; **2002** 39th; **2001** 73rd

"Now it's time for me to be a leader . . ."

ROBERTO HERAS (LIBERTY SEGUROS)

Three years with U.S. Postal Service were enough for the 30-year-old Spanish climber. Roberto Heras's departure from his role as *super-domestique* at Postal to lead the new Liberty Seguros team was one of the top stories of the off-season, but all parties seemed pleased with the outcome. Postal tapped José Azevedo to replace Heras in the mountains while Heras regained his freedom.

"Now it's time for me to be a leader," Heras said. "When I joined Postal, I wasn't ready, but now I am. Now I want to ride as a team captain and I knew that was never possible with Postal."

In three Tours with U.S. Postal, Heras never quite found the stride that carried him to a sensational 5th-place debut in 2000 with Kelme. He crashed in the 2001 Tour and was sick in 2003. But as a sign of his potential, his best Tour was 2002, when he sailed so fast up the La Mongie climb that Armstrong asked him to slow down.

Without Armstrong but with the support of the Postal team, Heras won his second Vuelta a España in 2003 after a dramatic uphill time trial win that erased a gap to Isidro Nozal. It was a victory that helped Heras reclaim his crown as one of Spain's top riders after he bitterly lost the 2002 Vuelta in a final-day time trial showdown with Aitor González. (At 132 pounds, Heras struggles in the long, flat time trials.)

Heras rode slowly into form in 2004, finding his legs just in time to win the Bicicleta Vasca in June. With the newly assembled Spanish team working for him under the watchful eye of veteran team director Manolo Saiz, Heras fully intended to take on his former boss in the mountains, and, with luck, in the Tour overall.

PREVIOUS TOURS: 2003 34th; **2002** 9th ; **2001** 15th; **2000** 5th

IVAN BASSO (TEAM CSC)

BASSO

The best young rider in 2002, Basso delivered on his promise last year to finish 7th overall. And he did it without much of a team; only Dario Cioni and Marzio Bruseghin made it past the first week that saw the rest of Basso's Fassa Bortolo team abandon with food poisoning. Basso did fine work to stay with the best in the mountains, but he lost ground in the two time trials.

With the departure of Tyler Hamilton for Phonak, Team CSC manager Bjarne Riis looked to Basso: a strong climber with room to improve in the time trial. Unusual for an Italian, Basso has never focused on the Giro d'Italia, so leaving the Italy-based Fassa squad for Riis's relentless crew fit in with his hope to break into the Tour's top placings.

Indeed, while his CSC teammates were racking up victories all spring, Basso set his eyes on the Tour. "I've trained and raced a lot this spring, but all the time I've focused on the Tour de France," Basso said. "I can feel that I'm in better shape now compared to the same time last year, and everything has gone according to plan."

The plan included Basso nudging into the top five and making strong progress in the race against the clock. In May, he and teammate Carlos Sastre traveled with Riis and a team mechanic to MIT in Boston for two days of wind-tunnel testing. Basso trained extensively for the first time of his career on honing his time trial position. As he and Riis looked forward to the Tour start, the days of Hamilton seemed far behind.

PREVIOUS TOURS: 2003 7th; **2002** 11th (best young rider)

CHRISTOPHE MOREAU (CRÉDIT AGRICOLE)

MOREAU

As the top French hope in the overall classification, Christophe Moreau gets more than his fair share of attention in the French media. In 2002, rumors of his early departure garnered pages of coverage before he finally pulled out of the race in the Pyrénées. Yet for non-French observers, there seems to be little in his résumé to warrant the attention.

True enough, Moreau proved surprisingly tenacious in the mountains last year and clawed his way to 8th overall for the second-best Tour of his career. But even five-time Tour champion Bernard Hinault was downplaying Moreau's chances before the start of this year's race. "How can I give him credit?" Hinault asked. "Aside from the Dauphiné Libéré, Christophe Moreau has never won anything. And now that he's 33 years old, I don't see him reversing that trend."

Moreau's checkered career included a stint on the ill-fated Festina team, whose doping scandal rocked the 1998 Tour. In 2000, he just missed the podium with a 4th-place finish as he gave way to his Festina teammate Joseba Beloki, then largely unknown. Moreau won the 2001 Tour prologue in a return to the good graces of the French public, but the rest of his race that year was ordinary.

Still, he carried the hopes of his country into the race this year. He was troubled with health problems early in 2004, pulling out of the Four Days of Dunkirk and the Vuelta a Asturias before bouncing back to win the Tour du Languedoc-Roussillon in May.

But with the retirement of Laurent Jalabert and no young French stars moving up, Moreau was pegged to be France's only hope in the GC. And Hinault was watching. "I don't want to be harsh," said the hard man from Brittany. "It's up to him to prove me wrong."

PREVIOUS TOURS: 2003 8th; **2002** DNF; **2001** DNF (prologue winner); **2000** 4th; **1999** 27th; **1998** DNF; **1997** 19th; **1996** 75th

SIMONI

GILBERTO SIMONI (SAECO)

After his disastrous 2003 Tour was salvaged by a Pyrénées stage victory into Loudenville, Gilberto Simoni had a grand plan for 2004 to arrive at the Tour with fresher legs and challenge Lance Armstrong in the mountains. The strategy called for the two-time Giro d'Italia champion to roll to a third *maglia rosa* in May.

Unfortunately for Simoni, he ran headlong into a teammate 10 years his younger. A frustrated Simoni could only watch Damiano Cunego roar to four stage victories and the overall Giro crown.

Simoni quietly regrouped for the Tour—minus the confident declarations of toppling Armstrong that backfired on him so publicly in 2003. At least Simoni wouldn't have to worry about Cunego; Saeco brass is shielding their gem from the Tour until 2006.

PREVIOUS TOURS: 2003 84th + stage win; **1997** 116th; **1995** DNF

YOUNG RIDERS WAITING IN THE WINGS

The Tour always seems to deliver surprises, especially in transition years when older riders begin to ride into the sunset, making room for a new generation. A crop of riders born in the late 1970s and early 1980s are now poised to take over. There are several rising stars that wouldn't start the Tour, including Alejandro Valverde (Comunidad Valenciana-Kelme), 2004 Giro d'Italia champion Damiano Cunego (Saeco), and Yaroslav Popovych (Landbouwkrediet-Colnago).

Topping the list of young up-and-comers for the 2004 Tour was **MICHAEL ROGERS** (Quick Step). The 24-year-old Aussie enjoyed a breakthrough season in 2003, hitting a pre-Tour winning streak that included the Tour of Belgium, Tour of Germany, and the Route du Sud. "I want to win the Tour," Rogers said then. "I hope to see myself in five years in that position to win the Tour. I hope to surprise myself and be in that position in two, three years. You never know. Cycling is a sport like that, full of surprises. He who works harder than the other guys takes the cake." Rogers survived his Tour debut in 2003 by finishing 42nd overall at 1:37:28 back. He remained quiet throughout much of the spring to save everything for the 2004 race, hoping that his five-year plan would see early dividends.

ROGERS

SCARPONI

Prior to this edition, **MICHELE SCARPONI** (Domina Vacanze) hadn't even raced the Tour, but many believed the 24-year-old would slip into the top ten if he could hang with the big boys in the mountains. The rail-thin Italian skipped the Giro d'Italia to focus on the Tour and became the first Italian to win the Peace Race in a tough edition in May. Scarponi is a scrappy climber who's improving in the time trial, but he was unlikely to see much in the way of support from his Domina Vacanze team, which was preoccupied with pulling its leader, Mario Cipollini, to the sprint finishes.

Russian transplant **DENIS MENCHOV** (Illes Balears-Banesto) won a tough Tour of the Basque Country in April and narrowly lost the Tour of Aragon on time bonuses in the final stage. A solid climber, Menchov won the best young rider's

MENCHOV

MERCADO

jersey in last year's Tour en route to finishing 11th. "Since last winter, I've been thinking about the Tour. I believe that I can defend myself well in three weeks," said the 26-year-old. Menchov has become thoroughly Hispanicized in five years under the tutelage of José Miguel Echavarri and Eusubio Unzue, Banesto's team manager and sport director, respectively. The same cohorts who led Miguel Induráin to win five consecutive Tours de France during the glory days of Banesto were hoping they'd found their new star. "We can't push him along too fast," Unzue warned. "Last year was a good test for him. We want to see him continue along this road for another year or two without pressure."

And leading a new generation of Spanish mountain goats was **JUAN MIGUEL MERCADO** (Quick Step), who was hoping for better results after suffering through last year's debut with a bad stomach in the Alps. Mercado, who turned 26 in the first week of the Tour, was to share leadership duties with Michael Rogers, though neither was expected to carry the heavy load of seriously challenging for the overall. Instead, Mercado wanted to get through the Tour with a solid ride. "I'm not going to say I can fight against Armstrong, against Ullrich; they are riders on another level from me," Mercado said. "What I will try to do is make something happen for me on a realistic level. A good objective for me would be top ten. For the second Tour, that's OK. If the GC is not going well, if I have a bad day, maybe I will try to win a mountain stage."

Chapter 5

How the Other Five-Time Winners Fell Short of Six

JACQUES ANQUETIL

Born: Jan. 8, 1934 in Mont Saint Aignan, France

Died: Nov. 18, 1987

Nickname: "Mister Chrono"

Career: The first rider to win five Tours, Anquetil also won two Giros d'Italia, one Vuelta a España, and the world hour record.

Tour stats: Anquetil won the overall title in 1957 and 1961–64, won 16 stages in eight Tours, and wore the race leader's yellow jersey for 16 days.

Jacques Anquetil helped usher in the modern era of cycling, becoming the sport's first superstar. The handsome and aloof Anquetil was one of cycling's greatest time trialists, and most of his major victories came thanks to his prowess in the race against the clock.

Anquetil had fluid style on the bike that Tour de France historian Jacques Augendre described as "quite simply the perfect aesthetic representation of a cyclist." His first major win came at the Grand Prix des Nations time trial, an event he won six times. A supreme strategist, Anquetil would use his mathematics acumen to win by just enough time to secure victory.

Anquetil won the Tour on his first try in 1957. He went on to win four consecutive Tours, all thanks to his time trial skills. An adequate climber, Anquetil could stay close enough to the other riders in the mountains and then gain time in the time trials, a strategy emulated three decades later by Miguel Induráin.

Anquetil's battle against rival Raymond Poulidor in 1964 is considered one of the classic Tours and helped cement Anquetil's reputation as a true champion. While Anquetil was cold and ill at ease with the press, Poulidor was the working-man's hero, known for his warmth and accessibility to the public. Much as Italy was divided between Gino Bartali and Fausto Coppi, the French took sides in the rivalry.

Poulidor was the better climber and saw his opening on the Puy de Dôme, an ancient volcano in the Massif Central. The two haggard riders rode side by side, their shoulders even bumping as they matched pedal strokes up the twisting climb. Finally, Anquetil cracked, and Poulidor thought he might take the jersey. But Anquetil limited his loss that day to 14 seconds and went on to take overall victory in his final Tour de France by 55 seconds after winning the final time trial.

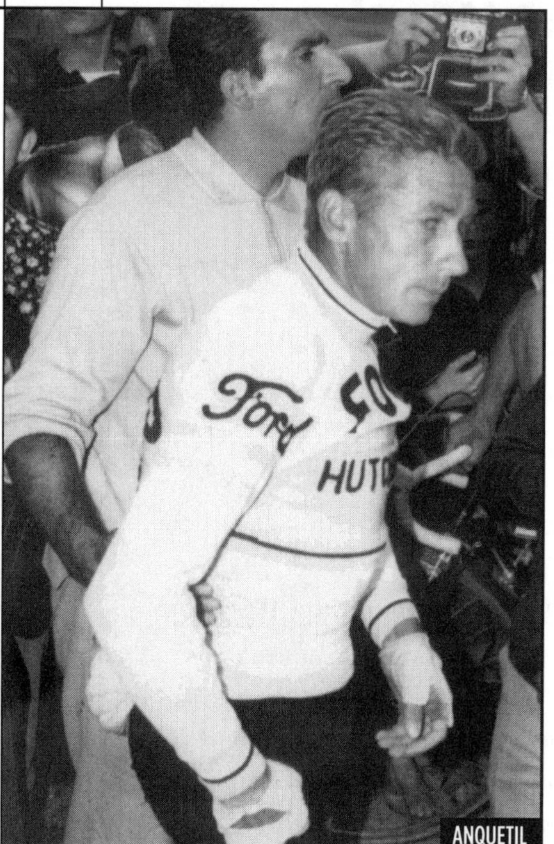

ANQUETIL

How he lost No. 6

After his dramatic fifth victory, Anquetil started to lose his dominance. He did not start the 1965 Tour but returned in 1966 to make a run for six. Anquetil was suffering from bronchitis and instead worked for teammate and eventual winner Lucien Aimar, relegating pre-race favorite Poulidor to the podium again.

Anquetil couldn't win a stage that year—not even in the time trial—and packed it in during the 19th stage. He never raced the Tour again. "I'm more embarrassing than useful now," he said.

Anquetil's legacy was somewhat marred by his open yet honest insistence that racers needed the help of doping products to compete in the grueling sport. In the 1966 Tour, he helped orchestrate a rider's strike against antidoping tests. He died from complications due to stomach cancer in 1987.

EDDY MERCKX

Born: June 17, 1945 in Meensel-Kiezegem, Belgium

Nickname: "The Cannibal"

Career: The winningest professional rider ever, Merckx won five Tours, five Giros, one Vuelta, three world championships, the world hour record, and dozens of one-day classics.

Tour stats: Merckx won the overall title in 1969–72 and 1974, won a record 35 stages in seven Tours, and wore the race leader's yellow jersey for a record 96 days.

Today: Eddy Merckx owns a bike company that builds high-end frames bearing his name.

Considered the greatest racer ever, Eddy Merckx holds just about every record in cycling, including a record of 525 career victories. Merckx was nicknamed "The Cannibal" because he rode every race to win, eating races and opponents alive on his way to a seemingly endless string of triumphs. During his heyday in the early 1970s, Merckx won 35 percent of all races he entered, including five of the seven Tours he started.

Merckx was both loved and hated for his authority. Connoisseurs of the sport often derided his lack of tactics, because Merckx was so strong that he could easily ride off the front to victory. In 1974, he became one of only two cyclists, along with Stephen Roche, to win the Tour de France, Giro d'Italia, and the world championship in the same year.

MERCKX

Merckx's dominance in his Tour de France debut in 1969 set the tone for his reign. He held a solo attack between the Tourmalet and Mourenx Ville Nouvelle for 130 kilometers and won by 8 minutes, a victory that earned him his nickname. Tour boss Jacques Goddet called him "Merckxissimo" as he went on to win by nearly 18 minutes and added the green jersey, the climber's jersey, and the team competition jersey to the maillot jaune.

In 1970, he dominated yet again, winning the prologue only to let teammate Italo Zilioli keep the jersey warm until the race reached the mountains. The Tour then saw the arrival of a young 22-year-old Frenchman named Bernard Thévenet, who won on La Mongie and seemed poised to steal Merckx's thunder in the mountains. However, Merckx won the polka-dot jersey again as well as eight stages.

By 1971, Merckx entered as the heavy favorite but faced stiff competition from Luis Ocaña. He all but lost the race when he let the Spanish rider take a lead of 8:42 out of the Alps. Merckx tried to counterattack in the Pyrénées, but Ocaña didn't crack. Both crashed on the descent off the Col de Mente in horrible conditions and Ocaña was hit by descending riders; his injuries forced an evacuation by helicopter. Merckx, who took over the lead, refused to wear the jersey the next day.

Ocaña was in poor form in 1972, and without his most dangerous rival, Merckx won his fourth successive Tour. Ocaña came back to win the 1973 Tour, but Merckx didn't race that year. The Belgian returned to win a fifth time in 1974, taking six more stages and holding off a good challenge from the aging Poulidor. Merckx also won the Giro and the world title in the same season.

How he lost No. 6

Gunning for his sixth win in 1975, Merckx grabbed the yellow jersey away from prologue winner Francesco Moser but was punched in the kidneys by a French fan on the Puy de Dôme climb. Despite the theatrics, Merckx held a 58-second lead on Bernard Thévenet going into the next stage to Pra-Loup.

Thévenet attacked on an early climb but Merckx held on and even mustered a counterattack coming off a descent to the base of the final climb to Pra-Loup. Thévenet didn't give up and finally caught and dropped Merckx in the final 3 kilometers to take nearly 2 minutes out of the Belgian. On the next day over the Izoard, Merckx lost more ground and Thévenet went on to win the Tour.

Merckx did not start in 1976, and he finished sixth in his final Tour in 1977 before retiring the following year with persistent back problems.

BERNARD HINAULT

Born: Nov. 14, 1954 in Yffiniac, France

Nickname: "The Badger"

Career: Hinault won five Tours, three Giros, two Vueltas, and one world title.

Tour stats: He captured the overall title in 1978–79, 1981–82, and 1985, won 23 stages in eight Tours, and wore the leader's yellow jersey for 78 days.

Today: Hinault currently works in public relations for the Tour de France race organization.

The last Frenchman to win the Tour de France, Bernard Hinault was known for his tenacious attacking style and stubborn intensity on and off the bike. Hinault was the *grand patron*, or big boss, of the peloton during his day, reigning with a ruthless authority intended to maintain his position atop the cycling world. A solid all-rounder, Hinault excelled in time trials and mountain stages.

HINAULT

Hinault has an extraordinary Tour record, winning five times in eight starts, abandoning only once, and never finishing worse than 2nd place overall. His 78 days in the maillot jaune and 23 stage victories are bested only by Merckx.

Like Merckx, Hinault won in his Tour debut. The 23-year-old was solid in the mountains but couldn't wrestle the yellow jersey away from the determined Dutch veteran Joop Zoetemelk until winning the final time trial at Metz. Hinault clashed again with the Dutchman a year later in 1979, when Zoetemelk unleashed an unexpected attack on the final laps on the Champs-Élysées. Zoetemelk finally got his lone Tour victory in 1980 after Hinault abandoned at the foot of the Pyrénées with chronic knee pain.

The Frenchman went on to win two more Tours, in 1981 and 1982, but his most dramatic victory came in 1985. At the time, Hinault was France's top sports star gunning for his fifth Tour, but the gifted American Greg LeMond was waiting in the wings. The pair rode together on the La Vie Claire team with LeMond coming off his promising 3rd-place Tour debut the previous year.

The duo agreed to work together behind the strongest man, which Hinault settled by winning the opening prologue. In the 75-kilometer time trial into Strasbourg, Hinault took 2:20 on archrival Stephen Roche and 2:34 on LeMond, but he broke his nose in a crash on the stage to St. Étienne.

As the race pushed into the Pyrénées, Hinault was, not surprisingly, having trouble breathing when Roche attacked on the mighty Tourmalet. LeMond, sitting 3:38 behind his team boss in the overall standings, was hot on the Irishman's wheel when La Vie Claire's assistant sport director pulled the team car alongside the fair-haired Californian to tell him to ease off his attack.

Could LeMond have taken the time on Hinault to grab the jersey and win the Tour? Probably; in fact, LeMond did win the final time trial at Lac de Vassivière to become the first American stage-winner. But Hinault won his fifth Tour by 1:42 over LeMond and promised to help the American win the next year.

How he lost No. 6

The chance to win a sixth Tour proved too tempting for Hinault and, after beating LeMond by 44 seconds in the first time trial, there were serious doubts about Hinault's intention to keep his promise.

Hinault attacked in the Pyrénées between Bayonne and Pau, leaving LeMond 4 minutes adrift. It looked as though Hinault might win a sixth Tour after all. The Frenchman struck again the next day between Pau and Superbagnères, but LeMond countered to recover most of the lost time and stood 40 seconds behind the Badger.

LeMond grabbed the yellow jersey for good at Sestriere in the Alps and a cease-fire was declared. Hinault led the way for LeMond as they climbed l'Alpe d'Huez, and the two riders crossed the line hand in hand with Hinault taking the stage victory.

But there was still the final time trial to negotiate, and LeMond was only 2:45 ahead of Hinault with a daunting 58-kilometer test against the clock standing between himself and the maillot jaune. Hinault exploded off the line and won the stage but, in a brilliant ride LeMond limited his loss to 25 seconds and became the first American Tour winner.

Hinault kept his word and quit cycling in 1986 at 32. Today, Hinault works with the Tour de France organization. During the event, you can find him every day on the awards podium, as one of his duties is to present the jerseys to the winners at the end of each Tour stage.

MIGUEL INDURÁIN

Born: July 16, 1964 in Villava, Spain

Nickname: "Big Mig"

Career: Induráin won five consecutive Tours, two Giros, the 1996 Olympic time trial gold medal, and the world hour record.

Tour stats: He won the overall title in 1991–95, captured 12 stages in 12 Tours, and wore the race leader's yellow jersey for 60 days.

Today: Now he enjoys a quiet retirement with occasional public appearances.

Looking at Miguel Induráin's first four Tours—two DNFs with 47th his best place—no one could have imagined that the tall, quiet, Spanish rider would go on to smother the Tour in such a dominant fashion.

INDURÁIN

Induráin won a stage in his fifth Tour, and in 1990 he quietly slipped into 10th overall, winning a mountain-top finish ahead of LeMond at Luz-Ardiden. Still, when the 1991 Tour started, three-time winner LeMond was the heavy favorite. Induráin won a 73-kilometer time trial on the 8th stage but only moved to 4th overall behind race leader LeMond. He rode steadily but not spectacularly for the next few days, and then, on stage 13, Induráin followed the attacking Claudio Chiappucci over the Tourmalet. The Italian won the stage, but Induráin slipped into the yellow jersey. Just like that, the LeMond Era was over and the Induráin Age had begun.

Nicknamed "Big Mig" for his large stature, Induráin was a humble rider who became a national hero in cycling-crazed, post-Franco Spain. With a corpselike resting heartbeat of 29 and the capacity to suck 8 liters of air into his huge lungs, Induráin's dominance soured fans beyond Spain. Save for his many fan clubs in the United States, he never became widely popular beyond the Iberian Peninsula.

Though Induráin was a relatively strong climber, it was his utter control in the time trial that delivered his unprecedented five successive Tour victories. Induráin won the Giro d'Italia in 1992 and 1993 en route to squashing the competition at the Tour. As with riders unlucky enough to race during the Merckx era, big names such as Gianni Bugno, Tony Rominger, and the diminutive Chiappucci were overshadowed by the soft-spoken Spaniard.

Induráin endured some stiff challenges in 1995 but held on to win his fifth straight Tour—a record few thought could be matched. That same year, Armstrong finished his only pre-cancer Tour in 36th place. The Texan won an emotional stage into Limoges in honor of fallen teammate Fabio Casartelli who died in a horrible crash on the descent of the Portet d'Aspet. Like many who doubted Induráin, there were few who believed Armstrong would one day come back from the brink to make the mark.

How he lost No. 6

Induráin again looked untouchable in 1996 after roaring to victory in Bicicleta Vasca and the Dauphiné Libéré a month before the Tour. Everyone expected him to win the record sixth Tour, and race organizers even scheduled a stage to roll past his hometown late in the race.

But Induráin's ambitions collapsed in the first mountain stage to Les Arcs on an epic day that saw Laurent Jalabert abandon, Johan Bruyneel skid off course, and Big Mig bonk on the cold, foggy climb. Eventual Tour winner Bjarne Riis took the yellow jersey two stages later after winning at Sestriere, while Induráin never recovered and finished 11th.

Induráin won a gold medal at the 1996 Summer Olympics in Atlanta, but he retired at the end of the season after being forced by his team to race in the Tour of Spain that fall. Today, Induráin keeps a low profile, making few public appearances during the racing season.

PART II

The 91st Tour de France

2004 Tour de France

Race Map

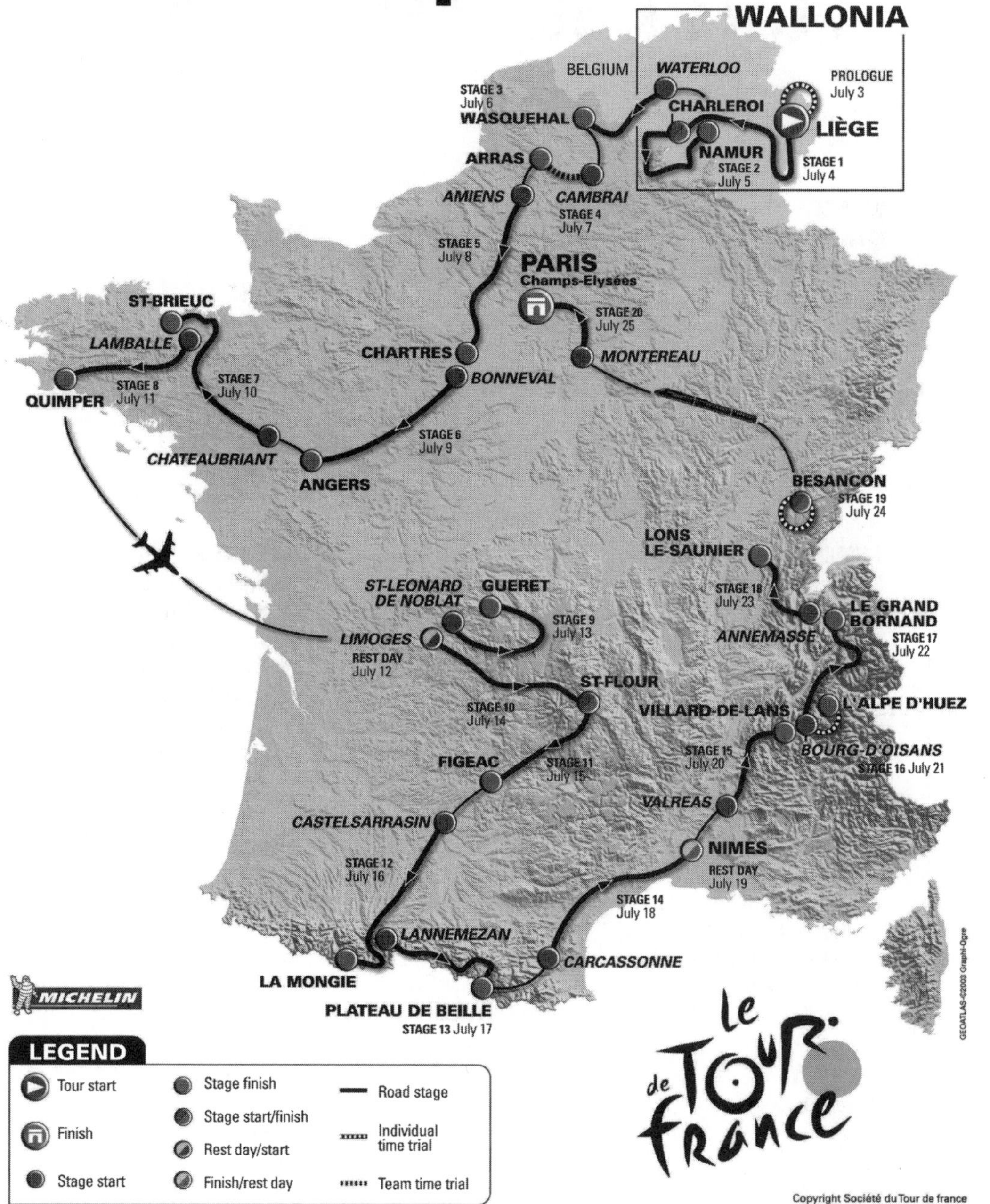

2004 Tour de France
Start List

U.S. POSTAL–BERRY FLOOR
(team manager: Johan Bruyneel)
1. LANCE ARMSTRONG (USA)
2. José Azevedo (Por)
3. Manuel Beltran (Sp)
4. Viatcheslav Ekimov (Rus)
5. GEORGE HINCAPIE (USA)
6. FLOYD LANDIS (USA)
7. Benjamin Noval (Sp)
8. Pavel Padrnos (Cze)
9. José Luis Rubiera (Sp)

T-MOBILE
(team manager: Mario Kummer)
11. Jan Ullrich (G)
12. Rolf Aldag (G)
13. Santiago Botero (Col)
14. Giuseppe Guerini (I)
15. Sergueï Ivanov (Rus)
16. Matthias Kessler (G)
17. Andreas Klöden (G)
18. Daniele Nardello (I)
19. Erik Zabel (G)

PHONAK
(team manager: Alvaro Pino)
21. TYLER HAMILTON (USA)
22. Martin Elmiger (Swi)
23. Santos Gonzalez (Sp)
24. Bert Grabsch (G)
25. José Enrique Gutierrez (Sp)
26. Nicolas Jalabert (F)
27. Oscar Pereiro (Sp)
28. Santiago Perez (Sp)
29. Oscar Sevilla (Sp)

EUSKALTEL-EUSKADI
(team manager: Julian Gorospe)
31. Iban Mayo (Sp)
32. Iker Camano (Sp)
33. David Etxebarria (Sp)
34. Unai Etxebarria (Vz)
35. Iker Flores (Sp)
36. Iñigo Landaluze (Sp)
37. Egoi Martinez (Sp)
38. Haimar Zubeldia (Sp)

FASSA BORTOLO
(team manager: Alberto Volpi)
41. Alessandro Petacchi (I)
42. Marzio Bruseghin (I)
43. Fabian Cancellara (Swi)
44. Juan Antonio Flecha (Sp)
45. Aitor González (Sp)
46. Kim Kirchen (Lux)
47. Filippo Pozzato (I)
48. Matteo Tosatto (I)
49. Marco Velo (I)

CRÉDIT AGRICOLE
(team manager: Roger Legeay)
51. Christophe Moreau (F)
52. Alexandre Botcharov (Rus)
53. Julian Dean (Nzl)
54. Pierrick Fédrigo (F)
55. Patrice Halgand (F)
56. Sébastien Hinault (F)
57. Thor Hushovd (Nor)
58. Sébastien Joly (F)
59. Benoît Salmon (F)

CSC
(team manager: Bjarne Riis)
61. Ivan Basso (I)
62. Kurt-Asle Arvesen (Nor)
63. Michele Bartoli (I)
64. BOBBY JULICH (USA)
65. Andrea Peron (I)
66. Jakob Piil (Den)
67. Carlos Sastre (Sp)
68. Nicki Sörensen (Den)
69. Jens Voigt (G)

ILLES BALEARS–BANESTO
(team manager: Eusebio Unzue)
71. Francisco Mancebo (Sp)
72. Daniel Becke (G)
73. Vicente Garcia Acosta (Sp)
74. José Iván Gutierrez (Sp)
75. Vladimir Karpets (Rus)
76. Denis Menchov (Rus)
77. Aïtor Osa (Sp)
78. Mikel Pradera (Sp)
79. Xabier Zandio (Sp)

GEROLSTEINER
(team manager: Christian Henn)
81. Georg Totschnig (Aut)
82. René Haselbacher (Aut)
83. Danilo Hondo (G)
84. Sebastian Lang (G)
85. Sven Montgomery (Swi)
86. Uwe Peschel (G)
87. Ronny Scholz (G)
88. Fabian Wegmann (G)
89. Peter Wrolich (Aut)

COFIDIS
(team manager: Francis Van Londersele)
91. Stuart O'Grady (Aus)
92. Frédéric Bessy (F)
93. Jimmy Casper (F)
94. Christophe Edaleine (F)
95. Jimmy Engoulvent (F)
96. Dmitriy Fofonov (Kaz)
97. David Moncoutié (F)
98. Janek Tombak (Est)
99. Peter Farazijn (B)

QUICK STEP–DAVITAMON
(team manager: Serge Parsani)
101. Richard Virenque (F)
102. Paolo Bettini (I)
103. Tom Boonen (B)
104. Davide Bramati (I)
105. Laurent Dufaux (Swi)
106. Servais Knaven (Nl)
107. Juan Miguel Mercado (Sp)
108. Michael Rogers (Aus)
109. Stefano Zanini (I)

LIBERTY SEGUROS
(team manager: Manolo Saiz)
111. Roberto Heras (Sp)
112. Dariusz Baranowski (Pol)
113. Allan Davis (Aus)
114. Igor González de Galdeano (Sp)
115. Jan Hruska (Cze)
116. Isidro Nozal (Sp)
117. Marcos Serrano (Sp)
118. CHRISTIAN VANDE VELDE (USA)
119. Angel Vicioso (Sp)

BRIOCHES LA BOULANGÈRE
(team manager: Thierry Bricaud)
121. Sylvain Chavanel (F)
122. Walter Bénéteau (F)
123. Anthony Charteau (F)
124. Maryan Hary (F)
125. Laurent Lefèvre (F)
126. Jérôme Pineau (F)
127. Franck Renier (F)
128. Didier Rous (F)
129. Thomas Voeckler (F)

ALESSIO-BIANCHI
(team manager: Bruno Cenghialta)
131. Magnus Bäckstedt (Swe)
132. Fabio Baldato (I)
133. Alessandro Bertolini (I)
134. Pietro Caucchioli (I)
135. Martin Hvastija (Slo)
136. Marcus Ljungqvist (Swe)
137. Claus Michael Moller (Den)
138. Andrea Noè (I)
139. Scott Sunderland (Aus)

AG2R PRÉVOYANCE
(team manager: Vincent Lavenu)
141. Laurent Brochard (F)
142. Mikel Astarloza (Sp)
143. Samuel Dumoulin (F)
144. Stéphane Goubert (F)
145. Jaan Kirsipuu (Est)
146. Yuriy Krivtsov (Ukr)
147. Jean-Patrick Nazon (F)
148. Nicolas Portal (F)
149. Mark Scanlon (Ire)

RABOBANK
(team manager: Erik Breukink)
151. LEVI LEIPHEIMER (USA)
152. Michael Boogerd (Nl)
153. Bram De Groot (Nl)
154. Erik Dekker (Nl)
155. Karsten Kroon (Nl)
156. Marc Lotz (Nl)
157. Grischa Niermann (G)
158. Michael Rasmussen (Den)
159. Marc Wauters (B)

FDJEUX.COM
(team manager: Marc Madiot)
161. Bradley McGee (Aus)
162. Sandy Casar (F)
163. Baden Cooke (Aus)
164. Carlos Da Cruz (F)
165. Bernhard Eisel (Aut)
166. Frédéric Guesdon (F)
167. Christophe Mengin (F)
168. Jean-Cyril Robin (F)
169. Matthew Wilson (Aus)

SAECO
(team manager: Giuseppe Martinelli)
171. Gilberto Simoni (I)
172. Stefano Casagranda (I)
173. Mirko Celestino (I)
174. Salvatore Commesso (I)
175. Gerrit Glomser (A)
176. David Loosli (Swi)
177. Jörg Ludewig (G)
178. Evgueni Petrov (Rus)
179. Marius Sabaliauskas (Lit)

LOTTO-DOMO
(team manager: Claude Criquielion)
181. Robbie McEwen (Aus)
182. Christophe Brandt (B)
183. Nick Gates (Aus)
184. Thierry Marichal (B)
185. Axel Merckx (B)
186. Koos Moerenhout (Nl)
187. Wim Vansevenant (B)
188. Rik Verbrugghe (B)
189. Aart Vierhouten (Nl)

DOMINA VACANZE
(team manager: Antonio Salutini)
191. Mario Cipollini (I)
192. Gian Matteo Fagnini (I)
193. Massimo Giunti (I)
194. Sergio Marinangeli (I)
195. Massimiliano Mori (I)
196. Michele Scarponi (I)
197. Francesco Secchiari (I)
198. Filippo Simeoni (I)
199. Paolo Valoti (I)

RAGT SEMENCES–MG ROVER
(team manager: Jean-Luc Jonrond)
201. Christophe Rinero (F)
202. Guillaume Auger (F)
203. Pierre Bourquenoud (Swi)
204. Gilles Bouvard (F)
205. Sylvain Calzati (F)
206. Frédéric Finot (F)
207. Christophe Laurent (F)
208. Ludovic Martin (F)
209. Eddy Seigneur (F)

Part II
Introduction to the Tour

Liège, a bustling city of 350,000 along the Meuse River in Belgium's Ardennes region, had never seen anything quite like the Tour de France. True, the city has hosted the annual start and finish of the Liège-Bastogne-Liège spring cycling classic since 1892. But popular as that race may be, it was nothing compared to the invasion underway for the "Grand Départ" of the 2004 Tour de France.

For days preceding the start of the race, racing fans from Europe, North America, Australia, Japan, and other nations had been pouring into the lively city. Bars were packed with rowdy cycling fans and the streets were alive with evidence of the Tour's arrival. Store windows were decorated with bike racing themes, temporary fencing was in place for the prologue, and large-format video screens were being erected around the course. The streets were choked with the buses, trucks, cars, and caravans of the Tour's supporting cast, the newspaper, television, and radio reporters, the team support members and sponsors, the Tour VIPs, and the rest of the cast of thousands who make up the rolling three-week carnival that is the Tour. There was a Friday night concert downtown and the anticipation for the start of the race on Saturday rocked and rattled the foundation of the old city.

The Tour is the world's largest annual sporting event, and it acts every inch the part. In size it is eclipsed only by the Olympics and soccer's World Cup, but those events are held every four years. The Tour is an annual assault on the senses and sensibilities of every millimeter of the continent that it touches—unavoidable, unstoppable, and often unbelievable. Millions of viewers watch it daily on live broadcasts in Europe, the Americas, and Australia. More importantly, an estimated 15 million spectators line the byways of France each July to watch the race and its associated spectacle zoom by. The Tour is indeed much more than a bicycle race; it has become a cultural and historic event for the passionate French public that in its own way defines a small part of what it is to be French. As much as the Tour takes over the country, the country gives itself to the Tour.

In the Tour's 101-year history, the race has been held every year since 1903 except when war interrupted in 1915–18 and again in 1940–46. In the 90 editions of the race through 2003, athletes raced an estimated 350,000 kilometers; it would be about the same distance to pedal to the moon. About 10,000 racers have competed in the Tour, with 250 different racers taking the maillot jaune, sometimes just for one day.

The Tour's immense size has made it a virtual city within itself, jumping from one host town to another in what is one of Europe's most colorful events. This roving village boasts a population of about 4,000 people. With 370 different press agencies, newspapers, magazines, and Web sites, 70 national and international radio stations and 75 television broadcasting channels beaming the images worldwide, the press entourage alone tops 2,200 journalists and support staff. Throw in each team's respective managers, sport directors, mechanics, drivers, soigneurs, physiotherapists, press officers, and chefs, and that number is bolstered by another 350.

The Tour de France organization also boasts its own platoon of staff, with 100 permanent and another 200 temporary staff members working the race. To help ensure safety, 45 motorcycle police from the *Gardes Républicains* patrol the race as it snakes down the roads. There are another 9,000 police and 12,000 *gendarmes* that work at some point during the course of the three-week Tour.

The publicity caravan—a fan favorite that plows ahead of the race dishing out 11 million trinkets and silly gifts to spectators lining the course—features 200 vehicles and stretches out for more than 20 kilometers preceding the race. In 2004, companies paid $25,000 each to have three vehicles in the caravan and there were 42 different businesses represented.

Each day, the Tour's support staff erects and tears down miles of fencing along the course as well as the temporary structures that make up the start and finish-line podiums and VIP villages at the start and finish. As soon as the riders zip away from a stage start, crews immediately dismantle everything, pack it into trucks and drive to the next day's start. At the finish, the process repeats itself and crews skip ahead to the next day's finish.

Of the enormity of Planet Tour 2004—the thousands of staffers and followers, the tons of equipment, the phalanxes of vehicles, and the millions of spectators—only 188 were actual bicycle racers.

Lance Armstrong doesn't like press conferences, even though most press hacks are quick to say he gives the best in the business. While many bike riders can be boring stiffs with little to say, Armstrong always has something on his mind, and almost everything he says is interesting, no matter the topic.

This year, however, Armstrong wasn't giving away much. Two days before the start of the prologue, a tanned, rested, and ready Armstrong reluctantly faced the world's press in a cramped convention center 5 kilometers north of Liège, and kept most of his comments to words of one syllable.

"I feel strong, I feel healthy. I feel stronger and healthier than previous years," Armstrong said. "It will be the hardest Tour yet. This race will be tight. It will be very hard to win. Right now I feel very good. Maybe in three weeks' time I'll have a different answer."

Despite his growing celebrity status, Armstrong was hesitant to make bold statements about his status among the deities of cycling. As he prepared his assault on an unprecedented sixth straight victory, Armstrong shied away from discussing his place in history.

"The word 'legend' is more than just six letters. That's a big, big word, and I'm not sure I'm ready to talk about that now," he said. "If July 25 comes around and I'm in the yellow jersey, we can talk about a record sixth, but for now that's a daunting task and one that I prefer to simplify and focus on day by day."

On the eve of the 91st Tour, many of Europe's top cycling gurus couldn't decide whether an American surpassing cycling's legends was a good thing or not. "I hope that Lance does not win the sixth Tour," said Walter Godefroot, the Belgian director of Jan Ullrich's T-Mobile team. "It wouldn't be correct that Armstrong wins because he comes from America, and there's not a rich cycling culture there. It would be unfair to the cycling fans in Europe who love the sport."

Armstrong has often butted heads with the conventions of European cycling. Everything from his preparation and attitude to his singular focus on the Tour while ignoring other important races such as the Giro d'Italia and the world championships have irked many traditionalists. Manolo Saiz, the Spanish manager of the Liberty Seguros team, said, for example, that Armstrong has done little to support cycling. "Lance is a great champion, but he's also selfish in his vision. He's taken a lot from cycling, but he's given very little back," Saiz told Belgian journalists. "It's the difference between European culture and the American way of thinking. Maybe I am wrong, but I hope that Armstrong is not the first to win six times."

Other insiders, though, did indeed believe Armstrong to be a worthy champion. Bjarne Riis, the Dane who beat five-time winner Miguel Induráin in the 1996 Tour, said modern cycling requires a different style of racing. "It's unfair to

TYLER HAMILTON—PHONAK

Getting Ready to Ride

June has been a little hectic. We started out the month in the Alps previewing the Tour de France climbs. Our training camp finished just in time for the challenging one-day Classique des Alps race, which I decided to sit out since I had done so much riding in the days preceding. But it was a successful race for our team, with four Phonak guys in the top ten. My teammate Oscar Pereiro won, which was a big victory for the entire organization.

So we headed to the Dauphiné Libéré a day later on a high note. My personal goal was to try and test myself as well as some new equipment in the prologue and in the time trial on Mont Ventoux. Both outings went okay, and I was happy to see my form was where it needed to be, if not a little ahead of schedule. It's difficult to come down off the spring season and then try to peak again for the Tour. Most guys don't want to show up for the prologue with 100 percent of their firing power. It's better to find the final percentage of your form during the race, getting stronger as it progresses. Otherwise, you will be suffering by the final week. That's my plan—90 to 95 percent at the start and 100 percent by the last week. I'll let you know how it goes.

This year's Tour is almost two races. The first 10 days and second 10 days are totally different. With all the serious climbing stacked at the end of the race, the final stages promise to be a bit of a suffer-fest. There are a number of favorites given the way the course

compare Lance to the other generations. Everything is different today," said Riis, who manages Team CSC. "Lance is the most professional, hardworking racer. You cannot say he doesn't deserve to win because he is the best right now."

For his part, Armstrong has never worried much about what others think. At the end of last year's Tour victory, Armstrong said he would be content to let the historians write about his place in Tour lore. He had more immediate concerns. At 32, Armstrong realized he'd reached an important milestone in cycling history. None of the previous five-time winners won after the age of 31. Jacques Anquetil, the first five-time champion, capped out at 30. For Eddy Merckx, a Belgian who won five Tours in seven starts, his last victory came at age 29. Bernard Hinault, the last Frenchman to win a Tour, was 30, while five-straight winner Miguel Induráin last won at 31.

Armstrong was undaunted. "My body's changed. I feel tighter," he said. "I'm not that old, I'm 32. I started young. I quit most of those early Tours I started, so I shouldn't count all of them. Four Tours before I got sick, then I rode five that were okay."

has been designed, so the race could be wide open going into the final week. As a fan, I can't remember ever looking forward to a Tour de France as much as I am this year. As a rider, well, let's just say, I'm glad most of my teeth are already capped. I think all the riders entering the race this year know they are going to be enduring a significant amount of pain . . . but I'm not going to dwell on that until I have to.

If you can't make it to the race but want to see some of the suffering live and on the big screen, the Tyler Hamilton Foundation, in conjunction with Regal Cinemedia and OLN, will be hosting a live showing of stage 13, which finishes atop Plateau de Beille in the Pyrénées. This should be a great stage to see, as it's the most difficult mountaintop finish prior to the Alps.

After the Dauphiné I headed to Italy to ride, test, and motor pace with my coach. He's a bit of a slave driver. Normally, when I'm motor pacing with my wife, I just yell to her to go faster or slower depending on how I'm feeling. But Cecco is in charge of the pace when you ride behind him. He has an SRM monitor on his scooter that reads my data, so he can track exactly how I'm doing as we go. He can see my watts, speed, heart rate, and cadence, so he knows when he has me at my limit, and he likes to keep me on the edge. He's amazing. He can do 6 hours of motor pacing without blinking an eye, although it would be safe to say by the end of one of our training rides, we're

continued ›

Each of the previous five-time winners who failed in their respective runs for the elusive sixth Tour victory succumbed to conditions much like Armstrong would face now—keener rivals, harder courses, and the overall weariness that comes from racing bicycles. In the past half century, just one rider, Dutchman Joop Zoetemelk, had won the Tour at any age older than 32, and he was 33 when he won in 1980.

But those close to the cancer-survivor-turned-sports icon said Armstrong had worked harder than ever to be ready for a chance to make history. "He wants to win this year bad," said longtime coach and trainer Chris Carmichael. "After what happened last year, he wants to return to the Lance we saw in 2000, 2001. The standard he holds for himself is higher than anyone can put on him."

Tyler Hamilton was the center of attention when Phonak held a press conference to mark its first Tour as a team. The Swiss hearing-aid company had invested heavily in Hamilton and in doing so had earned its first bid to cycling's marquee race. For Hamilton, there was no hiding his desire. "No question, I'm here to win. I'm

both pretty worked. He's dedicated beyond belief.

I returned home to Spain this week to a bit of a crisis. Our dog, Tugboat, has been a little under the weather lately and had to spend most of last week in the veterinary clinic. At the onset it looked as though he had developed a reaction to an anti-inflammatory he was on for arthritis in his hips. But now we are not sure. He has been bleeding internally and has lost more than half of his blood, which is very scary. He seems to be getting better but is still not 100 percent. Tomorrow he'll have to head in for an internal exam that will hopefully determine why he is so sick. We are keeping our fingers crossed the diagnosis will be stomach ulcers, which are very treatable and manageable. So it will be a stressful day around our house, especially since I'm scheduled to leave for the Tour later in the afternoon.

Our team is heading up north a couple of days early to ride the team time trial course together. It's always important to do this one more time before the start. The team time trial

here with a strong team, we're motivated, and they expect me to do well. There's more pressure, but I like that," he said.

Hamilton's star was on the rise. He had become a household name in 2003 after he won a stage and finished fourth overall despite breaking his collarbone in a stage 1 pileup. Now 33, he said Armstrong's troubles in 2003 were giving him and other rivals more motivation.

"A lot of guys are licking their lips and ready to attack," Hamilton said. "A lot of people believe they have a chance. To beat Lance, you have to be not stronger than he was last year, but two years ago. Last year, he showed he was human, yet he still managed to win. I know him well and he'll be back in fighting form, so that means I have to be better than Lance was two years ago."

Hamilton was often perceived as being a "gentleman" racer, a nicer, friendlier counterpart to the sometimes cold Armstrong. But that stereotype ignored Hamilton's ambition and willingness to suffer. When a Danish journalist asked the inevitable question of whether Hamilton was too nice to win the Tour, Hamilton replied with a smile: "I've got a mean streak in me, too."

Hamilton may have believed that, but few journalists agreed. In the pre-race synopses churned out by the busy press, each of Armstrong's main rivals had acquired shorthand tags, and Hamilton was the nice guy. No matter how he might try to cast himself otherwise, Hamilton was simply too charitable with his time, too kind to his rivals, too modest of his own skills, and too polite to the press to be seen any other way.

can be a tricky event, so it's good to get as much practice in as you can.

Our final team selection was somewhat of a gut-wrenching affair. We had ten guys for nine spots. But then, this has been the case with almost every team I have ever been on. This year Cyril Dessel was left off, which was a very difficult decision for the directors. Cyril battled back from injury this spring to ride strong in the Alps camp, Classique des Alps, and the Dauphiné. He even finished 2nd in the French National Championships yesterday. He is a really talented guy, and I'm confident he'll have many, many Tour de France rides in his future.

The Phonak roster includes: Oscar Sevilla, Oscar Pereiro (OP as we call him), José Gutierrez (Guti), Nicolas Jalabert (Nico), Martin Elminger, Santi Perez, Bert Grabsch, and Santos Gonzalez.

So we're almost there. It seems like a million details, issues, and decisions have been thought through, examined, weighed, and debated in the last couple of months. But what's done is done. As I say every year, it's time to take the test. ■

And then there was Jan Ullrich, the T-Mobile leader from Germany. Ullrich was another good guy with tons of potential to win the Tour. But you never knew which Jan Ullrich would show up for the race.

The highlight of any Jan Ullrich press conference is the gut check, but not the kind when someone's courage is tested. With Ullrich, it is a literal examination of his body fat. Would the 2004 Tour see the pudgy Ullrich who feasted on cake all winter and struggled during the Tour's first two weeks to burn it off? Or would the other Ullrich show up, the one who won the Tour in 1997 and the Olympic road race in 2000?

Back with the mighty German T-Mobile team for 2004 after a year of exile with a second-rate Bianchi squad, Ullrich greeted the press with no gut, just muscle and icy confidence. "I am determined to beat Armstrong this year," promised Ullrich, a runner-up five times since his single Tour victory. "I want to fight him man-to-man and I don't want to be second again."

Ullrich's low-key determination was an encouraging sign. If he was strong, the race would not be a runaway. Hamilton, nice guy or not, could also challenge Armstrong in the mountains and time trials, assuming he stayed healthy enough to get to those stages in one piece. And Armstrong would also face another half-dozen rivals capable of knocking him off the top step of the final podium. Topping the list was Spanish rider Iban Mayo, an explosive climber who had dropped Armstrong at l'Alpe d'Huez in last year's Tour. Mayo now arrived at the 2004 Tour with an extra dose of confidence, still glowing from his victory in the Dauphiné

Libéré race in June where he had taken nearly two minutes out of the Texan in a climbing time trial at the feared Mont Ventoux, widely considered the toughest mountain climb in Europe. The press was still buzzing from that feat, and seasoned observers gave Mayo the best chance, behind Ullrich, for victory.

Other threats to Armstrong's hegemony included former teammate Roberto Heras, Russian Denis Menchov, and Italians Gilberto Simoni and Ivan Basso. All were expected to give Armstrong trouble in the steep climbs of the Pyrénées and Alps.

His rivals' strength was one thing, but what interested Armstrong more was what they had been saying all spring. "I read all these people saying Armstrong is finished, washed up," Armstrong said. "That's all I ever read." But the talk didn't bother him; in fact, he hoped there would be more of it. "It's a perfect thought for them to have," he said. "I always come back to the fact that I'm not a retired racer sitting at the bar telling stories about my glory days. I'm still here, I'm still competitive and I think I can win another one. That's where I choose to focus."

"I read all these people saying Armstrong is finished, washed up," Armstrong said. "That's all I ever read."

Despite the long list of favorites, there were some notable absentees that would surely be missed. Alexandre Vinokourov (T-Mobile) had injured his shoulder in a fall at the Tour de Suisse. Joseba Beloki, the three-time Tour podium finisher, had been unable to reestablish his form following his harrowing crash in 2003 and ultimately left his French team Brioches La Boulangère in June when it became obvious he wasn't going to be in condition to race the demanding Tour. Also absent was Cadel Evans, a promising Australian who was left off his Tour team by T-Mobile, while Danilo Di Luca (Saeco) and the entire Kelme team were victims of the Tour's policy to rid itself of anything disagreeable surrounding doping, though neither Di Luca nor the Kelme team had been proven of doing anything wrong.

Back in October of 2003, the cycling world took its first glimpse of the route for the 91st edition of cycling's most important race. Armstrong was the focus of attention as cycling's biggest names filed into the Palais des Congrès in Paris for the course unveiling.

Many were surprised by what they saw, and "unconventional" was the word quickly used to describe the 20-stage, 3,391-kilometer course that pushed counterclockwise around France, hitting the Pyrénées and then the Alps. The prologue in Liège would be followed by three opening stages that paid homage to the spring classics. Indeed, the tricky third stage would roll over a section of cobblestones—the notorious *pavé* of Paris-Roubaix—for the first time in more than two decades. Obviously, this was not going to be an average Tour.

There were more surprises as soon as stage 4, a team time trial that would introduce controversial new rules to limit the losses of teams and score the time differences on 10-second intervals based on placement. Who had ever heard of that? The Tour route then pushed across the western flank of France toward Brittany, and the flat stages just kept coming and coming. Sprinters were salivating, but the favorites were squirming in their seats. Everyone knows how nervous and stressful the first week of the Tour can be when the order of the race has yet to be established. This course would only accentuate the nervousness, with no real hills in sight until the middle of the second week, when three stages would bump over the Massif Central. But the first true climbing stage wouldn't come until stage 12 to La Mongie, nearly two full weeks after the July 3 start.

And then things would get rough. Stage 13 to Plateau de Beille looked to be a killer, with seven rated climbs in a long 205.5-kilometer course across the heart of the Pyrénées. By the time the peloton hit the Alps it would be well into the third week, with just six days of racing before the finish on the Champs-Élysées. There would be three stages in the Alps, all of them difficult. One was a summit finish to Villard-de-Lans, and another was a 204.5-kilometer marathon over the Glandon and Madeleine peaks. And then there was the blockbuster—a time trial up the 21 hairpin turns of l'Alpe d'Huez, cycling's most famous climb.

Many were puzzled by the course. Limiting losses in the team time trial? No individual time trial in the first week? All the decisive stages packed into the final week of racing? The course seemed to favor an attacking rider like Iban Mayo over the all-rounders such as Armstrong and Ullrich. Were officials trying to stack the odds against Armstrong?

One could argue that was the case. Until the thrilling and down-to-the-wire 2003 Tour—one that saw Armstrong attacked at every turn, suffering through dehydration and crashes to take his narrowest victory ever by just 61 seconds—the Tour had been in danger of becoming Armstrong's personal playground. A Tour course that did not play to Armstrong's strengths was clearly desirable.

Tour officials, however, were quick to insist they weren't trying to set the stage for an Armstrong defeat. Their only goal, they said, was to deliver another nail-biter on par with the epic 2003 battle.

"After the centenary Tour we were afraid of creating an insipid, pretty Tour," said Tour director Jean-Marie Leblanc. "That's how the idea of a time trial up l'Alpe d'Huez came about. If Armstrong wins for a sixth time, it will be historical. If he's beaten, the man who succeeds will be a hero."

The one chink in Armstrong's armor was a perceived weakness in the third week when the rigors and stresses of racing across the narrow byways of France finally started to take their draining toll on the body and spirit. Armstrong had always enjoyed the protection of his loyal U.S. Postal Service teammates, but late in the 2000 Tour Armstrong struggled over the Joux-Plane climb high in the French Alps, essentially "bonking" after not eating enough when an angry Marco Pantani undertook a long solo attack on the stage into Morzine. Armstrong did his best to limit the damage, but lost 1:37 to Ullrich. Armstrong went on to win his second Tour by 6:02, but that day on Joux-Plane provided a glimpse of perhaps his only vulnerability. And now the 2004 Tour route was stacked much the same way.

"The last week looks really tough, the toughest we have ever done," Armstrong admitted. "It will be much better to have a stronger second half than a strong first half," he said.

But that was in October. Now the troops were assembled in July, and after months of talking, it was finally time to start racing.

Chapter 6: Week One
Ready for Blastoff

PROLOGUE

ARMSTRONG SCORES AN EARLY PSYCHOLOGICAL ADVANTAGE

In the rolling, three-week chess match that is the Tour de France, Lance Armstrong is the master tactician. His mind games begin months before, and once the firefight actually commences, his rivals often don't know what to think. This was certainly the case by the time Pierre Bourquenoud, a Swiss rider on the RAGT team, rolled down the start ramp at 4:01 p.m. in sunny Liège to kickstart the 91st Tour.

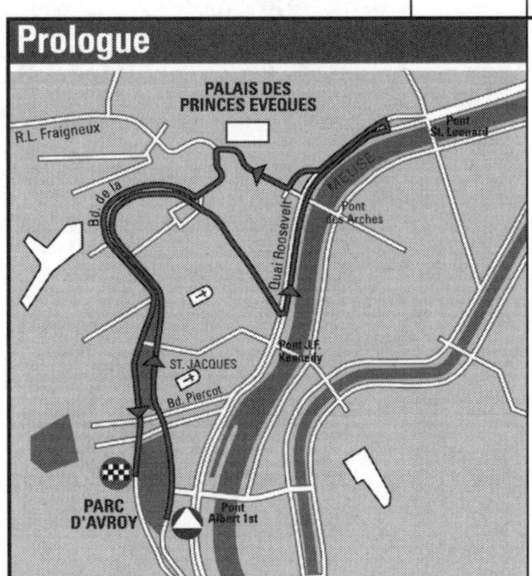

Bolstered by Armstrong's narrow, 61-second victory in 2003, nearly a dozen riders came to Belgium believing in their chances. Armstrong's nearly 2-minute loss to Iban Mayo in the climbing time trial at Mont Ventoux in June's Dauphiné Libéré raised further questions about his form.

Off the bike, Armstrong was fighting to shake doping allegations made in *L.A. Confidentiel: Les secrets de Lance Armstrong*, a controversial book written by veteran Irish journalist David Walsh and French sportswriter Pierre Ballester, published in France just two weeks before the start of the race. Armstrong, who has never failed a doping test, vehemently defended his name. "I can absolutely confirm that we do not use doping products," he said defiantly during a press conference in Maryland, where it was announced that Discovery Communications would take over for departing team title sponsor U.S. Postal Service at the end of 2004.

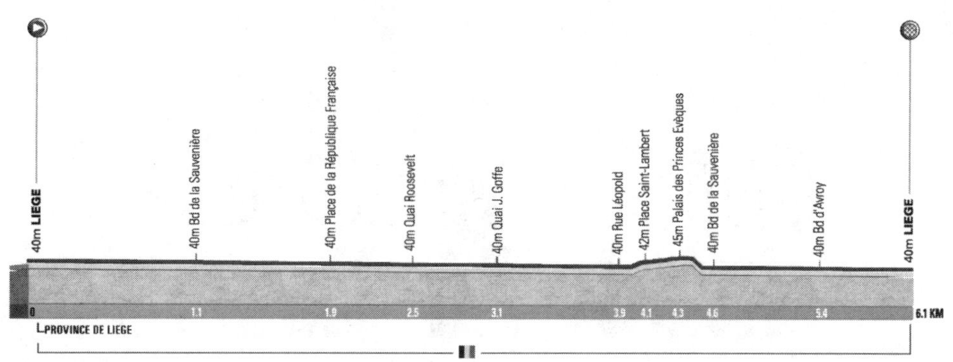

The weight of history was also tugging on Armstrong. None of cycling's mythic champions were able to win the elusive sixth Tour. As an upstart American was poised to break the record, some big names in the cycling community were openly wishing he wouldn't be able to succeed where Anquetil, Merckx, Hinault, and Induráin had failed.

So which Armstrong would show up for the flat 6.1-kilometer prologue? That soon became clear, as Armstrong pushed all the anger, frustration, and resentment of the previous weeks into his pedals and delivered a sharp blow to his rivals. While Tour rookie Fabian Cancellara, a 23-year-old Swiss rider for Fassa Bortolo, stopped the clock at 6 minutes, 50 seconds to serve up a fresh-faced winner, Armstrong roared across the line just 2 seconds slower—and 15 seconds faster than archrival Jan Ullrich (T-Mobile). Armstrong rode aggressively and wanted the win, smacking his right fist on his handlebars after crossing the line.

"I felt strong, my legs felt good. When I was warming up, I knew I was going to have a good day," Armstrong said. "I would have liked to have won, but the most important thing is that I felt good on the bike. I had good sensations."

While the time differences marked in a prologue might seem insignificant in the face of three hard weeks of racing, Armstrong's powerful ride let the world know just where he stood.

BUZZED IN LIÈGE

The Tour de France has a rich history in Belgium, and locals were making the most of the festive atmosphere. Crowds estimated at 200,000 lined the course, with many sitting in sidewalk cafés or quaffing beer along roadside stands to get lubed for only the third Tour to start in Belgium.

The Tour first ventured into Belgium in 1947 for two stages, from Lille to Brussels and from Brussels to Luxembourg. Since that modest start, 97 stages in 38 Tours have started or finished in the cycling-crazed nation of 11 million. The Tour has concluded 18 times with a Belgian champion—the most by any nation except France, which has 36. Five were won by cycling great Eddy Merckx, with the last coming with Lucien Van Impe in 1976. The green points jersey has been taken 18 times by Belgians and the polka-dot best climber's jersey 11 times. The Belgians have also won their fair share of stages, claiming 447 stage victories from 1909 to 2001, when three Belgians won one stage each.

Despite the rich culture, Belgian cycling has taken its lumps recently. Even with the last-minute inclusion of Peter Farazijn, only eight Belgians started the 2004 Tour, matching an all-time low set in the previous Tour. Following the retirement of Merckx and Van Impe, there hasn't been a Belgian podium finisher since 1981. The best in the past decade was 7th in 1993 by Johan Bruyneel, now the directeur sportif of Armstrong's Postal team.

"Look at Postal, everything is for Lance. That's how you win the Tour."

Despite some lackluster Tour results recently, Belgian fans still love their cycling, and they swarmed around the team buses as riders warmed up on rollers. At Postal Service, security guards fought in vain to keep fans behind fences, and crowds spilled over into the warm-up area of Gerolsteiner next door.

Udo Bölts, a former German pro who is now an assistant director for Gerolsteiner, pushed through the crowd to ask Armstrong to autograph a saddle. A former teammate of Jan Ullrich, Bölts said he believed Armstrong would take another yellow jersey. "Armstrong's strength is in his heart and mind. Everyone is talking about Ullrich being skinnier, but Armstrong's best advantage is inside," he said, before questioning T-Mobile's tactics. "I cannot understand why Erik Zabel is even on the team. He probably won't even win a stage and Jan will need help in the mountains. Look at Postal, everything is for Lance. That's how you win the Tour."

Postal Service had indeed arrived with a strong team, but in the prologue it was every man for himself. Once again Armstrong bucked Tour tradition, refusing to wear the maillot jaune as defending champion, instead preferring to fight for cycling's most treasured prize. "I haven't earned the yellow jersey," Armstrong explained. "I think it's right and fair to start in the blue jersey of Postal and try to earn the yellow jersey." He started last as defending champion, wearing an aerodynamic full bodysuit and a Giro helmet painted with the stars and stripes.

THE BATTLE BEGINS

Disaster can strike at any time in the Tour, sometimes even before it starts. Matthew White, an Australian on the Cofidis team who was anxious to make his Tour debut, broke his clavicle after crashing on some electrical cables lying across

TYLER HAMILTON—PHONAK

And We're Off!

It feels good to have officially started the race. The days leading up to the Tour always seem like such chaos. You never stop moving. There is always somewhere to be and someone who needs to speak with you. It's a hectic pace to keep when all you really want to do is rest. Three long weeks are ahead, so it's important to maintain a balance.

Our camp gathered a little early on Tuesday morning to do some last-minute previewing of the team time trial course together. It's always a bit of a challenge to figure out the riding order, so it was good to have the chance to fine-tune things a bit while riding on the actual course.

We also spent an afternoon previewing stage 3, which will feature two pretty significant sections of pavé. It's only a few kilometers of cobblestones total, but they are pretty tough, and I got blisters on my hands just riding them in training. I had to hold the bars tightly to keep control of my bike, which was bouncing all over the place. Everyone keeps talking about the second half of the Tour being where the real racing will be done, but there will be plenty of hurdles to jump before anyone can get to that.

Today's prologue course was pancake flat. Prologues are not always my specialty, and I tend to favor those that are a little more technical or feature a bit of a climb. I tried out some longer cranks thinking they'd help me go faster on the long straightaways, but in retrospect, they may have cost me too much in the corners. I would have preferred to have placed in the top ten,

the road while doing his warm-up before the prologue. White's last-minute replacement was Peter Farazijn, a Belgian rider who just happened to be the team member in closest proximity to the start.

With lead reserve Iñigo Cuesta in Switzerland, frantic team officials finally reached Farazijn, who was watching a car rally with his buddies near his home in western Belgium. Police motorcycles escorted the 35-year-old as he made the 200-kilometer drive across Belgium to reach Liège just in time for the start. Tour officials allowed him to switch start places with Jimmy Casper. After such an unexpected trip, Farazijn was forced to ride White's bike but managed to finish third from last.

More technical than last year's prologue in Paris, the Liège start featured sharp turns, a tricky section over cobblestones, and a long curving section that was ridden in both directions. Gusty winds buffeted the flat course, but sunny skies welcomed 188 riders from 21 teams despite forecasted rain.

Last year's prologue winner, Brad McGee (fdjeux.com), was starting as the favorite, but the Aussie had shed nearly six pounds since last year's winning ride, mak-

but I'm satisfied to have finished in the hunt—inside the top 20. There's a long way to go in this race, so it's not worth beating myself up over a few seconds lost today.

I was able to race on my new time trial bike this afternoon. It's a newly designed frame from BMC, custom made in Switzerland by a carbon fiber company that also works with teams from Formula One auto racing. The frame features an integrated fork design that eliminates the need for a stem, so it looks and feels pretty different. It's the most aerodynamic time trial bike I've ever ridden.

On behalf of my dog Tugboat, I want to extend a huge thank-you for the well-wishes, notes, and e-mails I've received regarding his recent illness. An endoscopy preformed early last week showed he is suffering from multiple stomach ulcers that developed after he had an allergic reaction to medication he was taking. He's still making daily vet visits for treatment but hopes to be well enough to catch a couple of the Pyrénées stages of the Tour.

I also want to send my condolences out to the family and friends of Stive Vermaut. Stive was a teammate of mine back on U.S. Postal, and I have great memories of racing alongside him. He supported me with the strength of two men in the Dauphiné Libéré in 2000; he was a big factor in my overall victory in the race that year. I'll never forget how hard he rode, and how much work he did to support me there. He was a very talented rider who surely would have accomplished great things had he not suffered from a hereditary heart condition. His career and life ended far too early. ■

ing him lighter in the mountains but potentially less powerful in the prologue. McGee, who spent all day Friday in bed with a crippling headache, back pain, and an attack of pre-race nerves, came through at 6:59—one of four riders under 7 minutes.

McGee's superb ride was expected, but the prologue delivered a surprise winner in the 23-year-old Fabian Cancellara. Starting 43rd from last, the Tour rookie used his time trial prowess to post the third-fastest time in Tour history at 53.561 kilometers per hour. (Chris Boardman holds the record at 55.152 kilometers per hour, set in 1994 on a 7.2-kilometer course in Lille.)

"I'm the happiest man in the world," beamed the exuberant Swiss, who last year won the opening prologues in the Tour of Romandie and the Tour of Belgium. "My aim was to go out there and win today, and I've done it. And beating Armstrong, I can't believe it."

Cancellara enjoyed some quality podium time, snatching up every jersey in the offing, the maillot jaune of the leader, of course, along with the green jersey and the white jersey of the best young rider.

MAGNUS BÄCKSTEDT, ALESSIO-BIANCHI

Back in the Saddle Again

I did a pretty normal prologue time trial today. I wasn't all that lucky with the wind and the weather. If you look at the results, it looks like the riders who went off early turned in better times than even some of the big specialists at the end. The first guys had a pretty nice tailwind going out, then things shifted a bit and it felt like it was either a headwind or a crosswind. I doubt I got 200 meters of tailwind throughout. Still, I have no complaints. It was a reasonable ride and 6 kilometers doesn't exactly create a huge gap, now, does it? I finished in 62nd, at 28 seconds. All told, I'm pretty happy with it.

For a lot of us who know him, the big news of the day is also the worst news of the day. I'm sure you already know that poor Matt White crashed this afternoon before the start and is out of the Tour. His team managed to get Peter Farazijn down here to replace him in time for the start, but Matt is out with a broken collarbone.

He's been wanting to ride in the Tour ever since he became a pro, and here he was, only to have it ripped away from him a couple of hours before the start. I feel so sorry for him, because I know how much he wanted this. It's one of those things that's just not supposed to happen.

It's been a tough time since the Giro for me. I had a little bit of a time of it trying to train. I've had some problems with my back, and I hadn't really been able to train at 100 percent until Route du Sud a couple of weeks ago. I sort of forced my way through that and then went up to Sweden to get my back looked at by a couple of specialists. They managed to get my back straight and sort my muscles out. I had been completely twisted on my bike. It was mayhem. This line of work does take a bit out of a guy sometimes.

Part of the problem, it turns out, was that the arches on my feet would

But as with any recent Tour prologue, the real interest lay in how a horde of favorites would stand up against Armstrong. Ullrich, Hamilton, Mayo, Leipheimer, Heras, Julich—these were the men, and their times against the clock would be used by many wags to predict the final outcome of the race.

Surprisingly, most wilted in the face of Armstrong's grim determination, with the Texan scoring some important psychological points on this first day of racing. "Now we're seeing the real Armstrong," Mayo told Spanish journalists as Armstrong sped past him in the finish zone. "I think Armstrong didn't try at Mont Ventoux. Everyone knows the Tour is the only race for this guy."

Tyler Hamilton (Phonak) and Mayo both lost valuable ground, with the New Englander finishing 18th, at 18 seconds slower, while Mayo was 26th, at 21

begin to collapse after an hour or two on the bike. One of the recommendations was to have insoles—orthotics some call them—made for my cycling shoes. That helped, but it took awhile to straighten everything else out.

Anyway, I feel pretty good right now and felt much better on the bike last week at nationals in Sweden. I was getting all the power that I had into the pedals and I felt good. I feel good this week, too, and even though I have fewer kilometers than I'd like, I think I can ride into the Tour and be up to speed quite soon.

Alessio-Bianchi has a good group here at the Tour. We have three GC contenders: Pietro Caucchioli and Claus Michael Moller, who are probably going to be our two main guys, and Andrea Noe'. I don't know what Andrea's form is like right now, but Caucchioli is riding really well; he looks good.

We also have Marcus Ljungqvist, my roommate from the Giro. Scotty Sunderland is back in the Tour, and he's dead keen on riding again. We have the Slovenian guy, Martin Hvastija, who is always, always, always riding strong, no matter what. He's always up there and always giving it large every single day. He's strong in the flats. He can do lead-outs. He can do pretty much everything. And Fabio Baldato is here and brings lots of experience to the team. All in all we have a solid crew, and we all have a good laugh when we're together.

My personal goal is to try and get a stage win here. We'll see how it goes these next few days. We are up in my territory and the wind, it seems, has been very strong, which should suit me. I will do what I can to get into a good break. If I manage that, who knows what can happen? Over these next couple of days—up until the team time trial—I will definitely give it everything I've got and try to do some kind of damage in the race.

Wish us luck. It's going to be a long three weeks. ■

seconds back. Roberto Heras (Liberty Seguros) and Gilberto Simoni (Saeco) didn't even make the first page of the results sheet.

"For all the people who had doubts about Lance Armstrong, I was one of those people, too," Armstrong said. "I had doubts after Ventoux, to lose 2 minutes to Mayo, to Hamilton, I was sitting at home thinking, 'What the hell happened?' So I don't blame anyone for thinking that. It was huge to have a big ride."

Of the other Americans, Rabobank's Levi Leipheimer (who got some extra energy during his warm-up listening to Limp Bizkit on his MP3 player) posted a solid ride to slip into the top 15. Bobby Julich was also happy to be back after being overlooked by Telekom for the 2003 Tour. The 32-year-old American stopped the clock in 9th at 7:02, and four Team CSC riders finished in the top 15.

CHRISTIAN VANDE VELDE—LIBERTY SEGUROS

At Last, We Begin

We finally started the Tour de France, thank god. It's been a long week for everyone, and we've all been sitting around the hotel waiting for dinner to come around. It's been a lot of hurry up and wait, wait and then hurry. The beginning of the week was even longer for me as I was waiting next to the phone. It came down to the wire whether I'd make the team. Given the spring that I had, I experienced some serious doubts up until Monday, when I finally got the call.

The week before the Tour, team members receive all sorts of new clothes, bikes, shoes, sunglasses, and often with new and different sponsors' names on them. So we have to make sure we're wearing the right stuff. We all received new bikes from BH. It's a Spanish bike with some serious technology going into it. It looks more like a time trial bike than a road bike, and a light one at that. We each got two of those. Most teams usually supply "climbing bikes" for their team leaders. They are a bit lighter and supposedly have better angles to make climbing easier. So everyone on the team received one of these as well.

Our mechanics haven't been bored. I've spent some time watching them

"I had a smile. I don't know if I had one on the outside, but I had one on the inside," said Julich, 3rd overall in the 1998 Tour. "It sure beat watching it on my couch like last year. Being older, I realized all the stress you put on yourself was wasted energy and you appreciate it a little more."

Armstrong, meanwhile, was hesitant to read too much into the differences, realizing that the short, punchy course favored him over riders such as Ullrich. Armstrong has won the prologue twice en route to five Tour titles while Ullrich has never won the event. "I'm a little surprised [in the time difference], but maybe it means that Jan's better prepared for longer, harder climbs, so we have to think about that," he said. "But the Tour is long. One good prologue doesn't mean you're going to win."

A strikingly lean Ullrich shrugged off the lost time, insisting the Tour will be won in the steep mountains, not on the narrow streets of Liège. Ullrich said he was coming into this Tour stronger than in any since his 1997 victory and he clearly wasn't going to sweat the losses. "I didn't want to take any unnecessary risks to avoid crashing," said the newly confident German. "This Tour will be won by minutes, not seconds. And those minutes will be in my favor, not Lance's."

For Armstrong, the strong performance marked a return to his comfort zone. After the harried 2003 Tour, he wanted to avoid the stressful battle that came

and I haven't learned a thing other than I'll never be a mechanic. These guys are machines, always changing something or swapping this with that or just putting together new bikes. Every day something has changed—different cranks, bottom brackets, cables, you name it. Our mechanic Manolo is crazy about working on the bikes and it shows.

The prologue came and went. I didn't exactly light the world on fire, but I'm happy to have the first day out of the way. Lance had a great ride and definitely started the Tour off on the right foot. Fabian Cancellara flew—almost 54 kilometers per hour. Not bad! His eyes were filled with tears and he was obviously overwhelmed with his performance. It was pretty cool to see. He deserved it today, as only Lance came close. Our team didn't have a great day, but we're definitely looking forward to the TTT.

The biggest bummer of the day was Matt White's crash. I flipped on the TV this afternoon after lunch and saw the unmistakable "baby-chick-yellow" hair of Whitey, and he was on the ground bloody. I was sick. He broke his collarbone and didn't get to start his first Tour. He will be missed by his teammates and maybe even more by the other English speakers in the peloton. I feel like I'm writing his obituary. He's still alive, but probably not happy. ■

down to the wire. As journalists and crowds pressed in on the Postal Service bus to catch a glimpse of the American hero, Armstrong stepped out after freshening up and sneaked a kiss to his girlfriend, rock singer Sheryl Crow.

The crowd cheered and Armstrong was all smiles. He hopped onto the trainer for a post-prologue cooldown and laughed as his inner circle joined him for a private moment, and 400 people craned their necks to see. Even when he doesn't win, Armstrong is still a crowd-pleaser.

PROLOGUE, LIÈGE: 1. Fabian Cancellara (Swi), Fassa Bortolo, 6.1km in 6:50 (53.6kph); **2. Lance Armstrong (USA), U.S. Postal–Berry Floor, at 0:02; 3.** Ivan Gutierrez (Sp), Illes Balears, at 0:08; **4.** Bradley McGee (Aus), fdjeux.com, at 0:09; **5.** Thor Hushovd (Nor), Crédit Agricole, at 0:10.

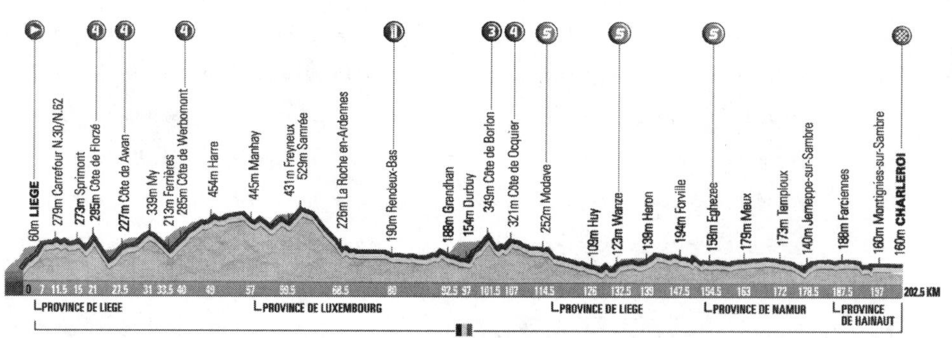

STAGE 1 | Liège to Charleroi

Opening-day jitters can have disastrous consequences at the Tour de France. A year ago, the 2003 Tour hopes of Levi Leipheimer and Tyler Hamilton were spoiled in a massive finish-line pileup into Meaux. Leipheimer was sent packing early with a cracked tailbone, while the gritty New Englander gamely fought on to finish 4th and win a stage despite riding the entire Tour with a broken clavicle.

Thankfully, the first stage of the 91st Tour didn't pack the same dramatic punch. There were no broken bones, but plenty of Tour souvenirs were collected in the forms of scraped elbows and bleeding knees.

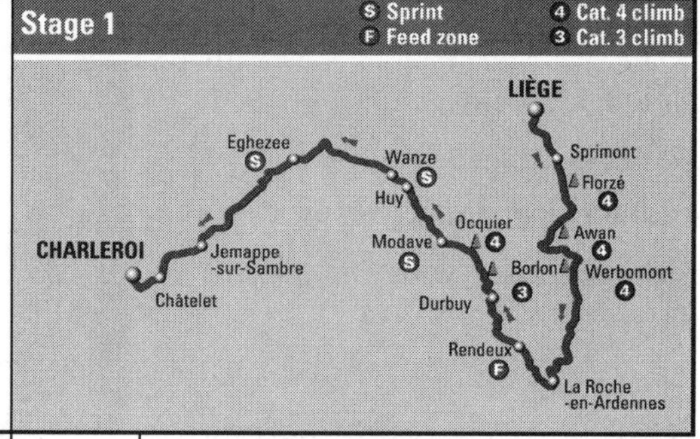

Hamilton was once again a victim of a crash, but this time it was much less serious. The 33-year-old Phonak leader came swooping into a right-hand turn with about 70 kilometers to go when he saw five riders sprawled on the pavement. His only option was to bury the bike into a ditch. "I finished the Tour's first stage better than I finished last year's stage, that's for sure," said a relieved Hamilton, who escaped with a scraped elbow and hip. "It was difficult, it was raining, it was windy, the peloton was very nervous. For a lot of riders, the first week is their only chance to win a stage, so a lot of guys are going full gas."

More crashes were in store, including two U.S. Postal Service riders, Manuel Beltrán and Benjamin Noval; three more Phonaks, Oscar Sevilla, Oscar Pereiro, and Nicolas Jalabert; Guillaume Auger (RAGT); Alessandro Bertolini (Alessio); and Nick Gates (Lotto-Domo). Gates, one of a record nine Aussies starting the Tour, crashed coming down the day's final climb and rode alone for the final 70 kilometers. Finishing the race in last place at 30:38 back, Gates was outside the time limit and eliminated by the race jury.

"The first 10 days is a race of elimination; you can't win the Tour but you can lose it," Hamilton said. "If you're already five minutes behind, it's a big problem if you want to be with the leaders by the time the race hits the mountains."

With only five minor climbs spaced along the first half of the 202.5-kilometer stage from Liège to Charleroi, riders were pressing steadily to open a gap on the rolling terrain. Prologue winner Fabian Cancellara (Fassa Bortolo) was keen on protecting his lead, and he would need to count on wile beyond his 23 years if he expected to keep the yellow tunic.

Meanwhile Bjarne Riis, the 1996 Tour champ and Team CSC director who promised that his squad would be an aggressor, quickly set his riders in motion. When French rider Walter Bénéteau (La Boulangère) made the 2004 Tour's first attack just 4 kilometers into the stage, Riis sent German rider Jens Voigt up the road.

The move was gobbled up, but Voigt went again on the Tour's first climb—the Category 4 Côte de Florzé, at 15 kilometers. Two-time World Cup champion Paolo Bettini (Quick Step), Janeck Tombak (Cofidis), Franck Renier (La Boulangère), and Tour rookie Bernhard Eisel (fdjeux.com) joined the party, and the 2004 Tour had its first serious breakaway.

The following two climbs came in quick succession—with the Cat. 4 Côte de Awan at 21 kilometers and the punchy Cat. 4 Côte de Werbomont at 33.5 kilometers—effectively slingshotting the break to a 3:45-minute gap at 55 kilometers.

Rain started to fall and temperatures hovered in the 60s, giving the stage a dark tone as the peloton drove west out of the Ardennes. Lance Armstrong, who started the day wearing the green points jersey, avoided the day's adventures and safely hovered near the front of the main bunch. "I was very nervous today because of the wind, rain, and crashes," Armstrong said. "These first days are always so nervous. Just your typical day of racing in Belgium."

Voigt, who started the day in 7th at 11 seconds back, became the road leader, while Bettini shot ahead to take the points over the day's final two climbs—enough to earn him the first King of the Mountains jersey.

The average speed for the second hour was 44.8 kilometers per hour, and riders were already struggling to match the unrelenting Tour pace. Last year's prologue winner, Brad McGee, and 2002 world champion, Mario Cipollini (Domina Vacanze), were dropped as the peloton chugged over the Borlon.

The 37-year-old Italian sprinter was struggling to regain his form after a serious crash in the Giro in May, while McGee, a decade younger than the Lion King, was enduring crippling back pain caused by, of all things, a gardening incident; he strained his back while planting olive trees in his garden a week before the Tour. "I felt like my back was cut in half. I couldn't feel my legs and I couldn't

CHRISTIAN VANDE VELDE—LIBERTY SEGUROS

It's All Relative

In a word—nervous.

I am, as is the peloton, and so are the directors—everyone is nervous. It made for a stressful first stage, and the rain didn't help. There were crashes all day, going up the hills, going down, in the flats, around corners, you name it. Allen Davis was counting his lucky stars at the end of the day. A rider crashed in front of him coming into a corner. He thought that it was curtains and was preparing for the inevitable. But the rider went down and continued with the same speed. Allen stayed behind him, and when they came into the corner he turned while the other rider went straight. Crazy. The race was hard all day long with everyone's nerves on edge. The last few kilometers were probably some of the easiest (everything is relative) as everyone was a bit spent.

Speaking of relatives, I met some of my long lost family from Belgium on the way back to the hotel. It was quite an experience to meet more or less my Grandpa's cousins. One of them was more than a little overwhelmed. He cried and kissed me and was, of course, not speaking a word of English, but I got the point. What would life be like if my great grandfather, good old Frank Vande Velde, hadn't jumped on a boat to Ellis Island? I know that I wouldn't be writing a Tour diary for *VeloNews* for sure, but maybe for *Het Volk*. ■

seem to get any power out of them," said McGee, who limped in second to last at 6:05 back. "Basically my hips have just fallen out of place. They just fall in and out of where they ought to be. Today, obviously, they were out of place."

Riders started to topple like dominoes on the rain-slicked roads. One of the worst falls involved Eisel, who clipped wheels with fellow escapee Tombak as he drifted back to speak with the team car. The 23-year-old Tour rookie instinctively shot out his left foot but slammed hard to the wet pavement, skidding off course on his back. "My team manager said, 'You go into an attack so you can get some seconds to chase for the young rider's jersey,'" said Eisel, one of 30 riders competing for the white jersey. "It was a little bit stupid because my team car was next to me and I had no place to pass the other rider, so I hit the car then the other rider."

Eisel shrugged off the fall to rejoin the Voigt move, but the peloton had awoken from its slumber. The sprinters could smell the finish line and the break was caught with less than 75 kilometers to go.

Cancellara faced a new threat to his jersey with the peloton together and two intermediate sprints still in the offing. Despite getting a lead-out from 2002 Vuelta a España champion, Aitor González, Cancellara succumbed to Thor Hushovd, the big Norwegian sprinter on Crédit Agricole.

Following his excellent ride in the prologue, Hushovd was the best-placed sprinter, starting the day in 5th at 10 seconds back. O'Grady took the points in the day's final sprint, with Cancellara in 3rd with 48 kilometers to go when Team CSC sent Jakob Piil on a flier. Catching his wheel was Belgian rider Marc Wauters (Rabobank).

This was just the kind of break that can sometimes stick. Both riders were former Tour-stage winners, with Piil winning into Marseille last year and Wauters taking an emotional victory and the yellow jersey on home soil in Antwerp in 2001. The pair nursed a 1:55 lead, but they saw it erode under pressure from Quick Step, Fassa Bortolo, and Lotto-Domo.

Alas, the duo was caught with just under 2 kilometers to go, and all eyes shifted to Fassa Bortolo and its sprinting ace Alessandro Petacchi. Everyone expected the 29-year-old Italian to pick up where he left off from his history-making run of nine stage victories at the Giro d'Italia in May. Petacchi's yellow-jersey-clad teammate, Cancellara, was at the front taking a hard pull, but the mighty Fassa Bortolo train inexplicably fizzled on the slightly uphill finish against a moderate crosswind. Without a train driving home the sprint, sprinters suddenly didn't know whose wheel to follow.

Making a bold move on the right side was 34-year-old veteran Jaan Kirsipuu (ag2r). The aging Estonian doesn't win as much as he used to, but his *palmarès* were bolstered by a nice victory ahead of Robbie McEwen (Lotto-Domo) and Hushovd. Petacchi managed a disappointing 8th.

It was Kirsipuu's fourth career Tour stage victory and the 114th of his career, ranking him as the third winningest active racer behind Cipollini and Erik Zabel. "It's not the number of wins you have, but the importance of the race you win," he said.

Cancellara survived the day in yellow thanks to smart riding, while Hushovd snatched the green jersey and clawed his way within four seconds of the young Swiss rider. The battle lines were already being drawn and this was only stage 1.

STAGE 1, LIÈGE TO CHARLEROI: 1. Jaan Kirsipuu (Est), ag2r, 202.5km in 4:40:29 (43.318kph); **2.** Robbie McEwen (Aus), Lotto-Domo; **3.** Thor Hushovd (Nor), Crédit Agricole; **4.** Danilo Hondo (G), Gerolsteiner; **5.** Jean-Patrick Nazon (F), ag2r—all same time
OVERALL: 1. Fabian Cancellara (Swi), Fassa Bortolo, 4:47:11; **2.** Hushovd, at 0:04; **3. Lance Armstrong (USA), U.S. Postal Service, at 0:10**

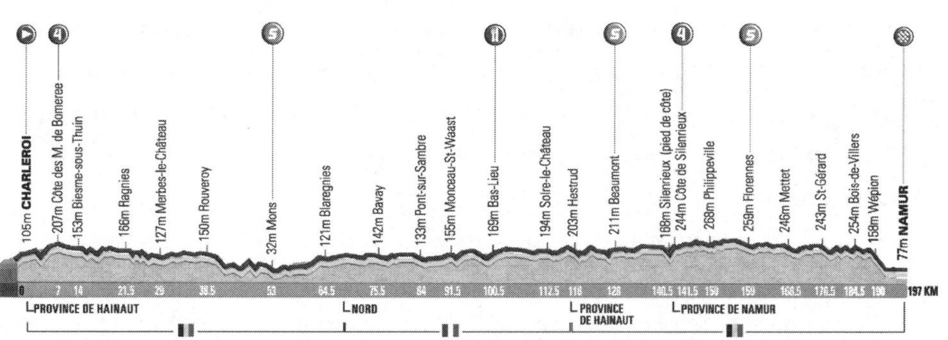

STAGE 2 | Charleroi to Namur

The third day of the 2004 Tour was a tale of two Norwegians. Thor Hushovd, a big, blond sprinter who won a Tour stage in 2002, became the first of his nation to wear cycling's most prized jersey, while Kurt-Asle Arvesen, a big, blond all-rounder on CSC, was sent hurtling to the pavement within sight of the finish line.

The 26-year-old Hushovd continued his upward trajectory that began with a fine 5th-place ride in the prologue. He chipped away at Fabian Cancellara's lead in the first stage when he grabbed the green jersey and then slipped into yellow thanks to time bonuses after finishing 2nd behind pocket-rocket Robbie McEwen.

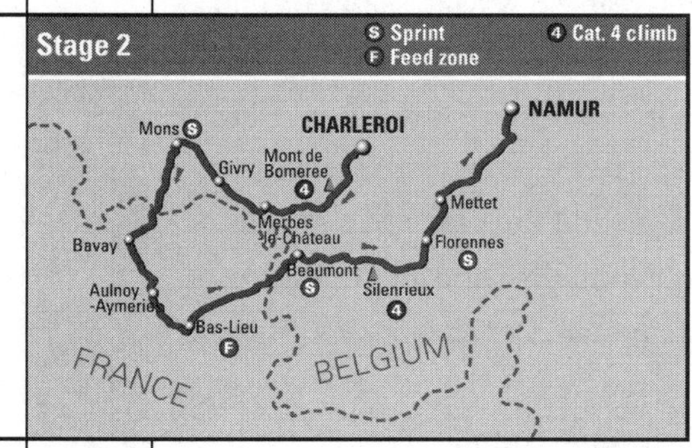

"It's the biggest thing that can happen in the Tour. I think it will change my life," said Hushovd, 4th in the green jersey competition in 2003. "I had two goals, to win another stage and win the green jersey. With the shape I have now, I will fight to keep it to Paris."

Arvesen, meanwhile, couldn't witness his compatriot make history because he was nose-down on the tarmac. Stage 1 winner, Jaan Kirsipuu, shot across the bunch to make a run for a second consecutive win and sideswiped Arvesen's front wheel in the heat of the sprint. Jimmy Casper (Cofidis) also fell. Arvesen, a former U23 world champion making his Tour debut, was left with serious cuts and abrasions to his elbow, hip, and knee.

"It was the greatest day in Norwegian cycling, but I crashed, so it wasn't so good for me," said Arvesen, who received treatments from the same osteopath who nursed Tyler Hamilton through last year's Tour. "But I'll come back, maybe make another good story."

Spills, and avoiding them, are an indispensable part of the first week of any Tour, and the Tour's hospital ward was filling up with victims. Andrea Peron, a

TYLER HAMILTON—PHONAK

Stress

The first few stages of the Tour de France are always kind of tough. They probably look easy on paper compared to the mountain stages of the Pyrénées and the Alps, but don't let the level terrain fool you.

There's no describing how nerve-wracking the opening stages of the Tour can be. For starters, there's a full field of nearly 200 guys all fired up about being at the year's biggest race. Add high speeds, rain, a bunch of crashes, spectators in the road, a good, hard chase to reel in a breakaway, and the madness that ensues before a field sprint, and you pretty much have the recipe for hard day at the office.

Stress is just as tough as any mountain pass; it'll leave you every bit as drained as riding a full day of vertical.

Road hazards

Yesterday's stage was nuts. If you saw the race on television then you already know the crowds were huge in some spots. And for some reason, there weren't barriers in every town like there usually are. This meant the folks on the side of the road were free to set up camp **in the road** while they waited for the race to come barreling through.

The peloton steamrolled through some towns like a wall stretched straight across the road. As it charged forward, fans were jumping back to get out of the way, seemingly one by one. People were literally springing from their lawn chairs at the very last second to run for safety, leaving their picnics, blankets, cameras, and whatever else behind as they did. I even saw one poor person in a wheelchair get abandoned as his companions darted for safer ground. It's a miracle no one got hurt.

Fair weather and hurtling the language barrier

Today the weather was a little more kind, which was a welcome change after

continued ›

last-minute replacement for CSC's climber Jörg Jaksche, who broke his elbow in training a week before the Tour, landed hard on his wrist but was able to finish.

The Tour ended at 156 kilometers for Gian Matteo Fagnini, once one of the best set-up men in the business. The Italian veteran was reunited with Mario Cipollini on the Domina Vacanze squad with hopes of reviving the Lion King's chances of a win this year, but Fagnini was knocked into a roadside ditch and broke his clavicle.

Super Mario Cipollini, cycling's most flamboyant showman, once dominated the roads of France, but he hadn't raced in cycling's marquee event since 1999, and he was maintaining a low profile in the opening days of the Tour. Cipollini

riding in the rain all day yesterday. The weather is funny in the north of France. It can be sunny, partly cloudy, and raining all at the same time.

This morning was a bit of a personal adventure for me. A reporter from Spain joined our team to interview me. He started out by asking "in English, right?" I am known for only speaking English—especially since I've always ridden on teams whose primary language is English.

I told the reporter he could ask the questions in Spanish, but that I preferred to respond in English. When he started interviewing me, though, I decided "what the heck, I'll give it a go in my 'Spanglishench.'" Why not? By the end, I had concluded an all-Spanish interview—a first for me. I'm not afraid to torture my teammates or the locals back in Girona with my Spanish, but this was the first time I was brave enough to bust out the language skills on television.

Spanish natives were probably suffering listening to me, but my teammates were impressed that I was trying. So now I probably won't be allowed to speak a word of English for the rest of the Tour without getting a little grief. On the bright side, I guess it's good that an old dog like me can learn a new trick or two every now and then.

Tomorrow will be another difficult day. It's the "Paris-Roubaix stage" of the Tour this year. I'm not a big guy, so I'm not really looking forward to riding the cobblestones. I'm glad we had a chance to preview the roads before the start of the race, so we know what's ahead and what we have to do to stay out of trouble. Now it's just a matter of doing it. Wasn't I just saying something about stress? ■

once showed up at the start of a stage in the 1999 Tour dressed in a toga and was pulled around by his similarly clad teammates in a rigged-up chariot. *Veni, vidi, vici* (I came, I saw, I conquered), Cipollini boasted after scoring four stage wins before promptly abandoning the race.

Cipollini made his Tour debut in 1992, winning 12 career Tour stages in seven starts and wearing the yellow jersey in 1993 and 1997. But at the start of the 2004 season, the 37-year-old sprinter was a shadow of his former greatness. After stage wins at the Tour Mediterranean and the Tour de Georgia, Cipo crashed out of the Giro d'Italia in the first week and went home without a stage win for the first time of his career.

"My season was based on the Giro and the Tour. The first aim was shattered," Cipollini explained before the Tour start. "This is not an ideal situation. I had an almost three-week-long break after the Giro and I clearly lack race days. I'll be going to the Tour not knowing how my form is," he continued. "I hope there'll be a couple of situations where it all falls into place, but hope is the best I can do."

A second reason for Cipollini's seemingly uncharacteristic gloom became clear once the race started. Unlike the Giro team, which was built solely around Cipollini's sprinting prowess, the nine-man Tour squad came with hopes of a strong placement in the overall classification with Michele Scarponi. Still, Cipollini was optimistic. "This year I've been in a team with a lot of climbers, but I think I'm sufficiently experienced to be able to sneak along," he said. "My aim is to win at least one stage. The green jersey is not an objective. I'll take it one day at a time."

While Cipollini considered his fate, the rolling 197-kilometer course dipped briefly into France, but quickly veered back into Belgium on a day tailor-made for a sprint. First came the obligatory breakaway: Jakob Piil, the dashing Dane who tore away late in stage 1, jumped just after the day's first of two Cat. 4 climbs at 10 kilometers, and five others followed the initiative. In the slipstream was Mark Scanlon (ag2r), the first Irishman to race the Tour since Stephen Roche.

In his 23 years, Scanlon has tasted the highs and lows of what professional racing has to offer. A junior world champion in 1998, the weight of an entire nation was thrust upon his shoulders. "After my junior title, I signed with Rabobank as an *espoir*, but I had an injured knee for six months, and because of the injury, I wasn't paid," he said.

MAGNUS BÄCKSTEDT, ALESSIO-BIANCHI

I Feel Like Crap

I don't know what is going on, but I feel like crap these days. I sure am not getting my legs to turn the way I want them to, and I am struggling quite a bit.

These are supposed to be my kind of days, and as I said, I am sort of on home turf, but it was all I could do just to stay in the field. If I knew what was wrong with me I'd be a happy man, because I could do something about it. As it is, I have no idea why I feel like I lack power and am struggling on the bike. It's really tough on my head. I want to get my body to do more, but it just doesn't seem to want to follow through.

I've never felt this poorly in a grand tour before. Heck, I've not felt like this in any race before. I don't know what you call it, but I feel like I am "pig rootin'" on the bike, just moving back and forth and my lungs seem to squeal . . . pig rootin'. I tried a few times to move up for the sprint toward the end, but I just didn't have the legs to do it.

Crazy finish

It was too bad about the crash at the finish today, but it wasn't anything like the troubles we had with some of those insanely dangerous finishes at the Giro this year. The road was plenty wide

continued ›

MB continued

enough, there were no hazards out there—nothing in the road blocking the approach, and the finish was pretty clean. Even that last corner was just a full-speed bend, more or less.

The troubles started when Tom Boonen had a problem with his gears, which slowed him down quite a bit. As that was happening, Kirsipuu almost ran into him, swerved, and switched sides to get past him. That happened just as Kurt-Asle Arvesen from CSC was coming through. Arvesen hit Kirsipuu's wheel and that was it. That's the sort of thing that you expect to happen in a bunch kick, though. As far as I am concerned, from a course perspective, it was a pretty safe finish.

A Scandinavian in yellow!

One thing that turned out well today, of course, was that Thor ended up in the yellow jersey. I know Thor, and he's worked very hard for this—he definitely deserves it right now.

It's a great thing for Norwegian cycling and good for Scandinavian cycling in general to have a guy in the yellow jersey, because it generates a lot of interest back home. Norwegian television is coming down to the Tour now and [a stage win] brings heaps more media coverage. It's awesome—absolutely awesome.

Back to the cobbles

So now this evening, after dinner and my massage, I want to get a good rest and be ready for tomorrow. Ordinarily I would be looking forward to the cobbles that we have to take on tomorrow, but as I said, I'm feeling a little off for that.

We'll see. Wish me luck. ■

Without a job, Scanlon retreated to his hometown of Sligo and worked as a milkman to underwrite the costs of extensive rehabilitation. He signed with the Linda McCartney team, but that squad folded before he ever raced with them. He then joined a French amateur team in 2001, and toward the end of the season arranged for a trial period with ag2r, which signed him to a professional contract in 2002. Two years later, he was in his first Tour breakaway.

Piil, meanwhile, was more interested in testing a groin injury he got during a pre-Tour warm-up race in June. The six drove for glory, but as happens so often, the peloton was hungry for another sprint. Quick Step and Crédit Agricole moved to the fore to squelch the move with just under 20 kilometers to go.

The sprinters' teams then fought for position on a long downhill run into Namur, a charming city at the confluence of the Meuse and Sambre rivers. The final run into the sprint came after a sweeping left turn with 400 meters to go and a final left turn 150 meters from the line. With the technical finish, Fassa Bortolo's silver train failed to position star sprinter Petacchi for the second day in a row.

McEwen, however, knew the race would be won on being first to the final corner. "I did have a good look at the race book in the finish, and I knew you couldn't see the finish line until 200 meters to go, so you have to start your sprint before the corner, which is not really easy when you're going 60 kilometers per hour," said the scrappy Australian.

The feisty 32-year-old from Queensland, who speaks Flemish and is married to a Belgian, felt like king for a day in his adopted country. He received a finish-line audience from Albert II, king of the Belgians, and cycling god Eddy Merckx. Talk about a royal reception.

STAGE 2, CHARLEROI TO NAMUR: 1. Robbie McEwen (Aus), Lotto-Domo, 197km in 4:18:39 (45.699kph); **2.** Thor Hushovd (Nor), Crédit Agricole; **3.** Jean-Patrick Nazon (F), ag2r; **4.** Danilo Hondo (Ger), Gerolsteiner; **5.** Stuart O'Grady (Aus), Cofidis—all same time
OVERALL: 1. Hushovd, 9:05:42; **2.** Fabian Cancellara (Swi), Fassa Bortolo, at 0:08; **3.** McEwen, at 0:17

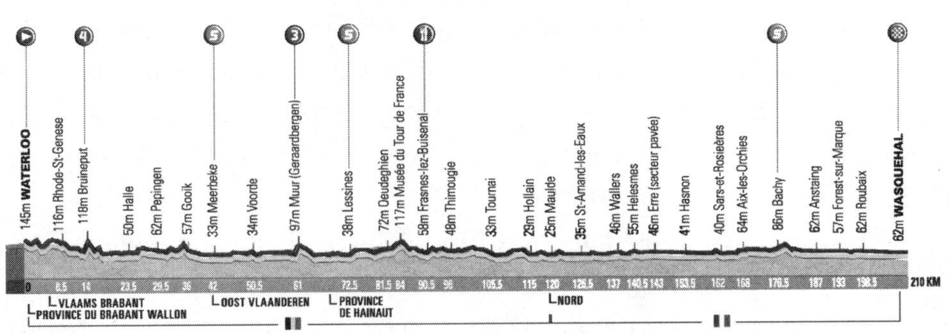

STAGE 3 | Waterloo to Wasquehal

The cobbles of northern France weren't about to become the Waterloo of Lance Armstrong. The third stage took its start in the Belgian town that saw the downfall of France's great Napoleon, who, despite overwhelming force, was outwitted by a smaller but craftier enemy.

Armstrong has ruled the Tour in imperial fashion since his now-mythic comeback from cancer in 1999, but unlike other dominators, he's yet to let his abilities descend into arrogance—at least in terms of how he prepares for and races the Tour. Armstrong is no Napoleon.

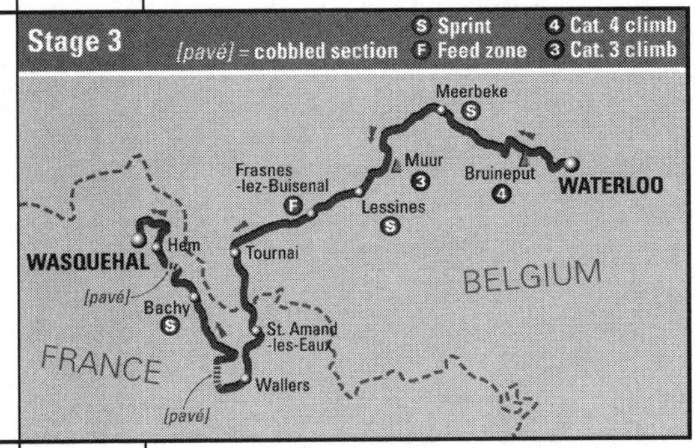

The Tour demands respect and Armstrong is always the first to show his reverence. So when Tour de France organizers decided to include two short *pavé* sections in the 210-kilometer third stage, Armstrong was ready. "I really think some people's Tour will be finished. And I could be one of those people," Armstrong said the night before the stage. "I'm not dumb enough to think that I couldn't be. And that would be a shame. But at the same time, the cobbles are a big part of French cycling. And if you look at Paris-Roubaix, they are what they are; they're a beautiful thing and so if you look at it like that, then they should be a part of the Tour de France." Armstrong was right about one thing. The cobbles were going to prove decisive.

Some people bemoaned the clear skies greeting the riders in Waterloo. The cobbles are always more dramatic in the rain, mud, and wind, at least for those standing alongside the road. The ancient, worn, cobblestone roads meander across much of windswept northern France and southern Belgium, and cyclists have been racing over them for more than a century. But before today, the Tour hadn't hit them since the 1980s.

Stage 3 would cross two relatively small sections of *pavé*. The first section, 2,800 meters at Erre, came at 146 kilometers into the stage. The second came 35 kilometers farther down the road, for a 1,100-meter stretch at Gruson. From there it was a 23.5-kilometer run into Wasquehal.

"It's not like riding Paris-Roubaix, because there you had another 20 sections, here you just have one more," said cobble-lover George Hincapie. Others, though, were questioning the wisdom of having the brutish pavement in the Tour at all. With growing concern for the cyclists' health, including the mandatory use of hard-shell helmets, some said taking featherweight climbers across the cobbled roads was hardly fair.

Magnus Bäckstedt, the big Swede with Alessio who won Paris-Roubaix in April, was not among the fragile lightweights in the peloton, but he predicted that it would be a difficult stage nevertheless. "It's going to be carnage, complete carnage," he forecast. "After the Arenberg [Forest, a famously nasty section featured each year in Paris-Roubaix], this is one of the hardest sections of cobbles. For riders who aren't used to the cobbles, they're going to have some trouble."

Knowing what lay ahead, Armstrong's U.S. Postal Service team left nothing to chance. All nine team members rode on wider, custom-made wheels shod with heavier, more durable tubular tires than usual to withstand punctures. Staff members were also to be deployed along the road at strategic intervals with spare wheels ready for quick changes.

At Phonak, there was quiet concern about getting Tyler Hamilton and Oscar Sevilla safely through the bone-chattering, cobbled roads, but the gritty New Englander simply said, "bring it on."

"That's what bike racing is all about—different terrain, mountains, flat stages, crosswinds, and this year, cobblestones," said Hamilton the day before. "We'll try to stay toward the front and try to stay upright, obviously. Our goal for the day is just safety."

As the race began Team CSC's energetic German, Jens Voigt, once again launched an immediate attack. The winner at Criterium International in March, Voigt, along with teammate Jakob Piil, had given the team plenty of TV time in the opening three stages with long, but ultimately unsuccessful, sorties. Voigt now jumped with Bram de Groot (Rabobank) at 8 kilometers.

It was a move that, though unlikely in its timing, looked more and more like one that could stick. By the halfway point, the pair had established a 6-minute lead, and the main bunch was getting jumpy. Adding to the nervousness in the peloton was a newly minted theory that Armstrong just might be vulnerable. Despite his show of power in the prologue, Armstrong's apparent weakness during his 2003 Tour victory now gave his rivals fresh motivation, each believing that he should race just like the Texan. It was creating havoc on the narrow roads.

"Now everyone has the blueprint of Lance and everyone is trying to copy that, everyone has the one leader to be in the front," explained Bobby Julich. As a result, he said, "it's been a little nervous. It's not just Postal, it's Euskaltel, Phonak, Liberty Seguros, it's just kind of crazy. Hopefully that will all mellow out, but I see a lot of people wasting a lot of energy for a lot of nothing."

Indeed, as the cobbles approached, things became even dicier. With about 20 kilometers to go, the main bunch was in an all-out sprint to hit the *pavé* first. Teams were fearful of getting caught behind a crash, so the safest place to be was nose to the wind.

"What was worse than the cobbles was the 60 kilometers per hour we made on the approach to the cobbles," said Team CSC rider Carlos Sastre, reflecting on the day's ride. "It was a full-on sprint and it was nervous."

Strong winds were buffeting the peloton as it plowed toward the first cobble section. After being near the front for much of the approach, Euskaltel's Iban Mayo drifted back to the left side of the road. It was a critical mistake and proved to be one of the decisive moments of the Tour. As a despondent Mayo later recounted, someone bumped into his handlebars, and before the slender Basque knew it, he had crashed—and the hopes of all of Spain had come tumbling down with him.

It was a real panic moment for Mayo. Ever since his breakthrough ride in the 2003 Tour, Mayo had put everything into being ready for July. His humiliation of Armstrong at Mont Ventoux during the Dauphiné Libéré in June had only whetted his appetite. Now the Tour hung in the balance and he was still a week away from his beloved mountain roads. With his shorts torn open at his left hip, Mayo scrambled onto his bike only to discover that none of his teammates had waited to help him chase back on.

Mayo's fall created a fracture in the main bunch, catching favorites such as Denis Menchov (Illes Balears) and Christophe Moreau (Crédit Agricole) out of position as well. Meanwhile, the Postal Service kept driving, and so did everyone else. Word of Mayo's crash was out, but the relentless force of the hard-charging peloton erased any chance for chivalry. Unlike the niceties shown during the 2003 Tour on Luz-Ardiden, when Ullrich waited for the fallen yellow jersey (or did he?), there was no stopping this train.

Others fell too, including Mayo's teammate Iker Flores, Benjamin Noval (Postal Service), Gerrit Glomser (Saeco), sprint set-up man Marco Velo (Fassa Bortolo) who abandoned with a broken clavicle, Paolo Bettini and Michael Rogers (Quick Step), and Thor Hushovd in the yellow jersey.

"A lot of those guys crashed at the worst possible time," Armstrong said later. "They crashed because it was incredibly nervous right before the *pavé*. There were guys going left and right, guys yelling and screaming. I've never seen anything like it in the Tour. At that point, the race is going, nobody stops, everybody wants to be on the *pavé* first. After that, the race just goes."

The lead group hurtled toward the cobbles in full flight, with U.S. Postal's classic strongmen Hincapie and Viatcheslav Ekimov leading the charge onto the dusty, bumpy *pavé*. Hincapie and Ekimov were clearly in their element (4th twice for Hincapie in Paris-Roubaix, 3rd in 2003 for Ekimov) and the pair drove hard against a strong headwind.

"We heard Mayo had fallen, but it didn't matter because we wanted to be at the front to avoid crashes," Hincapie said. "The first section is a tough one, there was a bit of headwind and we couldn't do too much damage. If there was a crosswind or a tailwind, it could have been better."

Armstrong had no problems on the cobbles and sat comfortably in Hincapie's and Ekimov's slipstream. Looking even more at ease was Jan Ullrich, who followed Armstrong's wheel as if attached by an invisible band. Ekimov and Hincapie took turns pulling, and their efforts caused a second split in the front group that dropped the likes of Levi Leipheimer, Roberto Heras, and Oscar Sevilla.

"There were guys going left and right, guys yelling and screaming. I've never seen anything like it in the Tour."

Once off the cobbles, the pace at the front slowed for a few kilometers as Hincapie and Ekimov caught their breath. The second group drove hard and rejoined the Armstrong-Ullrich-Hamilton group to create a pack of 91 riders.

Haimar Zubeldia, Mayo's quiet Euskaltel teammate who finished 5th in the 2003 Tour, wasn't caught up in the earlier crash but lost contact bouncing over the cobbles. Talk of rivalry between the two riders had filled the Spanish press all spring, but Zubeldia, sacrificing his own chances, sat up to try to tow Mayo back to the front. Mayo and Zubeldia were quickly joined by Crédit Agricole riders Moreau and Hushovd in an attempt to limit the damage. Despite riding as hard as they could, the group couldn't make up much ground. At the day's final intermediate sprint, with 33.5 kilometers to go, the difference to the Armstrong group still stood at two minutes. And after bouncing over the shorter but rougher cobbled section at Gruson, the chase group lost its resolve, forfeiting nearly two minutes more in the final 23 kilometers to the finish.

"We knew it was all over when we were chasing at 50 to 60 kilometers per hour and we weren't taking back one second. It's a feeling of helplessness, because you know it's slipping away," Mayo said. "The Tour can be lost in one day and that's what happened to me today. We have to reconsider the Tour. The podium looks difficult as well as it's too much time to make up. Now perhaps I can go for stage wins. I feel badly for the team because we came with more aspirations than ever. Now it's all lost. The Tour doesn't forgive."

By the time a dejected Mayo limped across the line, he had lost 3:48 to Armstrong and had fallen to 101st at 4:23. The damage was done. The Texan could scratch Mayo's name off his list of would-be usurpers to his Tour crown. Also losing time were Moreau, Menchov, Zubeldia, and Juan Miguel Mercado (Quick Step). Maybe Armstrong will reconsider his aversion to the cobbles.

But there was still the stage to fight for. Bad luck continued to plague Stuart O'Grady (Cofidis), the star-crossed, freckled, Australian sprinter who crashed on the second cobbled section. He was chasing hard with Pavel Padrnos (U.S. Postal Service) and Evgueni Petrov (Saeco) and was just 10 seconds off the back of the lead group when they came upon a train crossing with 18 kilometers to go. "Can anything else happen? Hopefully this is the last touch down [fall] in the Tour," said O'Grady, who waited for the train to pass. "It can't get much worse than this."

"I feel badly for the team because we came with more aspirations than ever. Now it's all lost. The Tour doesn't forgive."

Postal got some help from Phonak, T-Mobile, and Liberty Seguros to drive home the bunch. Voigt and De Groot (remember them?) were swooped up before the second cobbled section, and 91 riders slipped into Wasquehal to fight for the spoils.

Voigt earned the day's most combative rider award for his efforts and held the dubious honor of having spent 279 kilometers on the attack over the course of three days and a combined distance of 615 kilometers. But CSC Team boss, Bjarne Riis, couldn't hide his displeasure at the stage finish. "It wasn't a planned attack. Jens thinks he needs to be out there, but he has to ride smarter, measure his efforts," said the 1996 Tour winner. "We have the team time trial coming up. I don't want him out there. I'll stop him next time."

Many of the top sprinters safely cleared the cobbles, including German ace Erik Zabel (T-Mobile). The six-time green points jersey winner wasn't getting much attention from the press, which was more focused on Mario Cipollini and Alessandro Petacchi, but the Berliner still had some fight in him.

As the pack neared the finish, Jaan Kirsipuu, the Estonian winner of stage 1, took a hard pull to set up ag2r teammate Jean-Patrick Nazon for the sprint, but Zabel was hot on his wheel. Coming hard up the left was Robbie McEwen, the scrappy Aussie who had won the previous day. But McEwen started his sprint too soon, allowing Nazon to hold off Zabel and score his second Tour win, to go along with his final-day win in the previous Tour on the Champs-Élysées.

With Hushovd still out on the course, McEwen took the time bonuses and the yellow jersey, with a margin of just one second over prologue winner Fabian Cancellara. Capturing the yellow jersey is a career highlight for most riders, but for the hotheaded Aussie it was just another day at the office.

"I've always been interested in having the yellow jersey, but I don't think I've ever really, really chased it," said McEwen, winner of the green points jersey in 2002. "This is the first time I've taken it in a grand tour. Now I can tick that off the list of things to do.

"The thing with the yellow jersey is that it's great to have it, but if you are not going to be wearing it in Paris, there is not much difference between wearing it for one day or six," he explained. "It's more important for me to win a stage than to wear the jersey. That's what I'm paid to do."

STAGE 3, WATERLOO TO WASQUEHAL: 1. Jean-Patrick Nazon (F), ag2r, 210km in 4:36:45 (45.528kph); **2.** Erik Zabel (G), T-Mobile; **3.** Robbie McEwen (Aus), Lotto-Domo; **4.** Tom Boonen (B), Quick Step; **5.** Kim Kirchen (Lux), Fassa Bortolo—all same time
OVERALL: 1. McEwen, 13:42:34; **2.** Fabian Cancellara (Swi), Fassa Bortolo, at 0:01; **3.** Jens Voigt (G), CSC, at 0:09

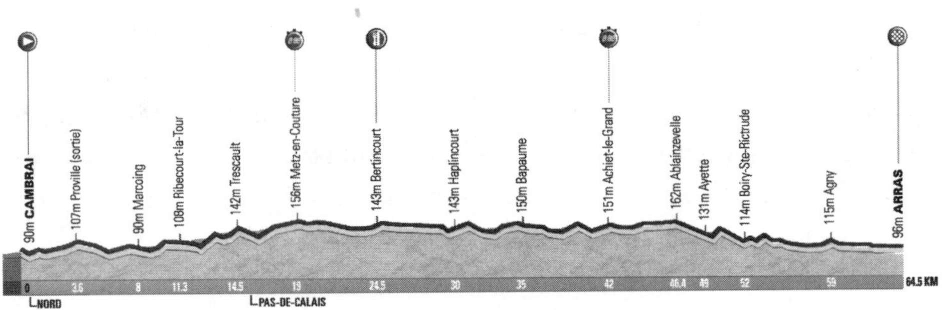

STAGE 4 | Cambrai to Arras

The race for the 64.5-kilometer team time trial began days before the cloudy, cool, morning start in Cambrai, a town of 35,000 that saw its first invasion of Planet Tour this year. The most advantageous spot in any team time trial is last—cycling's pole position—where teams can best watch the times of their competitors. With the decisive team race coming in the fourth day, U.S. Postal Service put in a full effort in the opening prologue to ensure it would get that leg up on the competition. Before the race began Armstrong said, "We had a meeting and we wanted everyone to have a really good prologue. It's important to start last [for the team time trial] and know all the time checks."

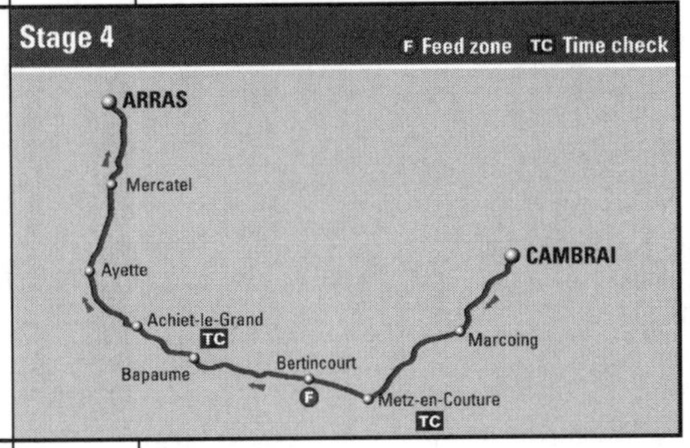

Tracking the times was important, but deciphering the rules proved more troublesome. Tour officials had introduced a new scoring system for this year's race designed to prevent a major team [insert U.S. Postal Service here] from blowing apart the race by taking a four-minute lead into the mountains against the climbing specialists [insert Liberty, Euskaltel, Illes Balears].

Initially, the rule was a time limit of 2:30, but once racers took a closer look at the rule book they discovered a scoring system based on placement, not time. Teams would be docked time at 10-second intervals starting with 20 seconds for 2nd, 30 seconds for 3rd, and so on.

The rule had some pre-stage favorites boiling. "I've never heard of a bicycle race that limited the amount of time you could lose," complained Bobby Julich of CSC, who won the team time trial in 2001 with Crédit Agricole. "The rules are pure idiocy. They shouldn't even have the team time trial if they're going to ruin it like this."

And for many of the contenders, the scoring system would indeed prove their ruination.

TYLER HAMILTON—PHONAK

Riding with Heart

Last night was pretty emotional for our team. In fact, the last couple of days have really put everyone to the test. And I don't just mean us, I mean everybody in the race.

Tuesday's stage from Waterloo to Wasquehal didn't make any liars out of those who predicted carnage by the conclusion of the day. I don't know if I've ever ridden in a peloton as aggra' as the one that headed into the first section of pavé. The fight for position started 40 kilometers in advance of the cobblestones, which meant we were going all out for nearly an hour before we reached the pavé. I can't believe there weren't more crashes given what the fatigue rate must have been by the time the bunch was hurdling single file across the dusty section of cobbles.

At least five GC contenders were caught in or behind the major crash of the day that wound up complicating Iban Mayo's Tour de France ambitions. I really felt for him after the stage. With a year's worth of training and sacrifice invested in readying for this race, he lost nearly four minutes due to an obstacle. That's tough to take when you've conditioned yourself to compete in an event of endurance.

The situation reminded me of the 1999 Tour when the peloton hit the Passage du Gois, a seaside road that was submerged under water during high tide. We rode through at low tide, but the pavement was slimy and slick, and half the peloton went down or got caught behind those who crashed. The second group lost 6 minutes that day. Alex Zülle was among them. He wound up losing the Tour by 6 minutes and 40 seconds that year.

continued ›

At the opposite end of U.S. Postal's pole position was ill-fated Euskaltel-Euskadi, still reeling from its disastrous day on the cobbles. To add insult to injury—Mayo awoke with a bruised hip and ribs—the UCI's dope-testing vampires came knocking before dawn for early morning blood tests. (All riders were declared clean.)

With their overall hopes in shambles, many observers expected another Euskaltel meltdown on the flat, windy course to Arras. But the orange-clad raiders showed their fortitude, finishing 8th as only one of four teams with all riders together across the line. "We know our chances of overall victory are over," said sport director Julian Gorospe. "But we can still try to influence the race. We're not going home."

Heavy winds gave way to an absolute downpour by the time the favorites hit the course. T-Mobile, Rabobank, and Phonak rode under adverse conditions.

Our team was happy to have made it through stage 3 relatively unscathed. My teammates rode incredibly well tactically and showed an impressive amount of strength. They took great care of me, and I was enormously grateful during and after the race.

We headed into the next day's team time trial with big ambitions. We have a lot of solid time trialists on the team so we were expecting a lot from ourselves. In addition, we had strong men like Nicolas Jalabert, who knew that this would be one of the key days where he would make a significant contribution.

The weather couldn't have been worse. It was pouring rain as we headed out of the start. The only consolation was that just about every other team had to ride under the same conditions. We had previewed the course and had done our homework. I knew we had a tough day ahead, but I was feeling a lot of confidence in the guys around me. Everyone was hungry.

And then all hell broke loose. We had three flat tires inside the first 20 kilometers. Nicolas Jalabert was the first victim, at the 10-kilometer mark. He flatted but we decided to keep going, and he wound up riding the final 50 kilometers by himself. Then Santos had a mechanical problem, so we lost him. Then Gutierrez flatted, which meant we had lost three critical guys pretty early on. We made the call to wait for Guti, even though we knew it would cost us 30 to 45 seconds. But we really didn't have a choice since we were down to six guys and had two- thirds of the race to go.

Eventually Santos chased back to within striking distance of us, so we

Rabobank's Levi Leipheimer slipped on a corner but wasn't seriously injured, while T-Mobile overcame a slow start to finish with seven of its nine, taking 4th.

Team CSC boss, Bjarne Riis, desperately wanted to win the team race. No discipline better reflects his singular view of bicycle racing, where the team always comes before individual interests. But his tall, balding brow darkened soon after his nine riders pushed off the start ramp. Big, German engine Jens Voigt punctured almost immediately, disrupting the team's rhythm. Then three riders fell on a rain-slicked corner, with Julich, Nicki Sörensen, and Ivan Basso skidding out. Basso later had to change his bike when it developed mechanical problems.

"Aagh, it's too bad," said Riis, the steam escaping his ears almost visible. "A flat tire, a crash, and a changed bike cost us 1:30. Take that away and we were with the best teams." Riis's temperature later rose from merely hot to truly broiling when it was revealed that team captain Carlos Sastre was docked his real time of 1:49 rather than the team's adjusted time of 50 seconds for finishing 5th. Under the complex scoring system, teams were given the adjusted time only if

slowed up again and waited for him.

At this point, we felt like the additional 25 to 30 seconds we were giving up to wait was insurance for what might lie ahead. It turned out to be a wise choice, because we lost Perez and Pereiro to two more flats. It was chaos. We were down to five guys—the minimum amount needed at the finish—and we still had a lot of ground to cover. At that point, I thought we were riding for pride.

I don't think there was a single guy on our team who didn't roll into the finish devastated. It was an awful feeling considering our ambitions for the day. We all boarded the team bus suffering from equal parts of frustration and sadness. Everyone on the team was deflated—from the mechanics who wanted to know what went so wrong, to the support staff that watched the race play out on television, to the riders themselves who felt like a big opportunity had just slipped through their fingers.

But then, at the end of the day, we had to feel good about finishing 2nd. On an afternoon when it seemed as though the odds were stacked against us, we managed to limit our losses. And to later realize that we actually got faster as the stage went on, and had made up as much time as we did with only five guys left, meant that we fought a good fight.

I'm really proud of this team. These guys are riding with a lot of heart. No one gave up in stage 4, and to me, that kind of commitment is just as important as winning. These guys care a lot about what we are trying to accomplish here at this year's Tour. Their efforts on the road, and the emotion they showed after the stage, proved it. I'm in good hands. ■

riders finished with the fifth man, where the official time was taken. Any rider losing contact with his team was scored with his real time.

Sastre's fine prologue ride and deft handling over the cobbles was now wasted. Instead of sitting in the top 20, he had plummeted to 36th at 2:02 back. "Yeah, we didn't even know about the rule. It's kind of bad to lose so much time because I was just being careful on the cobbles," said Sastre, who is remembered for popping his baby's pacifier into his mouth as he crossed the line a winner in last year's stage to Aix-3 Domaines. "Normally in the final meters of a race like that you don't lose the time. It's almost a minute, so it could be important later in the race. I hope not."

Sastre wasn't the only rider caught unaware. Two-time Giro d'Italia champion Gilberto Simoni saw his hopes dim dramatically when he crashed on the penultimate turn on a section of heavy, wet cobbles. The Saeco rider scrambled back on his bike but finished 6 seconds behind his teammates. Because of the rules, instead of scoring 1:30, Simoni's real time of 2:42 stood.

MAGNUS BÄCKSTEDT, ALESSIO-BIANCHI

Rain, Crashes, and I'm Feeling Good

I sure do feel a lot better than I have these past few days of the Tour de France, and there's nothing like a team time trial to get a big motor like me feeling back in sorts. No, it isn't a complete turnaround—I'm clearly not in top form—but it is definitely a step in the right direction. Team time trials are really what the early part of my racing career was all about. Being taller and stronger on the flats I offer up a pretty good draft, eh?

When you see teams like CSC and Phonak running into the troubles they had today, you begin to see how eventful the day was. The rain really does complicate matters. I had a major wheelspin just at the start and almost went down on the wet road.

Still, we got a really good start to things and even set the top mark at the time checks for awhile, but then we had two of our guys crash on a slick turn—the same one, it turns out, where CSC lost three guys. We came into the turn and Martin Hvastija and Fabio Baldato cooked it a little too fast and hit the ground. It's something that you have to be prepared for in a team time

"I can fight against bad luck, but I cannot fight against the rules. One hundred and twenty riders finished behind me, but I lost one minute more than them. It's a stupid rule," said Simoni, who lost the 2004 Giro to young teammate Damiano Cunego. "I came here hoping to win, but I've never liked the Tour. I'll carry on and we'll see, but it's frustrating when you fall within 400 meters of the line and lose so much. In theory, the team could have waited, but it was difficult with the wind, cobbles, and rain. My morale is in my boots."

Aussie sprinter Robbie McEwen, who took the race lead the previous day, enjoyed what was probably one of the shortest runs ever in the yellow jersey. His Lotto-Domo team wasn't exactly riding the turbos, perhaps to let the Aussie wear the jersey a little bit longer. In the end, his run in the maillot jaune lasted 1 hour, 17 minutes, and 22 seconds. "That doesn't count the hours I slept in it, does it?" he said.

For Tyler Hamilton, the team race was a badge of honor. After turning in a surprisingly flat prologue time, the New Englander was determined to solidify his position as a challenger. All season long Hamilton had been singing the praises of his underrated Swiss green machine. In fact, Phonak started the stage hoping to win and take the yellow jersey for José Enrique Gutierrez, who started the day 8th at 23 seconds back.

But the team encountered difficulties right from the start. First, Nicolas Jalabert, younger brother of cycling legend Laurent Jalabert, punctured at 13 kilo-

trial, especially on a day when it's raining like that.

That crash would have been okay, but we had a complete screwup in communication after that. The seven of us slowed down and waited for the two fellas to catch back on. And we waited . . . and waited. We waited around for quite a while—probably a minute, but it seemed like an eternity—and then all of a sudden the sport director yelled "Go! Go! Go!" even though we didn't have our guys back.

So the net result is that we paid the price of waiting around and then didn't get the benefit of waiting. It would have made sense to either wait completely or to go right away—we didn't do either. That was a lack of communication, or better yet, a failure to make the decision quickly. Fortunately, when I punctured with 15 kilometers to go, they made the decision to go and I rode into the finish on my own.

Still, I have quite a positive frame of mind today. I felt heaps better than I did even yesterday, which has really changed my attitude. It's hard to approach the Tour with enthusiasm feeling the way I had been. So right now I can take things day by day. I hope that tomorrow when I get on the road I have the legs to do something. ■

meters and was sacrificed by his team. Then the second disaster struck, when Santos Gonzalez broke his handlebars and had to ride a reserve bike. Then Gutierrez and Santi Perez had flats. All of this happened in the opening third of the race. It was a dicey situation. Hesitation could spell doom, but the strongest riders needed to be rescued. Sport director Alvaro Pino made the call to wait for Gonzalez.

"I almost stopped completely and I thought that was the end of everything," Hamilton said. "Everything was going crazy, but we never stopped fighting. In the first 25 kilometers we had four punctures and a handlebar problem. Afterward we kind of found our rhythm. We fought to the bitter end and I'm proud of what we did."

In a testament to the team's strength, Phonak, with only five riders intact, finished 2nd to Postal Service. While other teams lost riders in the final bumpy turns, the Phonaks fell back early, leaving just Hamilton, Gonzalez, Bert Grabsch, Gutierrez, and Oscar Sevilla to drive the team home. "I feel kind of sad because I know we could have won," Hamilton said. "My team has proven that it's strong and it can fight to the end."

A year ago, U.S. Postal had roared to a team time trial victory, launching Armstrong to a record-tying fifth title. Now the 2004 Tour was starting to look like a summer rerun as *les boys*, as the French sports daily *L'Equipe* called them, blazed out of Cambrai with victory in their sights.

As much as the team wanted to show its dominance and ride for the win, Armstrong, like McEwen the previous day, was reluctant to wear the yellow jersey so early in the race. Starting the day in 5th at 16 seconds back, he would take the jersey with even a 2nd-place ride. But as the Posties turned on the gas, a team win seemed inevitable.

Riding with peerless precision, the team erased a 37-second deficit at the first time check at 19 kilometers to take the lead from Illes Balears, which had been fastest team up to that point. Rain eased up for the second half of Postal's ride and the team again set the fastest time at the 42-kilometer checkpoint.

As the kilometers clicked by, the team rode stronger and stronger. Encountering a buffeting crosswind, the Postal quickly formed a double paceline, rapidly rotating riders off the front who drifted back alongside their teammates and slipped into place at the end of the line in textbook time trial form. Viewed from above in one of the Tour's helicopters, Postal's ride was an organic creature of stunning beauty.

Beauty is as beauty does, and the Posties' elegant display drove them home to a 1:07 win over 2nd-place Phonak. Despite heavy winds, rain, and wet roads, the team posted a speed of 53.71 kilometers per hour—the third fastest in Tour history.

"All day long I was the last guy in the corners; I didn't want to take any risks," Armstrong said. "We started a little slow—maybe some of the guys were nervous—but that's a sign of a strong team when you fight back. And look what happened in the end."

Viewed from above in one of the Tour's helicopters, Postal's ride was an organic creature of stunning beauty.

Indeed, whether he liked it or not, the Postal trouncing had nudged the Texan into the Tour's yellow jersey for the 60th day of his career, tying him with Spanish rider Miguel Induráin for 3rd on the all-time list. Eddy Merckx holds the mark with 96 days while Bernard Hinault wore the jersey for 77. "If it's going to be 60 days in the yellow jersey, that's almost two months," Armstrong said. "When you count it like that, it's a lot of days. It hits home."

While Postal Service was nearly flawless, its Tour rookie Benjamin Noval was having trouble. Already a victim of two crashes, the Spanish rider lost contact with the blue train about 20 kilometers into the stage. "I know what it's like to be dropped; it happened to me a few times as a rider," said team director Johan Bruyneel. "It was very hard on Noval, but we knew he would probably have problems. He had fallen already twice."

A year ago, following Postal's victory in Saint Dizier, team member Victor Hugo Peña became the first Colombian to don the yellow jersey. Peña had ridden alongside Armstrong for three of his Tours, but his place was taken on the 2004 team by Noval, who Armstrong said was simply too strong not to bring. Now, however, some were questioning the wisdom of the move.

Armstrong was not concerned. He and his teammates were already celebrating their victory when Noval sheepishly rolled across the line 13 minutes, 16 seconds later as the last rider on course. Crestfallen, Noval broke down in tears under the pressure and hid his face in his hands, but Armstrong went to his side and consoled his young charge before returning to his familiar position atop the Tour de France podium. Things were looking very good for the five-time winner despite the limited gains the day's format allowed him to make against his rivals.

"That's the rule, we can't change it. If they say it's 20, we get 20 seconds. It is what it is," said Armstrong, referring to the difference to the 2nd-placed team Phonak. "If there is one consolation, we know our team is the strongest. Those guys were incredible today."

Compared to his problems in the opening week of last year's Tour—when he endured stomach problems before the prologue, got caught up in a crash in stage 1, and suffered tendinitis due to new shoes and equipment—the 2004 Tour was smooth sailing so far. While Armstrong was only 10 seconds ahead of his teammate Hincapie and 16 seconds ahead of Landis—putting Americans in the top three slots for the first time in Tour history—his first real challenger was Hamilton, in 8th at 0:36. Jan Ullrich was 16th at 0:55, and Roberto Heras had fallen to 34th at 1:45 back. Just like last year, the team time trial had catapulted Armstrong toward victory. More than ever, he was feeling confident.

"Ever since I was a junior, this was the race that's always been my favorite event," Armstrong said. "We've always come close in Motorola, but we were always upset and we never won. Last year we won and it was probably one of the highlights, if not the highlight, to win the team time trial. This year was even stronger. I was just smiling on the bike. It was like a dream."

STAGE 4, CAMBRAI TO ARRAS: 1. U.S. Postal Service, 64.5km in 1:12:03 at 53.71kph; 2. Phonak, at 0:20 (+1:07); **3.** Illes Balears, at 0:04 (+1:15); **4.** T-Mobile, at 0:40 (+1:19); **5.** Team CSC, at 0:50 (+1:46)
OVERALL: 1. Armstrong (USA), U.S. Postal Service; 2. Hincapie (USA), U.S. Postal Service, at 0:10; 3. Floyd Landis (USA), U.S. Postal Service, at 0:16

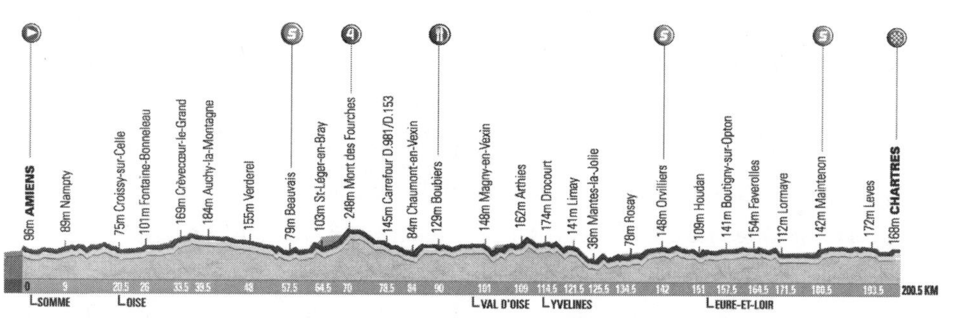

STAGE 5 | Amiens to Chartres

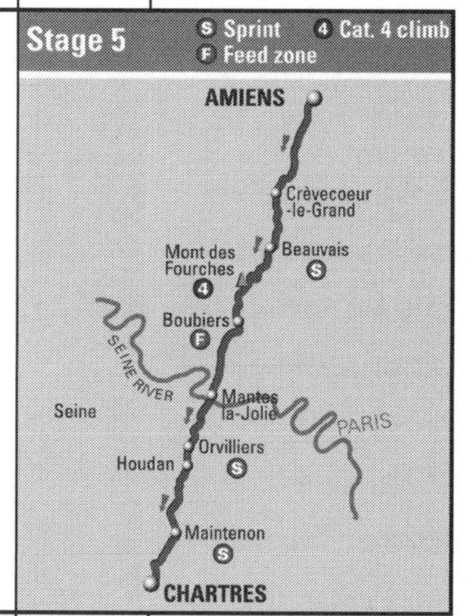

Nearly a week into the Tour, it became clear that everyone wanted to be like Lance. Teams with any rider capable of finishing within eyeshot of the podium were keeping their cyclists in check and conserving their strength for the battles waiting in the mountains, still more than a week away. It was making for a very nervous peloton and a rash of painful crashes.

"It's tough when you have nine Euskaltels, nine Phonaks, nine Postals, nine CSCs, nine riders from the leading team—the road is only so wide," said Armstrong, referring to rival teams fighting for position to protect their leaders. "There are guys here who think they can win, so their team puts a lot of pressure on them to stay out front and stay out of trouble," he continued. "I think the Tour needs a time trial in the first week. It's safer for the event to establish some order. We're still a week away from figuring out who's going to be at the front."

For his part, Armstrong promised to give up the jersey to anyone willing to make a run for it. Defending the jersey would put extra pressure on Armstrong's eight U.S. Postal Service teammates. They'd have to work hard to chase down dangerous breakaways, keep Armstrong protected from the wind, and steer him away from trouble. Who needed all that bother? As huge crowds gathered around the Postal Service bus to greet him moments after taking the jersey in the team time trial, the Texan said his boys in blue were in no mood to unnecessarily defend the jersey. "It would not be in the best interests of the team," he said. "It's a hard race to defend the jersey all the way to Paris. We're not going to sacrifice the team to defend the yellow jersey in the north of France. The time to defend begins in the Pyrénées." As word of Armstrong's intentions spread, many teams reached the same conclusion: If the Texan indeed was indifferent to holding his lead, stage 5 would be wide open.

Every day so far in the Tour, there had been a breakaway that tried and failed to escape the clutches of the peloton. And one team—Team CSC—was present in each of the major escapes to liven up the race. It was no surprise that the Danish-based, American-sponsored team was ready to go on the assault despite the inclement weather in the rolling, 200.5-kilometer stage that pushed south from Amiens, skirted the western reaches of the Paris suburbs, and plowed across the lush farm country into France's heartland.

"It's all part of our strategy for the first part of the week," explained team boss Bjarne Riis. "We're not chasing the team classification; that's not so important to us right now. We want to animate the race, force others to chase, be aggressive."

Riders knew they were in for a miserable day on the bike. Strong headwinds buffeted the peloton and rain fell intermittently throughout the day. Last year riders were baking in 100-degree temperatures; this year it was more like spring in Belgium than summer in France.

It didn't take long for Team CSC to put the hammer down. At 16 kilometers, Jakob Piil slipped away with four other riders: Sandy Casar (fdjeux.com), Stuart O'Grady (Cofidis), Magnus Bäckstedt (Alessio-Bianchi), and Thomas Voeckler (La Boulangère). With U.S. Postal Service more than happy to let them ride away, the quintet soon built up a seven-minute lead over the next 27 kilometers.

Voeckler, the freshly crowned French national champion, was the best-placed rider, starting the day in 59th at three minutes back, and he soon gained the elusive *virtuel* Tour lead. "We were trying to put guys in the breaks early in the stage, but I went with the right move," said Voeckler, who was born in Alsace and raised on the Caribbean island of Martinique, where his mother still lives. "I didn't even know I was the best-placed rider in the bunch until my sport director called it in later. It was a pleasant surprise and gave me a little more motivation to ride hard."

Each rider had something to gain, so the quintet collaborated to widen the gap by another 8:35 over the next 37 kilometers to a margin of 15:40 over the main bunch. Strong winds and a steady downpour were perfect ingredients in their recipe for success. In fact, the conditions of the race were eerily similar to stage 8 into Pontarlier in the 2001 Tour, when Armstrong let 14 riders, including Andrei Kivilev and François Simon, gain 35:54. Armstrong was later forced to fight hard through the Alps and into the Pyrénées before capturing the yellow jersey.

This time around, Postal was again content to let the jersey ride away—as long as it didn't stray too far. The team stayed at the front with Ekimov, Padrnos, Landis, and Hincapie setting a steady tempo that held the move to just over a 12-minute gap with 40 kilometers to go. "I didn't want to kill the team to chase

MAGNUS BÄCKSTEDT, ALESSIO-BIANCHI

All in All, a Good Day

I told you I was feeling better.

I had a good day today. I knew I was feeling okay after yesterday's time trial, and this morning circumstance allowed me to take advantage of that and get into one of those rare little breaks that actually manages to stay away. Sure, I am disappointed I didn't win today, but at the same time, I am really happy that my legs are feeling good.

There were attacks from the gun. We all knew there would be, especially after we saw Armstrong speaking last night about how he and the team really had no reason to defend the jersey at this stage of the Tour, because it was going to cost his riders too much energy. With that in mind, you just knew there would be a lot of attacks early on, so I did my best to stay near the front from the start.

One group got off the front at maybe 2 kilometers and it was just too big, with too many good climbers in the mix, so the Postal team was not going to let them go. Sure enough, that group was pulled back quickly.

At about 10 or 11 kilometers, the four guys who I ended up in the break with got away. Now this was the one time in the Tour where I was both close to the front and felt like I had good legs, so I gave it a shot, bridging the little gap. It was actually quite easy, so that put a positive spin on my outlook for the day. We worked really well together as a group. In fact, it didn't take all that long for us to start building up a nice gap. There was no question about anyone not taking his share of pulls.

I have to tell you, one of the guys, Thomas Voeckler, has had an incredible month now. He's the French national champion, has been winning race after race, and now he's in the yellow jersey. He's got a heck of a future in the sport, I'd say.

a breakaway of five riders," said Bruyneel later. "It's a comfortable position for us to let another team take the jersey. It means less work for us."

As his fdjeux.com teammate Casar was making headway in the break, Brad McGee was losing contact off the back of the main group. McGee's troubles began a week before the Tour when he strained his back planting olive trees in his garden near Nice on France's Cøte d'Azur. Now, riding with severe back pain, and struggling to keep up, the Australian unclipped from his pedals at 102 kilometers. His Tour was over.

"It has nothing to do with the wind and rain, I just couldn't keep up. Simple. It's like I've got one leg," he said. "I've never been in this position before, never thought I would be, either. I have to get some experts to take a look at it and see where I am. When you win races and they ask how you feel and it hasn't sunk in

Anyway, we were out there, the gap was getting bigger and bigger, and it started becoming clear that we stood a real chance of pulling it off. You never know with those things. Back in 2001, Stuart was in a break that gained 35 minutes on the peloton, and then last year he got caught in the final kilometer after having been on the attack all day. You never know, but that's the Tour de France.

With about 50 kilometers left, we still had 16 minutes, and it looked like we were good to go. Postal surely wasn't interested in chasing, and when my director came up and said that it was only Postal at the front of the peloton, I was sure there wasn't going to be any chase. It was a good thing for us.

So heading toward the finish, we knew that the race was going to come down to the five of us—it was all that was on our minds. We just eyed each other, and then the attacks started. Voeckler was especially aggressive, but Stuart was the most experienced, and he looked like he had plenty of kick in him, too.

Honestly, those last 5 or 6 kilometers were just done on pure willpower, because I was totally spent after being out there for 188 kilometers. I kept trying and trying, mostly because I held out hope that I could pull something off. Coming into Chartres, there were three or four times that I was convinced it was more or less over for me, but I figured that, having come this far, I should give it my best. I kept getting dropped and coming back, and it took a lot out of me.

At about 1.5 kilometers, I got dropped and thought "well, that's it," but then the guys up front slowed down and I managed to reconnect at about 500 meters from the line. With the four guys stopped up there, I thought I'd make one, last, desperate attempt to come up on them. I figured my best bet would be to swing out to the right and launch

continued ›

yet—it's the same. I have to get my head around it all first. What is really disappointing for me is that I know I can push through anything, but I just don't have the legs. It makes it hard to accept."

Also struggling was French rider Maryan Hary, who was having a day quite unlike that of his Boulangère teammate Voeckler. Hary gamely fought on, riding alone through the rain and wind with stinging pain in his Achilles' tendon. He would end up finishing last at 40:07 back—out of the time limit. His Tour was over as well.

Crashes, spills, pileups, and accidents were creating a slow boil in the main bunch. Nerves were frayed as riders jockeyed for position on the narrow roads. Rudi Aldag, one of Ullrich's tough bodyguards, crashed at 70 kilometers. Then several riders folded like a house of cards on a sweeping turn at 101 kilometers,

MB

continued

an attack while they were busy looking at each other, and if I got a gap of 20 or 30 meters I might get the stage.

Unfortunately, just as I was making the jump, Stuart sort of looked over at Sandy Casar and I came into his field of vision. So he did exactly the right thing and got straight onto my wheel. I figured at that point I would just try to ride it out and see if one of the four of them was even more spent than I was. But as you know, the guys were really strong. They all got past me on the way to the line, and I ended up 5th. Still, I have to be happy with it.

So here I am, 4th overall in the Tour de France. We'll see how long that lasts, but I do have to say that I'm a much happier man than I was a few days ago. My legs feel so much better than they have been, though it may take a few kilometers to work out the kinks tomorrow morning. ■

leaving Alessandro Petacchi facedown on the wet pavement and four of Armstrong's Iberian contingent—Spanish riders Chechu Rubiera, Benjamin Noval, and Manuel Beltran, and Portuguese cyclist José Azevedo—sprawled on the tarmac as well. Michael Boogerd (Rabobank), Roberto Heras and Angel Vicioso (both Liberty Seguros), and green jersey Robbie McEwen also crashed.

It wasn't going to be Triki's day. Beltran crashed again, with McEwen, Paolo Bettini, and Matthias Kessler (T-Mobile), at 171 kilometers. Beltran later stumbled across the line with his left elbow badly cut, while Rubiera suffered punctures to his calf after falling onto another rider's pedals. Both riders received stitches as Tour de France souvenirs. "I hate these flat stages," Beltran said. "Everything is so nervous; I can't wait for the roads to get steep. Then I won't have anyone around me."

The break started to believe in its chances when it hit the day's final points sprint at 180.5 kilometers with more than 14 minutes in hand over the main bunch. O'Grady had deftly picked up 18 points by taking 1st in all three sprints, thereby repositioning himself in the hunt for the green jersey. Three times runner-up for the green points jersey competition, O'Grady had started the stage 61 points behind his compatriot McEwen.

Of the five riders in the break, Piil and O'Grady were the strongest sprinters while Voeckler was a lock on the yellow jersey. That left Bäckstedt and Casar with few options for victory. A fresh douse of rain fell as the quintet plowed under the 10-kilometer banner, and the big winner of Paris-Roubaix shot the first volley.

Not surprisingly, Bäckstedt's move did not stick, but to everyone's surprise, Voeckler jumped just as the big Swede was reeled in. With multiple feints under way, Casar followed the wheels as Piil made two attacks and Voeckler initiated three more over the next 4 kilometers. O'Grady shot ahead with 3 kilometers to go and opened a gap, but Voeckler and Piil fought hard to bring him back. Piil and O'Grady then attacked on a short, uphill section and looked to have gapped the others, but Bäckstedt clawed back and even led out the sprint with 450 meters to go.

Alas, a move that worked for Bäckstedt in April's Paris-Roubaix would not work in July's Tour de France. With Piil blocked on the inside, O'Grady came around Bäckstedt and powered to the finish, easily holding off Casar to take his second career Tour victory.

It was an emotional win for O'Grady, a popular Australian who endured a spring from hell to come back to the Tour and snatch an uplifting win for his beleaguered Cofidis team. In April, O'Grady broke a rib in a spill at Ghent-Wevelgem. A few days later, his Cofidis team decided to voluntarily stop racing after a police investigation into doping allegations within the team threatened to overwhelm the sport.

"The days we stopped competing were the worst in my life," an emotional O'Grady recounted. "I had lost my grandfather, and my wife went over to Australia with my baby to support my parents. I was alone at home, lower than ever in my life. I was hoping for the team to continue. I came to France because I love cycling, because I love the Tour de France."

Following its terrible spring, Cofidis started the Tour without world time trial champion David Millar or French rider Cedric Vasseur, both charged in the ongoing doping scandal. Things looked even bleaker when O'Grady's compatriot Matthew White couldn't take the start after breaking his collarbone while warming up for the prologue. Then Frenchman Frederic Bessy called it quits in the third stage due to a knee injury, and O'Grady crashed three times in the opening stages.

"Every night in my hotel room I was telling myself luck would turn our way, that it could not get any worse," O'Grady said. "I knew I should go for it, and this victory is all the more emotional as it is for the team and all the people who worked for it."

Armstrong crossed the line 12:33 back as the main bunch rumbled steadily down the finishing stretch. The Texan was more than happy with his day. "It was perfect for us to have the break go clear because it made the final part of the stage less nervous," said Armstrong, who slipped to 6th overall. And he seemed just as pleased with the whereabouts of the maillot jaune. "Tactically, it's a great move. Voeckler is a good young rider. He's French and I think it's a good thing."

For nearly any rider, wearing the yellow jersey is a career highlight. More than that—it defines who you are. Wear the maillot jaune for a day and you'll never have to buy drinks again in France, it's said. But for Armstrong, the golden fleece was becoming a standard part of his wardrobe, and he was confident he'd regain the lead when the Tour hit the decisive mountain stages in the Pyrénées.

"The team was great today," Armstrong said cheerfully. "I kept telling them they wouldn't have to work for a week and so they were probably happy to hear that."

For Voeckler, taking the jersey capped a dreamlike day. "All the teams listened very carefully to Lance Armstrong when he said he wasn't going to defend the yellow jersey, so today we decided to go with all the breakaways," said the 25-year-old. "The weather was so bad, but it helped us to make it to the finish."

With the jersey on his back, the next question had to be how long would he wear it. Could he take it into the Pyrénées? Well, Voeckler has shown he's no slouch in the mountains, winning a tough stage in the Route du Sud two weeks prior to the Tour. He also won the Tour of Luxembourg in 2003. And the weekend before the Tour, he attacked his way to the French national championship against heavy favorites Sylvain Chavanel and Didier Rous. Despite his diminutive size, Voeckler seemed to have the legs and the will to defend the maillot jaune.

But the Posties weren't worried about the head start they had just given away. "Our plan was to give up the jersey or let someone like George take it over, but T-Mobile kept chasing him every time he tried to get away," Armstrong said. "We did enough work to keep the gap down to 12 or 13 minutes. That's fine." When asked whether he was worried about Casar, who finished 11th in the Giro d'Italia two years ago, the Texan seemed unfazed. "This is the Tour, not the Giro," Armstrong said as he stepped into a team car and sped away to his hotel.

STAGE 5, AMIENS TO CHARTRES: 1. Stuart O'Grady (Aus), Cofidis, 200.5km in 5:05:58 (39.30kph); **2.** Jakob Piil (Den), CSC; **3.** Sandy Casar (F), fdjeux.com; **4.** Thomas Voeckler (F), La Boulangère; **5.** Magnus Bäckstedt (Swe), Alessio-Bianchi—all same time
OVERALL: 1. Voeckler, 20:03:49; **2.** O'Grady, at 3:13; **3.** Casar, at 4:06

159m BONNEVAL · 144m Dangeau · 166m Logron · 150m Courtalain · 154m Droue · 152m Mondoubleau · 95m Sarge-sur-Braye · 56m Besse-sur-Braye · 40m Ruille-sur-Loir · 52m Château-du-Loir · 25m Vaas · 30m Le Lude · 42m Savigne-sous-le-Lude · 64m Carrefour D.817/D.139 · 42m Baugé · 34m Fontaine-Millon · 12m Corne · 26m St-Barthélemy-d'Anjou · 28m Angers (entrée) · 25m ANGERS

0 · 6.5 · 13 · 26 · 33.5 · 51.5 · 59.5 · 74 · 90 · 108 · 117.5 · 132 · 139.5 · 147.5 · 154.5 · 168 · 178 · 187 · 191 · 196 KM

EURE-ET-LOIR · LOIR-ET-CHER · SARTHE · LOIR-ET-CHER · SARTHE · MAINE-ET-LOIRE

STAGE 6 | Bonneval to Angers

It was late Thursday evening when Mario Cipollini slipped into a Domina Vacanze team car and made tracks for Paris. The Lion King was leaving the Tour, probably never to return. The flamboyant Italian was a shadow of his former self, with his best finish a 10th into Namur in what had become nothing less than a disastrous return to the Tour after a five-year absence. "My physical condition was deteriorating and I could not keep my focus. I've not felt well since Wasquehal," Cipollini said, referring to the Tour's third stage. "I hate to abandon the Tour de France. It's a race I dearly love." Ironically, it was in Wasquehal where Cipollini won a stage of the 1996 Tour, wearing the tricolored jersey of Italian national champion.

One of the most prolific winners of his generation, the 37-year-old Cipollini had been struggling with a leg infection from an injury he sustained in a crash in May at the Giro d'Italia. More crashes during the first week of the Tour aggravated the wound. "He fell twice, two days ago and yesterday, and the wound reopened," said team spokesman Gilberto Petrucci. "He will need 15 stitches on his left thigh."

Cipollini's countryman Alessandro Petacchi was in equally bad shape following a hard crash in stage 5, where, he said, his shoulder had popped out of its socket. A year ago the mild-mannered Petacchi won four stages before pulling out at the foot of the Alps, and this year he had vowed to make it to Paris. Now, a few hours before the start of the 196-kilometer run to Angers, the fastest man on two wheels was leaving the Tour with his left arm in a sling and his head hanging low.

"I suffered during the night," said Petacchi, who won nine stages in this year's Giro d'Italia. "I had a lot of pain and finally got to sleep at about four o'clock. The big problem is that I've got a ligament problem and I cannot move my arm. My Tour is over."

Just like that, the race had lost two of its best sprinters and two of cycling's biggest stars.

For the 179 riders taking the start in the small town of Bonneval, the day was also going to be a difficult one. Dark clouds were already piling up in the western skies and a strong wind guaranteed some heavy miles.

But you could have sworn it was a sunny day outside the Brioches La Boulangère team bus. Shining brightly in the yellow jersey was Thomas Voeckler, who looked a bit overwhelmed by the weight of the Tour's golden tunic. "After I won the French championships, I got a lot of interview requests, but I can see that with the maillot jaune, it will be even more," he said.

The press hounded the young man to capture a shot for the next day's papers. These days, a Frenchman in yellow is usually reserved for the middle part of the race. A record 81 Frenchman have held the yellow jersey, but none have won the Tour since Bernard Hinault's fifth victory in 1985.

"I didn't realize the effect of having the yellow jersey on my shoulders," Voeckler continued. "Everyone was patting me on the back, and giving me support from the side of the road." Voeckler was enjoying the attention, even patiently waiting while a nervous fan fumbled with a lens cap before snapping a picture.

Meanwhile, over at U.S. Postal Service, Triki Beltran and Chechu Rubiera were checking their wounds as Armstrong quickly slipped out of the bus for the mandatory morning sign-in, stopping briefly to sign a few autographs as well. Without the yellow jersey to worry about, things in the Postal camp were almost calm. Unfortunately, the calm didn't last.

There's no such thing as an easy stage in the Tour. Friday's ride across the rolling wheat fields southwest of Paris was supposed to be a routine day in a week-long march to the mountains, but it was far from uneventful. At just 7.5 miles into the stage, as rain began to spatter down, Armstrong fell atop a group of riders in a pileup that included Voeckler. "Three guys went down in front of me. I just went right over the handlebars," said Armstrong, who quickly remounted his bike. "It was just one of those typical early stage crashes," he shrugged.

Armstrong and the others donned arm warmers and vests during what looked to be an arduous push southwest toward the Loire Valley. Casar, Laurent Dufaux (Quick Step), and Axel Merckx (Lotto-Domo) crashed at 24 kilometers as three riders—Alessandro Bertolini (Alessio-Bianchi), Carlos Da Cruz (fdjeux.com), and Marc Lotz (Rabobank)—zipped off the front. Kurt-Asle Arvesen, the Norwegian rider from Team CSC who crashed hard in the second stage, chased and caught on at 26 kilometers. Two more riders—Jimmy Engoulvent (Cofidis) and Juan Antonio Flecha (Fassa Bortolo)—bridged to make it a sextet.

Thus began a race against time, incentive, and distance. The six riders carved out a four-minute lead at 85 kilometers, but after letting a break stay away the previous day, the sprinter teams led by ag2r and Gerolsteiner started chipping away at the gap.

Engoulvent attacked the lead group with about 30 kilometers to go, but that was going nowhere. Neither was the break. Arvesen and Bertolini lost interest with 22 kilometers remaining, while Flecha hung until the final kilometer. As the peloton surged up to swallow him, Flecha lazily drifted back into the middle of the bunch. Then all hell broke loose.

Tyler Hamilton must be cycling's unluckiest rider. Or perhaps he's the luckiest, depending upon your perspective. He's unlucky to crash, but luckier still to be able to carry on. As the sprinters were revving up their engines for the final slingshot to the line, the peloton was pedaling furiously to stay in contact and avoid losing time if the group broke up. As the pack reached warp speed, there was a horrific crash right in the middle of the bunch. Some thought it was caused by Flecha easing up, while others said dangerous moves by sprinters caused someone's tire to clip. Whatever the cause, riders fell like trees.

The stage was an eerie replay of the opener last year into Meaux—a dangerous finish with narrow barriers, reckless sprinters, and desperate challengers fighting to hang on. More than a dozen riders went down, and the tangle of bikes and bodies cut the bunch in two.

"The road got narrow and guys had nowhere to go but into each other," said Hamilton, who crossed the line with a bloodied jersey and cuts to his back, hip, and elbow. "I went over the handlebars and somehow landed on my back. I kind of lay there for a second to see if I was okay. It was under the 1-kilometer-to-go banner, so I knew we couldn't lose time," he added, referring to a rule that awards all finishers the same time when a crash occurs within 1,000 meters of the line.

Three other Phonak riders crashed, and Hamilton's key helper, Oscar Pereiro, was taken to a local hospital for X-rays, which revealed that his pinky finger was not broken, as feared. "It was similar to last year's stage 1 where I cracked my collarbone," said Hamilton, whose helmet was now broken in three places. "I lost a lot of blood, some bruises, road rash. *C'est la vie*. I'll survive," he said, as only one who has survived many crashes can.

Other victims included Leipheimer, who suffered minor cuts and scrapes to his arm, and Julich, who was slow to get up, having injured his hip and the lower part of his back. "It was a strange crash, and I wound up landing on my back on top of the base of one of the barriers lining the course," Julich said. "I couldn't move my leg for a few minutes, but then after the initial shock, it started to

MAGNUS BÄCKSTEDT, ALESSIO-BIANCHI

Avoiding Disaster

One step at a time. One day at a time.

I know that my "legs" and whether I "have them" or not has been a recurring theme here this Tour. I tell ya, it's a big deal coming to the Tour de France feeling like death warmed over and it's an even bigger deal when you start feeling good. And I feel pretty good all of a sudden.

Yesterday's long break certainly gave me a confidence boost. Today I felt ready to do it again and did my best to get in an early break. As it turned out there were a lot of attacks, and the one that finally stuck included my teammate Alessandro Bertolini.

We were pretty sure that we'd see another break go to the finish again today, but the sprinters' teams seemed intent on keeping this one in check. As soon as this breakaway group went, the peloton didn't really give those guys much time, and the break had to really work to get the gap up to 4 minutes or so. For us yesterday, it took a lot of work, too, but our gap grew out to around 16 minutes, so it was clear that the chase was on today.

Alessandro was definitely keen on going in a break today, and he was ready to jump from the gun. I told him it would do him good to wait a little. Normally, the first four or five attacks don't work, then finally everyone gets tired of chasing and the break goes. Alessandro managed to get into the right one. He's the kind of guy who loves being out there on those long ones, too, so this worked out perfectly. He was happy. He eventually got tired in there and was one of the first two who got caught, but it didn't matter because the peloton swept up all of them by the end . . . all of them, that is, except for Juan Antonio Flecha.

loosen up so that I could walk. I got some treatment from our physical therapists, but I am going to be really sore tomorrow."

Julich rolled across the line with the last group that also included Bernhard Eisel, the young Frenchman who crashed in the first stage, and green jersey holder McEwen. Two-time Giro champ Gilberto Simoni was knocked flat on his back, but his Saeco team rallied around, and together they rode in slowly several minutes later. Worst off was Rene Hasselbacher, an Austrian on the Gerolsteiner team, who was knocked unconscious and later diagnosed with three broken ribs and a broken nose, ending his Tour.

Armstrong was able to avoid the melee and rolled across the line some 40 seconds later under the watchful eye of faithful lieutenant George Hincapie. "The barriers were really tight there and everyone was going 40 miles an hour; I don't know what the hell they were thinking," said Armstrong, who remained 6th over-

This evening we finally got to watch him on television, and it was absolutely amazing. Flecha was unbelievable. He had those guys sitting right on his wheel for almost a kilometer and then he just rode them off. It was a phenomenal and very gutsy ride. Good on him.

So, as you know, the big crash of the day happened almost at the same instant we caught him at the 1K-to-go flag. I was lucky. I was sitting pretty far up there, on the right-hand side of the peloton, and was just about to move up to see if I might contest the sprint. Things were going pretty well, too. But to my left, I heard this big bang and half the peloton came down. That's the awful thing about a crash in the final kilometer—it takes a lot of riders out.

I was lucky, though. I wasn't anywhere near it. I figure I was one of the last guys to get out of there before the whole field came crashing down. I could hear it start on the left of me and I just naturally accelerated and moved to the right. I never saw what happened or even who went down. I am glad I managed to avoid that mess.

Going into that sprint, I knew that it wasn't really my forte. It was uphill—about 4 or 5 percent—and had a couple of corners, neither of which was going to be particularly easy for a guy my size. At the same time, I did want to be up near the front, just in case I had the chance to do something. Obviously, it makes sense to stay close to the front coming into the finish, if for nothing else but to avoid the crashes.

All told, it was a good day. I figure now that I am running at about 85 percent, and I'm keeping my fingers crossed that I've put the sluggishness I felt at the start behind me and will keep moving toward 100 percent. ■

all. "We're lucky the crash was within the final kilometer or else we could have lost time," he said, echoing Hamilton's observation.

Also shooting clear of the pileup was Jan Ullrich, who hadn't kissed the pavement yet in the first week of this Tour, which seemed to be turning into a NASCAR race. "I was lucky to get through without crashing," said the 1997 Tour champion. "I heard it behind me but in those moments you can only concentrate on not crashing yourself. It's been so nervous this week. I cannot wait for the mountains."

One rider who could easily wait for the hills was Tom Boonen, the 23-year-old Belgian who's been anointed as the successor to classics king Johan Museeuw. Boonen, who finished 3rd in the 2002 Paris-Roubaix while racing for the Postal Service team, was now riding for his home country's Quick Step squad and had confirmed his status as rising star after racking up a string of wins in one-day races and minor stage races all spring long.

Tall, friendly, and direct, Boonen worked hard in the off-season to improve his bunch sprint. His efforts paid off handsomely with 13 wins coming into the Tour, including victories at Ghent-Wevelgem and EP3 Harelbeke, and overall titles at the tours de l'Oise and Picardie. Boonen desperately wanted to win one of this year's Tour stages in Belgium, but he lost his chain in the final sprint in stages 1 and 2.

He had no such problem on the rising finish into Angers. Jumping first was O'Grady, but without his usual snap—still tired, perhaps, from the day's previous efforts. The big Belgian roared past him to take a win in his Tour debut. "The last kilometer was hard, but I like sprints like that," Boonen said. "You had to be strong today to win here, and I was strong. I've been very confident. I think the other sprinters had been doubting my ability. I had those mechanical problems at the start of the Tour and maybe they were beginning to think I was using that as an excuse, but without that I would probably have won another couple of stages."

Despite finishing second, O'Grady captured a significant consolation prize. With McEwen caught up in the crash, O'Grady was now the proud bearer of the green points jersey. "It's not the best way to take it, but that's the way the race goes," he said. As one who finished three times runner-up in the hunt for the coveted points mantle, he could afford to be philosophical. "Robbie had a bit of bad luck today, but I've fallen three times already in the race and lost points," he said. "It's just the way it goes."

Before the start of the stage, Armstrong had summed up the feelings of everyone: "In this race, I'm always scared, always nervous. The last two or three days for me, personally, have been really, really nerve-racking," he said. Now, with the first week finally over, he and the rest of the contenders could only hope that the peloton would settle down in preparation for the long slog to the mountains.

STAGE 6, BONNEVAL TO ANGERS: 1. Tom Boonen (B), Quick Step, 196km in 4:33:41 (42.969kph); **2.** Stuart O'Grady (Aus), Cofidis; **3.** Erik Zabel (G), T-Mobile; **4.** Danilo Hondo (G), Gerolsteiner; **5.** Baden Cooke (Aus), fdjeux.com—all same time
OVERALL: 1. Thomas Voeckler (F), La Boulangère, 24:37:30; **2.** O'Grady, at 3:13; **3.** Sandy Casar (F), fdjeux.com, at 4:06

60m CHATEAUBRIANT — 87m Le Bourgneuf — 63m Teillay — 83m Bain-de-Bretagne — 13m Poligne — 60m Bourg-des-Comptes — 82m Guichen — 84m Goven — 41m Bréal-sous-Montfort — 24m Talensac — 15m Montfort-sur-Meu — 93m Irodouer — 147m Becherel — 37m La Roche-au-Borgne — 56m Calorguen — 65m Côte de Dinan — 110m Tréfort — 43m Plancoët — 35m Saint-Potan — 3m Port-à-la Duc — 62m Côte de St-Aide — 57m Cap Frehel — 15m Sables-d'Or-les-Pins — 74m La Couture — 88m St-Alban — 35m Les-Ponts-neufs — 0m Yffiniac — 80m Côte de Langueux — 73m SAINT-BRIEUC

0 6.5 14.5 25.5 31.5 38.5 46 52.5 58.5 67.5 71.5 85 91 97.5 107.5 113.5 119 129.5 138 148 149 157 166 174.5 182.5 190 195,5 199 204,5 KM

LOIRE ATLANTIQUE — ILE-ET-VILAINE — COTES-D'ARMOR

STAGE 7 | Châteaubriant to Saint-Brieuc

The opening week of the 2004 Tour saw a youth movement. Thirty riders started the Tour contesting the best young rider's category, and many quickly left their mark on the race. The surprises started early, with 23-year-old Fabian Cancellara winning the opening prologue. The Swiss rider has established a reputation for taking prologues, winning several in 2003 including the Tour de Suisse. Tom Boonen, the 23-year-old Belgian Tour rookie, won into Angers, and Thomas Voeckler, the 25-year-old French national champion, was sitting pretty in yellow. A new generation was knocking at the door. "That's the best news we had in the first week," said Tour race director Jean-Marie Leblanc. "To see hopefuls like Cancellara, Boonen, or Voeckler shine is my greatest satisfaction."

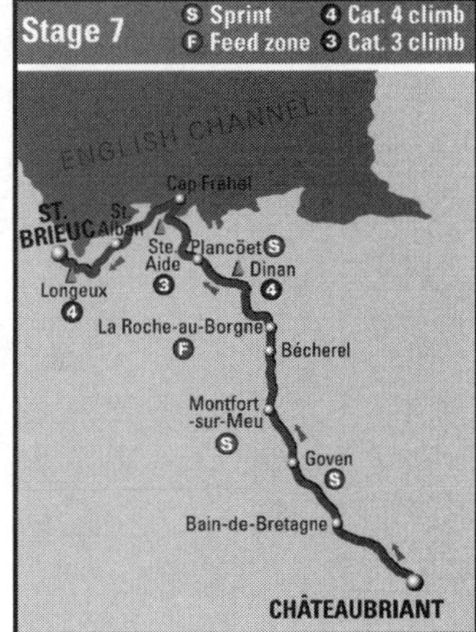

The fight for the white jersey, awarded to the best-placed rider aged 25 or under, was sure to be heated. Riders don't necessarily race for the category but will defend it once they find themselves in position to hold it, as it is one of only four special jerseys awarded during the Tour. The 25-and-under category was introduced in 1975, when Italian Francisco Moser won. Greg LeMond and Andy Hampsten both wore the jersey in their day, and Laurent Fignon became the first Tour winner to lead the category in 1983. Jan Ullrich holds the record with three consecutive white jerseys from 1996–98, while last year's winner was Russian Denis Menchov.

There was some commotion even before the race rolled out of Châteaubriant, a small town lost among rolling hills and dense forests. Each morning before the day's race, team buses park together in an impromptu maze that becomes a beehive of activity as fans scurry about hunting autographs from their favorite riders. Today, however, Lotto-Domo wasn't in the mix. Instead, the team had parked alone on an access road on a ridge high above the main expo area.

TYLER HAMILTON—PHONAK

Rain and Chaos Theory

Greetings from the rain-drenched Tour de France.

I don't think we saw a single drop of water throughout all of last year's Tour, but 2004 is shaping up to be a battle against Mother Nature, among other things. So much for that old theory that the first half of the Tour is always boring. The first week has been full of all kinds of action. Unfortunately, all of the excitement has been more about things outside of the riders' control than the race itself, although one could argue that weather is a major part of the Tour every year. Last year's heat wave was no treat. So far this year, it's been rain and wind wreaking havoc on the peloton.

When the streets are full of water, everything washes up from the gutters and the sides of the road, so you are constantly riding over pebbles and debris. I think our team has had more than 20 flat tires in the last four stages. It's been crazy.

Friday's finish was eerily reminiscent of stage 1 last year, when more than 40 riders hit the pavement with 500 meters to go. There is always a chance of a crash when the peloton comes charging in for a sprint finish, especially during the first week of the Tour, when there is so much at stake and huge pressure on every rider in the race. That's why I think—out of respect for the riders—every stage with the potential of finishing in a sprint should do so down a big, straight, wide boulevard.

Maybe this doesn't make for great television, but the number of roundabouts, medians, islands, lefts, rights, crowds, and narrowing roads we've needed to navigate through the finishing kilometers of the last few stages borders on irresponsibility. Expecting nearly 180 riders to barrel down a finishing straight that narrowed by the meter yesterday was a big miscalculation by the technical directors. It was as crazy as the hard right that brought down the peloton last year.

The team had reason to feel apart. Belgian Christophe Brandt had been kicked out of the Tour for failing a drug test taken after the second stage. Urine tests revealed traces of the banned substance methadone, a drug typically used to help recovering heroin addicts, but one that can also be used as a painkiller. The 27-year-old Brandt became the first rider to fail a dope test on this year's Tour and the first since 1999 to fail a test for anything other than banned blood boosters.

"I don't understand. I have never heard about this product," Brandt told Belgian reporters. "Maybe tests should be made on the vitamins I took in recent days, but I never took methadone." A second sample would be analyzed before Brandt was officially sanctioned, but his Lotto-Domo team suspended him immediately after the initial test results were received. "It's a shame and a pity, espe-

The number of guys riding in bandages at this point might be unprecedented. I've never seen so many guys beat up at the same time. Our team is no exception—almost all of us went down in the crash yesterday. Oscar Pereiro got up off the ground with his little finger bent straight out at a 90-degree angle. It looked awful but was not broken, just dislocated. He lucked out.

I went over the handlebars and landed on the back of my head, scraping up my shoulder blades and my spine. I was pretty sore at the start this morning, but all in all, I think I was pretty lucky. Hopefully I'll feel better in a couple of days.

Today's final kilometers were a bit crazy as well. Although the finishing straights were a little more generous than yesterday, there was a close call about 10 kilometers from the finish. The crowds were in the streets and some kind of flare was burning on the left side of the road. The smoke made it difficult to see padded barriers in the center median, and some guys just barely missed them. All this was going on just as we were heading full speed into a roundabout, so it really is amazing no one got seriously hurt.

These have been some tough days at the office, but our team does try to relax every night after dinner. Before we eat, we're all caught up in the hectic scheduling of massage, chiropractic work, getting bandaged by the doctors, and so on. No one has a free second until well after 10 p.m. But by late night, we all try to regroup outside. Our team bus is pretty comfortable, and it has become a tradition that we wind down our days here at the Tour watching a movie or race highlights, or just hanging out together out in the parking lot. It sounds kind of funny, given all the time we spend in the bus transferring to and from the starts and finishes. But I guess it's the closest thing we have to home at the moment, so it's kind of become our rolling clubhouse.

Tomorrow is going to be another long, windy ride. Hopefully, we'll see some sun. ■

cially coming from a rider we know well, but his team director took the right decision," Leblanc said. "That's what we expected."

Over at Saeco, there was another hullabaloo. Gilberto Simoni, the 33-year-old, two-time Giro d'Italia champion and winner of a Tour stage last year, was not a happy camper. Banged up and bruised from falling hard the previous day, and even angrier for losing minutes in the team time trial, a fuming Simoni sat in the team car and stubbornly refused to race.

Eventually, Saeco sport director Giuseppe Martinelli literally prodded his reluctant rider to the line. Simoni struggled during a fast opening two hours that averaged more than 45 kilometers per hour. After surviving the 204.5-kilometer stage, he rolled across the line *sans* helmet and surrounded by his teammates—a

MAGNUS BÄCKSTEDT, ALESSIO-BIANCHI

A Big Split, an Interesting Finish, and a Looming Sense of Dread

It really does pay to pay attention.

That's easy to say, but over the course of a 5- to 7-hour stage it's easy to let your attention lapse and miss something important. Fortunately, I was keeping an eye on things as we headed toward the coast of the English Channel today.

I was a hurting a bit on the day's Category 3 climb. Just before we reached the Channel, I noticed the CSC boys all moving up front together. We were riding into a heavy rain then, so I thought for sure that as soon as we hit the left turn along the water they were going to try something—put it straight in the gutter and just go for it. I figured that I needed to get up to the front myself then, too. I started making some crazy moves past people, working my way up there, and I got fairly close to the front just as they put the hammer down. The split in the field happened right behind me—I was the last guy to make it—and I figured that I made a lucky move.

For 20 kilometers the guys up front really put in a huge effort. We were just flying down the road on these little hills—up and down and up and down—running along at 60 kilometers per hour at times (all of it in this driving rain). The roads were slick, and the rain and road spray were such that you couldn't see anything.

It turned out that Stuart O'Grady—a guy who usually reads a race really well himself—was caught out by the split. There were a few others back there, too, Moreau being one of them. Still, all of the biggies—Armstrong, Hamilton, Ullrich, even Mayo—made the cut. And that may have been why all of a sudden—

mobile barrier in case he tried to do a runner. "I almost quit; it was fifty-fifty but in the end I decided to carry on," said Simoni bitterly as his long day wound down. "I'm hurting from my crashes and I am so angry from the time I lost in the time trial I could vomit."

Last year, Simoni was forced to eat crow after finishing a disappointing 84th, more than 2.5 hours behind Armstrong. Earlier in the 2003 season, he had loudly promised to derail the Texan, but under the Tour's relentless heat, he'd wilted. Simoni salvaged that Tour with a victory in stage 14 in the Pyrénées, but he arrived in Paris both angry and diminished.

Things were little better this year for the emotional Italian. Simoni came into the 2004 Tour on the heels of a humiliating loss to his younger teammate Damiano Cunego in the Giro d'Italia. Although he'd started the Italian grand tour as the heavy favorite, Simoni quickly found himself outflanked by his 22-year-old teammate. The chance for redemption at the Tour propelled him to continue

just as we got out of the rain—everyone suddenly stopped riding up there.

The split took a lot of effort on CSC's part, even with help from Postal. With that much effort, you have to hope for a return and neither team really was going to benefit from it if all the GC guys were up in the front group with them. You can imagine what would have happened if, say, Ullrich or someone else had missed the cut. They would have driven all the way to the finish like that. It pays to pay attention. So Moreau and Stuart and the others lucked out as the peloton regrouped after 20 kilometers, and then everyone's attention turned to the final kilometers and the finish.

Today's finish was a nice change of pace, with rolling hills all the way toward the line. Still, a lot of guys were really hurting once it got to a sprint—including me. It was quite an interesting finish. These days you don't see a lot of groups getting away in the last 5 or 10 kilometers like you did today. Usually if things regroup with 10 or 20 kilometers to go, you know it's going to be a bunch kick, but today the guys managed to get away and hold it all the way to the finish. That makes for quite a nice end to the day, really.

The team is holding up nicely. Boldato is starting to come around a bit after a couple of crashes this week. Scott Sunderland is starting to ride exceptionally well. He was in the mix all day and was still going well at the finish. He even managed 9th place today, I believe. That's a good sign, as he never really tries for the sprint unless he's got phenomenal legs. Caucchioli is riding very strong, always up there in the first 10 or 15 guys and always riding clever. We are really hoping that he can do something

continued ›

training after his infuriating Giro loss, but now his prospects were nil after so many opening-week difficulties.

"I'm going to keep going because I can't waste all the hard training that I've done and all the sacrifices I've made to get ready for the Tour," he said. "I hope that I can make it to the rest day on Monday so that I can recover and then think ahead to the mountain stages. Hopefully my Tour will start in the mountains."

Once the peloton rolled out, it didn't take long for the fireworks to begin despite the soggy conditions. It was no surprise when Team CSC tried to animate the stage as the course pushed west into Brittany, which featured the Cat. 4 Côte de Dinan climb at 114 kilometers and the Cat. 3 Côte de St. Aide at 149 kilometers.

Phonak kept the lid on until Cancellara, Massimo Giunti (Domina Vacanze), and Karsten Kroon (Rabobank) tore away before the day's first intermediate sprint, but their break lasted only a few kilometers. And when Erik Dekker

MB

continued

when we get to the mountains. He tells me he's feeling good.

All told, I felt a little bit less energetic than I did yesterday, but I still feel okay on the bike. I figure the stage on Tuesday—after the rest day—will suit me quite well, and maybe that's a day when I can try my hand. It will have to be then, because Wednesday is going to be a nightmare. Look at that profile. The thing is 240 kilometers long and there are a million bloody climbs in there! It never stops. There will be a lot of people suffering that day—it's going to be awful. Nine categorized climbs!

Those days are the worst. With so much on the road, you can't allow yourself to sit up until you get to that last Cat. 2 climb before the big Cat. 1. If you stop riding hard before that, you won't make it in with the gruppetto, you won't make the time cut, and your Tour will be over.

But in the meantime, we have a couple of easier stages and a rest day. Let's enjoy those. ■

(Rabobank) and Thierry Marichal (Lotto-Domo) shot off the front at 54 kilometers, the bunch was happy to let them go.

By 97 kilometers the gap was up to 8:30, and a steady dose of rain and wind made for yet another miserable day. With the nerves, the crashes, and the poor weather, riders were wondering if it was ever going to end. "Everybody is sick and tired of the rain," Armstrong agreed. "But anything over last year, when it was 35 degrees [Celsius], is better. It was so hot you couldn't sleep."

Rain continued to spit as Dekker and Marichal pushed farther west, but the peloton was waking out of its slumber. Having missed the break, Team CSC was not about to lie still. The big, red machine moved to the front just as the course edged near the blustery Baie de Saint-Brieuc, making a hard left turn as it followed the coastline.

Team CSC's acceleration quickly put the hurt on the main bunch, causing a split with about 40 kilometers to go. Getting caught in the second group of about 40 riders was O'Grady in the green jersey. The aggression made for a tough run into the finish for the Aussie. "I had pretty heavy legs after the last few days. It was very hard to come back," O'Grady said. "The guys rode their asses off and I was lucky to get back up," he confessed.

Eventually, Dekker and Marichal wilted under the pressure, and then Team CSC launched Piil with 25 kilometers to go. Hot on his wheel was Evgueni Petrov (Saeco), Vicente Garcia Costa (Illes Balears), and Cancellara. They built up a short-lived gap before the reassembled peloton caught them with 8 kilometers to go.

▶ Tour rookie Fabian Cancellara (Fassa Bortolo) surprised the favorites to take the first yellow jersey after a dominant performance on the streets of Liège, beating five-time defending champion Lance Armstrong (U.S. Postal Service) by two seconds.

▼ Estonian veteran Jaan Kirsipuu (ag2r) shot to his fourth career Tour stage victory in an unorganized sprint into Charleroi, making it the 114th win of his career and ranking him third among active racers behind Mario Cipollini and Erik Zabel.

⊙ Aussie pocket-rocket Robbie McEwen (Lotto-Domo) elbowed his way to victory in the tricky downhill run to Namur, ⊙ while Thor Hushovd (Crédit Agricole), right, finished second but grabbed the yellow jersey, the first by a Norwegian.

⊙ (OPPOSITE) Italian Marco Velo (Fassa Bortolo) clutched his left clavicle after breaking it during a decisive crash on the approach to the first cobbled section in stage 3. In the background, Iban Mayo received help from an Euskaltel-Euskadi teammate to remount his chain, but the damage was done. The Basque climber lost 3:48 on the day.

Škoda
robobank
rabobank.nl
159

Despite trepidation, most riders got across the cobblestones in stage 3 without too much difficulty. Australian Stuart O'Grady (Cofidis) was one of the few who crashed and later was caught up behind a passing train as he tried in vain to chase back on to the leading group.

Tyler Hamilton led the way for Phonak in the team time trial race. Despite a string of mechanical problems and crashes, the Swiss team finished second to U.S. Postal Service and positioned the American for a run for the podium.

BMC
BELL
BMC

▲ Viatcheslav Ekimov led the U.S. Postal Service to victory in the team time trial race for the second year in a row. The victory put Lance Armstrong into the yellow jersey for the sixtieth day of his career.

▼ The rainy stage 5 saw the Tour's first breakaway stick, with Stuart O'Grady shaking off his fellow escapees to grab an emotional victory. French sensation Thomas Voeckler (Brioches La Boulangère) slipped into the yellow jersey, giving the French something to cheer about.

▼ Tom Boonen (Quick Step) couldn't be happier after scoring his first Tour stage victory into Angers on a day that saw sprinting stars Mario Cipollini (Domina Vacanze) and Alessandro Petacchi (Fassa Bortolo) each leave the Tour winless. Boonen's victory, meanwhile, harkened a new generation of stars making their presence felt in the Tour.

The rolling terrain in the final kilometers prompted a string of attacks, first by David Etxebarria (Euskaltel), Spanish national champion Francisco Mancebo (Illes Balears), and Paolo Bettini (Quick Step). That didn't stick, but moments later a group of seven broke free that included Mancebo, Bettini, Iker Flores (Euskaltel), Filippo Pozzato (Fassa Bortolo), former world champion Laurent Brochard (ag2r), and Michele Scarponi (Domina Vacanze).

They didn't get much of a gap, but the windy and climbing finish worked in the break's favor. Scarponi, a Tour rookie who won the Peace Race in May, attacked with 3 kilometers to go, and Brochard dug deep to hang on. Flores, Pozzato, and Mancebo clawed their way to a narrow gap as they roared under the 1-kilometer banner. The 22-year-old Pozzato, the youngest rider in the Tour, made easy work of his two rivals and scored a victory a week into his first Tour.

"Since Petacchi gave up, all the riders are free to try to win the stage," said Pozzato, a winner last year of Tirreno-Adriatico. "Now the Tour is very different for us. Scarponi attacked, but I didn't want to go with him because it's not good for Italian riders to attack each other. Then the Spanish rider attacked and I followed him." Pozzato's win made Leblanc even more cheerful. The Tour had its third win in a week by a Tour rookie.

Nicknamed "Pippo," Pozzato seconded Leblanc's hope that a new generation was knocking on the door. "Boonen, Cancellara, Pozzato—yes, it's a new generation," Pozzato said. "This year with Cunego in the Giro, the new generation is here. The old champions are still there, but I think we need two or three more years before taking their place."

The main bunch caught Scarponi just as he crossed the line, 10 seconds behind the first finishers. For the sprinters in the hunt for the green jersey, the mad rush for the points was almost as important as the stage victory. Norwegian Thor Hushovd (Crédit Agricole) surged to take 8th place in a finish worth 18 points.

Behind him, frantically fighting to defend his jersey, was O'Grady, whose Cofidis team had given everything to bring him back when Team CSC forced the split. With his sprint rival McEwen out of position, and a straight shot to the line in the offing, O'Grady was horrified, then angered, to discover compatriot Scott Sunderland (Alessio-Bianchi) suddenly in front of him. When the stage has already been won, the G.C. riders typically step aside to the let the green jersey contenders make a clean run to the finish. Yet here was Sunderland, a 37-year-old veteran making just his second Tour start, mucking up O'Grady's sprint. Barely avoiding a collision, an angry O'Grady gave Sunderland a sharp shove after they crossed the line.

O'Grady kept the jersey by one point over McEwen, who was boxed out and finished 13th. Later, O'Grady wouldn't name Sunderland specifically, but he vented his anger. "There are always problems with other riders in the finish," he said. "It's hard, people get in the way. It does get a bit messy. There's lots of desperation with desperate riders doing desperate things."

Armstrong, meanwhile, rolled through 55th to remain 6th overall behind leader Voeckler. Nearly a week into the Tour, Armstrong was feeling the stress. "Nervous, dangerous, not easy, every day has been pretty long, every day has been 200 kilometers, that starts to grind on everyone," Armstrong said of the Tour's first week. "I think guys are tired, stressed from all the crashes."

Crashes and avoiding them had become a major theme. The French sports daily *L'Equipe* counted 99 crashes in the opening six stages, and riders openly complained about narrow roads and tricky finish-line approaches. Hamilton took that question to race director Leblanc before the start of Saturday's stage. "At least half the peloton is bleeding, if not more," said Hamilton, who had crashed hard the previous day. "I think we deserve safer finishes. There have been a lot of changes for the rider's health, so what about safer courses?"

Stage 7 had its victims. Sven Montgomery, the big Swiss rider on Gerolsteiner, went down in a crash at 127 kilometers and broke his right clavicle. With teammate Rene Hasselbacher not starting, Gerolsteiner was down to seven riders.

But the day was not without its charms. With 10 kilometers to go, the peloton had roared through Yffiniac, home to five-time winner Bernard Hinault. "His name was painted all over the road," Armstrong recalled.

Nicknamed "the Badger," Hinault is the last Frenchman to win the Tour and remains a national hero. After retiring in 1986, Hinault retreated to his farm in the rolling hills of Brittany. He kept to himself for a few years and then reemerged as a member of the Tour entourage, where today he works as a presenter of prizes on the podium. It was Hinault who shook Armstrong's hand following the Texan's fifth victory and said, "Welcome to the club."

"He's a legend," said Armstrong. Mulling over Hinault's career, which was built on stunning victories in the mountains far from Brittany, Armstrong added, "I don't know how the hell he became such a good climber growing up around here. I'm still trying to figure that one out."

STAGE 7, CHÂTEAUBRIANT TO SAINT-BRIEUC: 1. Filippo Pozzato (I), Fassa Bortolo, 204.5km in 4:31:34 (45.182kph); **2.** Iker Flores (Sp), Euskaltel-Euskadi; **3.** Francisco Mancebo (Sp), Illes Balears—same time; **4.** Laurent Brochard (F), ag2r, at 0:10; **5.** Sebastian Hinault (F), Crédit Agricole—same time

OVERALL: 1. Thomas Voeckler (F), La Boulangère, 29:09:14; **2.** Stuart O'Grady (Aus), Cofidis, at 3:01; **3.** Sandy Casar (F), fdjeux.com, at 4:06

Chapter 7: Week Two

Texas Chainring Massacre

Lance Armstrong enjoyed what he described as a "nearly perfect" opening week of the 91st Tour. Despite one minor spill, Armstrong put the cycling world on notice with a strong prologue and an absolutely dominant team time trial in stage 4.

Some of his key rivals weren't so lucky, and many entered the second week with both hope and trepidation as they prepared for the looming climbing stages in the Massif Central and Pyrénées. The walking wounded included Hamilton and Mayo, two of Armstrong's top rivals who were caught up in unlucky crashes that seemed to put a pall on their Tour aspirations.

If there was any consolation for the nervous peloton, it could be found in the three upcoming stages in the Massif Central. The constant climbs and descents over France's celebrated midsection would likely put an end to the massive sprint finishes of the first week, and thus reduce the chances for the chain reaction pile-ups that had put the hurt on so many riders. After a short stage 8 into Quimper in Brittany, the riders would board an evening flight to Limoges for a rest day. The race would then head into the hills, and also, most likely, into better weather, another welcome change for the rain-weary troops.

So far, the Tour had delivered an engaging opening series of tests. With each stage yielding a different winner, the Tour had already seen five riders embrace the yellow jersey in seven days. A new generation led by Pozzato, Boonen, and Cancellara butted heads with established stars Armstrong, Kirsipuu, McEwen, and O'Grady. Only one breakaway had stuck, but teams such as Team CSC were putting pressure on the peloton every day with long sorties. Despite the early departures of Cipollini and Petacchi, the sprints were heated and wide open.

Taking the yellow jersey into the second week was Voeckler, the young French champion who was growing in credibility by the kilometer. His Brioches La Boulangère team rose to the occasion to defend the golden tunic for their young charge, who was rapidly becoming the media darling among the French newspapers. Despite his 9:35 advantage over Armstrong, however, many assumed the untested Voeckler would fold in the Pyrénées.

But after the jumpy, pent-up battle of nerves across Belgium and northern France, it was still hard to judge the strength of the favorites. Apart from Armstrong's brilliant performances in the prologue and the team time trial, and the handicaps issued to Hamilton and Mayo due to spills, the state of the other contenders was largely unknown. Ullrich looked menacing and sounded confident. Heras lurked like a quiet assassin awaiting his opening. Basso, Mancebo, and Menchov were full of potential, but no one could say whether that potential would blossom until the battle was joined in the Pyrénées.

A look at the "virtual" standings revealed that Armstrong already boasted useful time gaps over his rivals, with Hamilton sitting 36 seconds adrift and Mancebo at 43 seconds. Ullrich was 53 seconds behind and Basso was 1:17 back. None of those deficits was insurmountable, but putting time into his rivals would freshen Armstrong's confidence—if he needed the boost.

So stages 9, 10, and 11 would provide the first clues as to who might have the legs and mental fortitude to challenge the Texan. It all would depend on how the stages were raced. If one of the major contenders dropped the hammer, the humps and bumps of the Massif Central could have major consequences for the final outcome.

But most eyes were glued on the Tour's two summit finishes towering atop the Pyrénées. If the Alpe d'Huez time trial wasn't counted as a true summit finish because it was one against the clock, then stage 12 to La Mongie and stage 13 across the heart of the Pyrénées to the grueling summit at Plateau de Beille could be the decisive battlegrounds for the yellow jersey.

That was the conventional thinking at the first break, anyway. As it turned out nearly a week later, though, few had truly imagined what lay in store when the peloton rolled out of Castelsarrasin for the start of stage 12.

90m LAMBALLE
111m Le Vau Jaune (Brehand)
143m Montcontour
247m Plemy
165m Le Poncet
246m Carrefour D.35/N.774
246m Carrefour D.35/D.53
209m Carrefour D.35/D.69
130m Mur-de-Bretagne
294m Côte de Mur-de-Bretagne
213m Pied de côte
297m Côte de St-Mayeux
220m Corlay
155m Plounevez-Quintin
228m St-Lubin
210m Mael-Carhaix
167m Carhaix-Plouguer
94m Port-de-Carhaix
140m St-Hernin
67m Ar c'hanol
136m Côte de Ménez-Kuz
115m Châteauneuf-du-Faou
58m Canal de Nantes à Brest
247m Côte de l'Enseigne Verte
152m Briec-de-l'Odet
158m Waterloo
55m Quimper (entrée)
89m QUIMPER
0 7.5 14 18.5 23.5 30 35.5 40 47.5 51 53.5 54.5 61.5 73.5 84.5 92.5 104 111 115 126 131 136.5 142.5 150 157.5 163.5 168 KM
COTE D'ARMOR
FINISTERE
127.5

STAGE 8 | Lamballe to Quimper

More rain and wind greeted the 176 remaining riders at the start of the hilly, 168-kilometer stage across the heart of Brittany. Despite the inclement weather, thousands of rabid fans turned out to stand in the villages and by the roadsides—not uncommon in the rugged, verdant heartland of French cycling.

With the first of two rest days coming up on Monday, Tour planners had mapped out a relatively short stage from Lamballe to Quimper over a smattering of Cat. 3 and Cat. 4 humps and bumps. That evening the riders would be whisked away by plane to Limoges to enjoy their day off, rather than make the six-hour drive that awaited the rest of the Tour entourage.

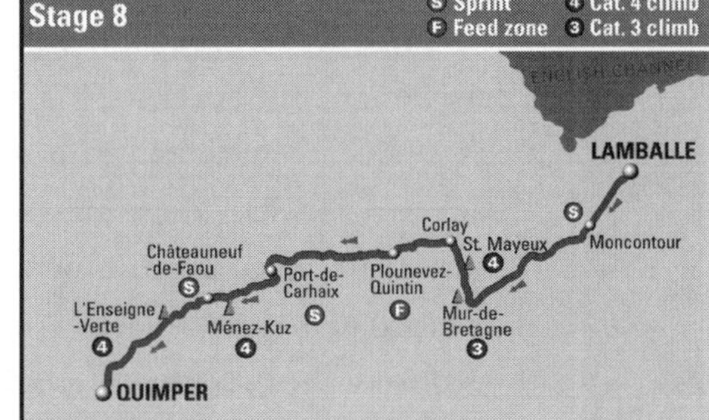

The clouds couldn't dampen the spirits of Michele Scarponi (Domina Vacanze), a bright-eyed Italian making his Tour debut. "It's been so rainy here I think I should race with an umbrella," Scarponi joked before the start. "I skipped the Giro to get ready for the Tour. I want to try to win a stage. I know it will be hard, but I am going to give everything I have. I don't want to get to Paris with anything left in my legs."

After some early moves, none other than Mr. Breakaway, also known as Jakob Piil (CSC), was back on center stage. In the first week of the Tour, Piil couldn't keep still. This time around, the 31-year-old Dane found company with Kaarsten Kroon (Rabobank), Ronny Scholz (Gerolsteiner), and Matteo Tosatto (Fassa Bortolo).

Each day in the opening eight days of the Tour, Piil had been sticking his nose in the wind. It was all part of Team CSC's strategy to light up the Tour de France. Team CSC manager Bjarne Riis surmised that the sprinter teams weren't as strong this year and thought some early pressure would force the other teams to do more work than they wanted. He assigned Piil, Kurt-Asle Arvesen, Michele Bartoli, and Jens Voigt to make sure the CSC red jersey was present in every break.

"It's just been lucky that the moves I've covered have stayed away," said Piil, a winner of a Tour stage last year into Marseille. "Most days you get caught, but it's a gamble that you have to try. It's a combination of factors, depending on the motivation of the other teams, the riders present in the break, and sometimes just luck."

Most of Piil's adventures ended short of the finish line, but in stage 5, the gamble paid off and the lead break he was in made it into Chartres, where he lost to Stuart O'Grady (Cofidis). The easygoing Dane said he preferred to be on the attack, even if it meant some extra legwork. "I actually feel a little safer in the breakaway," he explained. "When you're in the peloton, you really have to fight to keep your position and it's very stressful. At least when you're up the road you don't have to worry about anyone else."

Roughly five minutes behind Piil and Co., the main bunch suffered through the rain. Fans stood five deep on the moderate climbs that punctuated the day's rolling course, so much so the peloton had to snake through massive crowds atop the Cat. 4 Côte de l'Enseigne Verte with 24 kilometers to go.

Crédit Agricole and Quick Step collaborated to chip away at the lead the Piil group had worked to build. With 10 kilometers to go, the break gave way to the peloton, but the Dane had earned a dubious honor: In the opening eight stages, he'd been on the attack for 551 kilometers out of the 1,449 kilometers raced.

With 8 kilometers to go, a dog ran on the course and caused a crash near the back of the bunch. Worst off were Samuel Dumoulin, a French rider on ag2r, and Janek Tombak, an Estonian on Cofidis. Both ended up with cuts and scrapes but managed to finish the stage.

Facing the prospect of another bunch sprint, Quick Step's Paolo Bettini shot away with just over 1 kilometer to go on a short climb. The two-time World Cup champion had been wearing the polka-dot best climber's jersey all week, perhaps keeping it warm for teammate Richard Virenque, but he still hadn't been a decisive player in the Tour. Quick to mark Bettini's wheel was Robbie McEwen (Lotto-Domo), who sensed the scrappy Italian might stay away. The pair opened a short gap on the fast-charging bunch, but the Australian refused to come around and take a pull. The pair was gobbled up short of the line and exchanged words unfit for print.

"He wanted me to ride, I wanted him to ride, so neither of us rode," McEwen explained later. "You don't win the stage by riding at the front with someone else; that's the way it is." And after that? "I was legless at the finish," he said.

With McEwen swallowed up, Kim Kirchen (Fassa Bortolo) made a stab for glory, but he couldn't hold off the big motor of Thor Hushovd (Crédit Agricole). In the final 100 meters, the Norwegian national champion chugged past the Luxembourg national champion to win his second career Tour stage. "The Vikings have returned to Brittany," Hushovd joked after the win. "I want to thank Julian Dean, who really worked hard to get me into position over the final hill. Without him, I couldn't have won the stage."

Despite the wasted effort earlier, McEwen rebounded to take 4th ahead of O'Grady's 8th. His finish, along with the four points he won by taking 2nd at the day's first intermediate sprint, meant that he had recaptured the green jersey. Meanwhile, farther back, Thomas Voeckler's bakery boys had kept him well protected. The young Frenchman was able to pack the yellow jersey for the flight down to Limoges.

After eight stages, 1,449 kilometers, and 33 hours of racing, Lance Armstrong and the rest of the overall contenders were relieved to get through the opening week in one piece. Unlike last year's bumpy Tour, which began with Armstrong struggling through dehydration and injuries, the defending champion enjoyed a nearly flawless start to his run for a record sixth Tour title. "It was close to perfect," Armstrong agreed. "I can't complain. We're in a good position. I feel good, I feel healthy. Now we start the next part. We would have been better off without the new regulations, better off without the crashes. It could have been worse. There could have been some splits in the final kilometers; we didn't have that."

"The Vikings have returned to Brittany!"

Armstrong's rivals, meanwhile, were just as ready to leave northern France behind for three potentially explosive stages in the Massif Central. Hamilton was still sore following Friday's finish-line crash. Working with a physical therapist, the New Englander was also undergoing acupuncture treatments to help alleviate the pain. "Considering all the problems we had in the last couple of days, I'm happy we finished today," said Hamilton, who rolled over the line 36 seconds behind Armstrong. "A couple of days ago, we had problems with the crash. I was lucky we had a couple of flat stages to recover."

Iban Mayo, the Spanish rider for Euskaltel who humbled Armstrong on Mont Ventoux in June, smashed his right elbow into the barriers in Friday's crash. X-rays revealed no fracture, but it made life even more difficult for the Basque contender. "The elbow is better and even more important is the morale," said Mayo, who was sitting 5:27 behind Armstrong. "We see the American is strong, but we will attack once we get to the Pyrénées."

Jan Ullrich, meanwhile, had avoided crashing, but entered the rest day nearly a minute behind Armstrong. "The team has ridden well, but Jan is farther back than we'd like," said T-Mobile's team manager Walter Godefroot. "Armstrong's strength is no surprise to us. We knew he'd be ready for the Tour."

On Tuesday, the Tour's terrain would change significantly, leaving the flatland behind in favor of the Massif Central's medium mountain climbs over narrow, twisting roads. It would be an appetizer for the first major climbing stages in the Pyrénées.

STAGE 8, LAMBALLE TO QUIMPER: 1. Thor Hushovd (Nor), Crédit Agricole, 168km in 3:54:22; **2.** Kim Kirchen (Lux), Fassa Bortolo; **3.** Erik Zabel (G), T-Mobile; **4.** Robbie McEwen (Aus), Lotto-Domo; **5.** Andreas Klöden (G), T-Mobile—all same time
OVERALL: 1. Thomas Voeckler (F), La Boulangère, 33:03:36; **2.** Stuart O'Grady (Aus), Cofidis, at 3:01; **3.** Sandy Casar (F), fdjeux.com, at 4:06

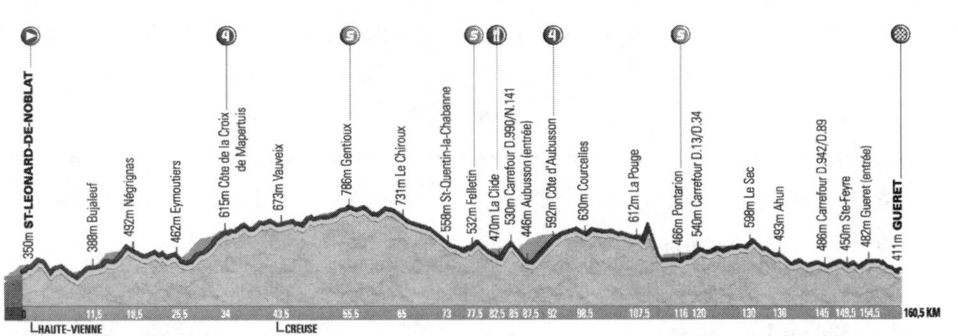

STAGE 9 | Saint-Léonard-de-Noblat to Guéret

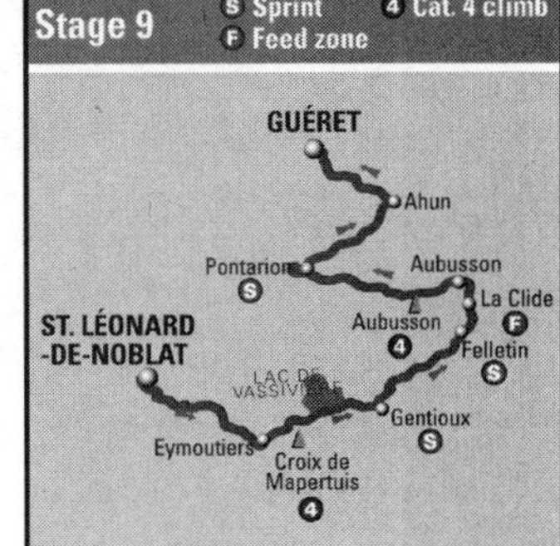

Lance Armstrong enjoyed a relatively quiet rest day, going on a two-hour morning ride with his teammates and otherwise relaxing around the team hotel on the outskirts of Limoges. Tuesday's stage 9 opened the door to three potentially tough days in the Massif Central, and all the teams were looking forward to putting the nervous first week behind them.

Armstrong was comfortably poised going into the Tour's second week, holding a 36-second margin over Hamilton, 55 seconds over Ullrich, and more than 5 minutes on Mayo. Armstrong had reason to be happy. "I'm glad we have a bit of a cushion on those guys," Armstrong said. "I would not want to be in the reverse position and have to make up a minute on Ullrich. We have a bit of a cushion and we can be more conservative in the mountains and we'll see what happens. We'll still attack if we have to attack."

Following the long transfer, the Tour's shortest road stage was scheduled a day before the longest. The 160.5 kilometers from Saint-Léonard-de-Noblat to Guéret would roll over two Cat. 4 climbs and through three sprint points, giving everyone something to savor. Gone was the rain, the wind, and the nervousness that dominated the opening week. Riders were looking ahead to the coming mountain stages with mixed feelings.

"From today on it's going to be really nasty," predicted Liberty's Christian Vande Velde, back at the Tour for the first time since 2001. Race leader Thomas Voeckler was particularly wary of Wednesday's stage, the toughest the peloton would face before the Pyrénées. "I'm scared. I'd be lying if I said otherwise," he admitted. They all knew it was going to be difficult, but almost anything was better than what they had endured across Belgium and northern France.

There was a special buzz in the start village as the stage assembled in the hometown of Raymond Poulidor, one of France's most beloved sportsmen, who captivated an entire nation for gutsy performances that inevitably came up short. Despite riding 14 Tours, from 1962 to 1976, Pou-Pou, as he is affectionately known to the French, never wore the yellow jersey. "Poulidor has almost become a noun, meaning second. There is a Poulidor of politics, a Poulidor of boxing," Poulidor told the French daily *L'Equipe*. "Of course I have regrets. I think I deserved to win it, really. But I'm not losing sleep over it."

"Poulidor has almost become a noun, meaning second. There is a Poulidor of politics, a Poulidor of boxing . . ."

His Tour record aside, Poulidor won nearly 200 races in his career, including the Vuelta a España, Paris-Nice, Milan-San Remo, and the Dauphiné Libéré. In what was something of a misnomer, Poulidor became known as the eternal runner-up. Even then his three 2nd-place finishes and five 3rd-place finishes were outdone, as Joop Zoetemelk finished 2nd a record six times. But Zoetemelk also won once, in 1980, something Poulidor was never able to do.

Before the racing could get under way, news from Belgium revealed that Christophe Brandt's second B-sample test confirmed the presence of methadone. Brandt had been yanked from the race by his team before the start of stage 7, after failing a test in Namur at the end of the second stage. "We have looked everywhere in the team for methadone. We have made tests and checks on power bars and nutritional products we use. But we did not find anything," Lotto-Domo team director Claude Criquielion told Belgian journalists.

The rest day also saw the forced departure of Stefano Casagranda, an Italian on Saeco, and Martin Hvastija, a Slovenian on Alessio-Bianchi, who were kicked off the Tour after doping allegations were brought to the attention of the race organizers. "We received a letter from financial investigators from the [Italian] city of Padova advising us that the two riders are under investigation on doping grounds," Tour director Jean-Marie Leblanc told a news conference. "We have told their team directors that they were no longer welcome on the Tour de France."

Casagranda, 31, and Hvastija, 34, were both caught up in the infamous San Remo raids of the 2001 Giro and linked to Italian doctor Enrico Lazzero. Leblanc pledged to exclude any rider from the Tour involved or charged in a doping investigation, a strict new policy that had kept Danilo Di Luca, David Millar, and Cedric Vasseur from starting. "We had asked the teams about the riders concerned before the start in Liège and they told us everything was fine," Leblanc said. "But now there is no doubt and we cannot let riders suspected of doping pollute our race."

In an attempt to leave his own doping scandal behind, Filippo Simeoni hoped to erase a career's worth of bad memories at this year's Tour and found what he thought was the perfect opportunity. Simeoni, a journeyman with Domina Vacanze, joined Euskaltel-Euskadi's water-carrier Iñigo Landaluze in a breakaway just 4 kilometers past the day's first of two Cat. 4 climbs, and he threw all of his anger, frustration, and hope into his pedals.

Prior to the Tour, Simeoni had been garnering more headlines off the bike than on it. He'd collected a modest seven victories in his 11-year pro career—hardly headline material—but had seen his name splashed across the front pages after he'd figured highly in court cases for alleged doping within the ranks of Italian cycling. In 1999 he told an Italian judge he had taken the banned blood-booster EPO. He gave his testimony, he said, because he was ashamed of his actions. Rather than encourage his honesty, though, the Italian Cycling Federation handed him a six-month racing ban (later reduced to four by cycling's international governing body, the UCI).

Then in 2002 he was back in the news after giving testimony during the trial of Armstrong's personal coach Michele Ferrari, claiming that Ferrari had given him doping substances. Later that year, Armstrong retaliated by openly questioning Simeoni's integrity and, in a 2003 interview with the French daily *Le Monde*, called Simeoni an "absolute liar."

That was too much for Simeoni, who decided to file a defamation of character lawsuit in an Italian court against Armstrong. Simeoni said he was pursuing the case against Armstrong "because he can't abuse his power and go unpunished. I just want him to publicly recognize his error," he said in an interview with French journalist Philip Brunel. "I'm not even making it into a question of money. If I win damages, I'll give the money to charity."

Seemingly away from his troubles, and finally riding the Tour, the 32-year-old rider churned his pedals to try to expunge those demons from his soul. "I attacked today for my pride," Simeoni said. "I've dedicated my life to cycling but I've been unfairly treated, so there's a lot of anger and desire for revenge in my heart."

Landaluze, meanwhile, was racing with *sangre fria* or cold blood, as the Basque riders like to call it, and he had every intention of winning the stage. Working smoothly with Simeoni, the pair sped up and down the rolling hills to build a lead of 9:45 with 70 kilometers to go.

As the end of the stage drew near, the sprinter teams, led by Cofidis, Crédit Agricole, and Quick Step, finally came to life and joined Boulangère's efforts in the chase. The lead came down rapidly. With 35 kilometers to go, the gap was trimmed to 5:25, and then to 1:25 with 10 kilometers to go. It was going to be close.

MAGNUS BÄCKSTEDT, ALESSIO-BIANCHI

Attack of the Speed Demons

Man, this was a tough day.

Like I've said here for a few days, I am feeling a whole lot better on the bike, and I sure needed to be, because this stage was tough!

I have to say I've never suffered as much on the bike as I did during the first 40 kilometers of this stage. I just cannot remember ever doing a stage this fast on terrain like that. It was unbelievable today—absolutely unbelievable. Everyone in the peloton was just sprinting flat-out for the first 40 kilometers. Every attack drew some kind of response from the field, and people just kept attacking and attacking. The terrain made it absolutely brutal. It was 2 kilometers up and 2 kilometers down and just kept on going like that the whole time. Even during the KOM—about 4.5 kilometers in length—the peloton seemed like it was hitting 40 kilometers per hour on the climb.

The whole time it was up and down, up and down. I would lose a few spots on the climb and then ride like crazy—diving into corners hard and trying to make up whatever places I'd lost. Finally, it eased off—it had to—and Igor Landaluze from Euskaltel and Felippo Simeoni of Domina Vacanze got off the front. They managed to get away just as everyone in the peloton was sitting up, mostly because everyone was just too wasted to move.

Right before they went—and while we were all still pushing it like crazy—I glanced around, and everyone I saw looked ready to explode. It had been like that from the start; everyone seemed to be riding at 100 percent just to to stay on the wheel in front of him. It was absolutely incredible.

Then these two guys just sort of drifted off the front. Of course, they really had to put in a lot of work to get away and build up any kind of lead, but they timed it perfectly. When they left

At the 8-kilometer mark, there was a heavy crash when Spaniard Mikel Pradera (Illes Balears) plowed into a road sign and cartwheeled into the path of Kurt-Asle Arvesen. Both riders went on to finish. Not so fortunate was Jaan Kirsipuu (ag2r). The Estonian sprinter who won the Tour's first stage abandoned the race early in stage 9.

After zipping under the 1-kilometer red pennant, Simeoni and Landaluze held a 15-second lead but their escape was still no sure thing. Simeoni kept checking back as Landaluze remained glued to the Italian's wheel, intent on timing his sprint just right. He needn't have bothered. New Zealander Julian Dean gave teammate Thor Hushovd a nice lead-out coming up the slightly climbing finish, and they, along with the other sprinters and the following peloton, swept past the pair in the final 50 meters like a wave engulfing two small stones on a beach.

there was a bit of a pause, and then everyone let out this big sigh of relief and looked happy to see them get away. Everyone sat up, caught his breath, got a drink, stopped to take a piss, and recovered a little.

However, once those two hit 10 minutes, the sprinters' teams moved up front and started driving it just as hard again. We were doing 60 kilometers per hour at times. It made for an unbelievably tough day, but not nearly as tough as it must have been for those two poor guys, getting caught like they did with less than 100 meters to the line.

What can you say? It's just not fair. I mean, if they'd have been caught with even a kilometer to go, I'd say, "All right, fair enough," but that close has got to rip your heart out.

I do need to respond to the many questions I've received about the Tour's decision to eject my teammate Martin Hvastija. From my perspective, it was unfair of the Tour to suddenly decide to throw him out after eight days of racing. Martin has never been caught using anything, never been caught in possession of anything, and he has not tested positive for doping. I respect the Tour's decision to apply a stricter standard, but in Martin's case, the whole thing is based on a taped conversation from three years ago.

What's more, the organization knew about this before the Tour started and said that it was not serious enough to keep him out. Then, after eight days of racing, they come and tell him, "No, you can't race anymore," and that is what makes it absolute bullshit as far as I am concerned.

It's a three-year-old case, and if the charge was that serious, then they shouldn't have let him start in the first place. If it wasn't serious enough to keep him from starting, then they should have allowed him to finish. But that's just my point of view. At the end of the day, the decision is made by Jean-Marie, and we can't do much about it. So I'll just focus on the task at hand and ride my bike. ■

"I didn't hear a thing as the peloton approached; it was all rather surreal," Landaluze said. "There was no sound at all. I couldn't hear the fans, nothing, then suddenly I saw riders to my left and to my right. Had I known the peloton was approaching so close I would have started my sprint at 300 meters. Instead, I started at 150 meters because I was sure I was going to beat the Italian."

For Simeoni, it was another cruel blow. At the team bus after the race, he recounted the finish choked with emotion. "With a kilometer to go it seemed like we'd stay away, but destiny stepped in and didn't want to help us stay clear," Simeoni said. "Losing like that really hurts. It's terrible to be caught so close to the line, but I've got to accept it because losing, just like winning, is part of cycling. Unfortunately it didn't come off, but I'll try again."

McEwen caught his fellow sprinters by surprise, shooting a half-wheel ahead of Hushovd and O'Grady to win his second stage and widen his hold on the green jersey. "I don't want to sound like I'm a one-legged man," said McEwen, who complained of injury. "It's a great victory after the crash and injury I suffered three days ago. In the sprint, I gave all the energy I had left in my body." McEwen's win earned him 35 points at the finish line, with 30 going to Hushovd and 26 to O'Grady.

McEwen had widened his lead on the powerfully built Norwegian champion by 18 points, but the Aussie admitted that tendinitis in his left knee kept him wondering whether he would be able to continue in the Tour. "After the crash in Angers, I was covered in bruises all over and my muscles really tightened up, but the main problem is that I landed right on my kneecap when I fell," McEwen explained. "I've also got a sore gluteus, which means that my whole way of riding has had to be modified. The physio has tried to work through the problems, but where he's putting his hands, there's no skin there, so it's quite difficult. Honestly, coming into today the most important thing was just to stay in the race. You can ask any of my teammates, I had to stop six times yesterday when I was out training because my knee was hurting so much. So I wasn't thinking about the green jersey; it was more about survival."

Armstrong wasn't about to take the bait offered up by Simeoni. U.S. Postal Service did what it had to do during the stage, letting Brioches La Boulangère defend the jersey until the sprinter teams were ready to take over the final chase. "We just stayed on the wheel and we didn't have any responsibility," said Armstrong, who remained in 6th place overall. "The speed today was just flying. I'm surprised we caught those guys."

The peloton was already looking ahead to the monster awaiting them in the tenth stage to Saint-Flour—the Tour's longest. The course would hit tough climbs along the way, including the 5,243-foot Col du Pas de Peyrol, a Cat. 1. "These stages are hard, but they're not the high mountains," said Johan Bruyneel, director of Armstrong's U.S. Postal Service team. "I don't think the major challengers will lose much time, but anyone who is not strong will have a hard time to stay on."

Armstrong would be counting heavily on new teammate José Azevedo as the Tour approached the decisive climbing stages in the Pyrénées and Alps. The 30-year-old Portuguese rider, who had joined Armstrong's nine-man team over the winter, was known as a *super-domestique*—a strong rider who had the ability to shine on his own but instead had chosen to sacrifice his chances to further his team leader's cause. "To help Lance win a sixth Tour would be the greatest achievement of my career," Azevedo said during Monday's rest day. "Lance is very easy to work for. He encourages you and demands the maximum, but you know your efforts are paid back when he wins."

Azevedo finished 5th in the 2001 Giro d'Italia and 6th in the 2002 Tour, and he had signed on with Postal Service to replace Roberto Heras, who had departed at the end of the season to lead the Liberty Seguros team. Losing Heras was tough, but Armstrong said the arrival of Azevedo made his Postal Service team even stronger. "Roberto is a great rider, but to be honest, Azevedo fits in the team much better," Armstrong said. "I think his personality and mentality is a better match for this team than Roberto. Roberto is probably destined to be a leader and it's good [for him] to be where he is."

Indeed, Azevedo's tireless climbing power and modest personality fit right in with the Postal brief, complementing the skills of his teammates nicely. And as the Postal machine clicked off the kilometers toward the mountains, the strength of Armstrong's team became more and more apparent.

STAGE 9, SAINT-LÉONARD-DE-NOBLAT TO GUÉRET: 1. Robbie McEwen (Aus), Lotto-Domo, 160.5km in 3:32:55; **2.** Thor Hushovd (Nor), Crédit Agricole; **3.** Stuart O'Grady (Aus), Cofidis; **4.** Jerome Pineau (F), La Boulangère; **5.** Erik Zabel (G), T-Mobile—all same time

OVERALL: 1. Thomas Voeckler (F), La Boulangère, 36:31:31; **2.** O'Grady, at 2:53; **3.** Sandy Casar (F), fdjeux.com, at 4:06

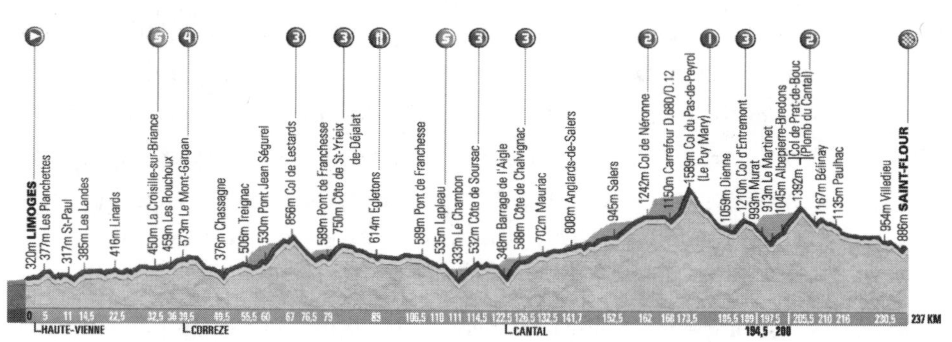

STAGE 10 | Limoges to Saint-Flour

After nine nervous stages, the favorites were looking forward to stretching their legs. The 237-kilometer, nine-climb course drove straight across the heart of the Massif Central—hilly, undulating country that's seen some of the greatest moments in Tour history.

Huge crowds turned out in downtown Limoges to watch the rollout of the 91st Tour's longest stage. It was Bastille Day, France's national holiday, and with businesses closed thousands of fans pressed in on the team buses as riders welcomed sunny skies for the first time in a week.

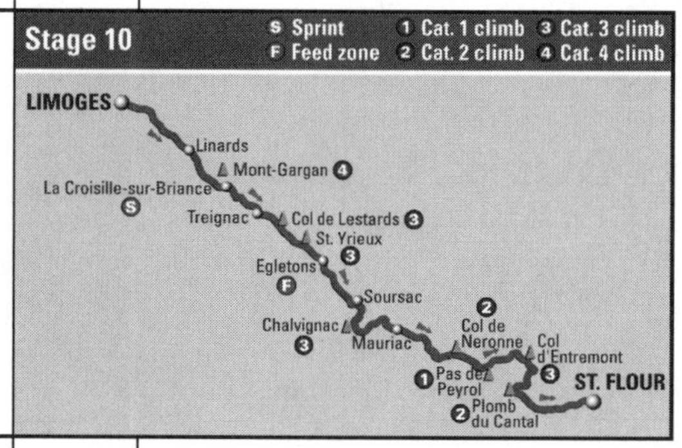

Nothing could cheer up Tyler Hamilton, however, who was tucked away inside the Phonak team bus after a dreadful night that saw him catch only intermittent sleep. The gritty New Englander, who had carved a reputation for enduring mind-numbing pain, was a wreck after a tearful good-bye to his golden retriever, Tugboat.

The dog had been an integral part of Hamilton's struggle through pain in the 2003 Tour, when he broke his collarbone in the first stage. Hamilton's wife, Haven, had traveled with Tugboat from their European home in Girona, Spain, to nurse Hamilton through the difficult moments. Tugboat slept at the foot of Hamilton's bed, and each morning before starting the day's stage, Hamilton would talk to Tugboat, stroking the dog's head, to help take his mind off the searing pain in his shoulder, back, and ribs.

A year later, Hamilton was banged up yet again from a crash, but Tugboat would no longer be there for him. The retriever's nine-year-old body was riddled with cancer, and Haven had brought him to Limoges on the rest day to let Hamilton say good-bye. Haven returned to Spain to have the dog put to sleep while

MAGNUS BÄCKSTEDT, ALESSIO-BIANCHI

Life in the Slow Lane

My responsibilities have changed.

We're in the mountains, so my job has changed from trying to win a stage to slipping down into "suffer mode," grinding it through, and making sure I don't miss the time cut. These are the days that my director gives me something of a free hand. The other guys have responsibilities themselves, of course. The big job is to do as much as possible to protect and help Pietro Caucchioli and Andrea Noe'.

It was an even tougher day than I had anticipated. The first days into the mountains are always a struggle for me; it takes time for my legs to get used to the stiff climbing. On top of that, the weather was—for the first time in this Tour—fairly warm, so I felt like I was suffering right off the bat.

I had hoped to make it a little farther, but I found myself struggling a bit on Col de Neronne, a Category 2, and then really had a tough time on that Category 1, the Col du Pas de Peyrol. I slipped back, chased on the descent, reconnected, and then found myself in a little gruppetto with Robbie McEwen, Thor Hushovd, and a few other guys. We worked to catch a bigger group ahead of us, then that group teamed up and chased on to another bigger one, and so forth.

Robbie was looking good today. He, too, is sort of on damage control right now. Robbie and I used to spend a lot of time together in the grupetto back when I was riding for Crédit Agricole. So things haven't changed much, except that these days a lot of the English-speaking guys we used to have back there with us—guys like Stuey and such—are now up front.

At one point, our group was about 3 or 4 minutes behind the big gruppetto on the last Category 2 climb (the Col de Prat-de-Bouc) and we chased fairly hard. But it was fine, because I can

continued ›

Hamilton faced the longest day of the Tour. "A lot of people probably don't understand, but Tugboat for me was a family member," Hamilton said. "I'd rather ride with two broken collarbones. I'd rather do it a hundred times than lose Tugboat."

Despite the long road ahead, riders wasted no time attacking once the course hit the green hills east of Limoges. There was only one strategy that would work for Postal Service: Keep Voeckler in the yellow jersey and force Boulangère to control the race.

An early group of nearly 18 riders tried to slip away. Postal's José Luis "Chechu" Rubiera covered the move, but Bruyneel didn't like its size and sent Viatcheslav Ekimov and George Hincapie to the front to chase it down. Boulangère had its own ideas and tried to put rising star Sylvain Chavanel into

MB
continued

usually make up 3 or 4 minutes on these guys on the descent.

It was hard work today, but there was no real stress about it. The time limit is so big on a long, hard stage like this one, we really were never in any danger of missing it, so the pace was fairly relaxed and we came across around 25 minutes after Virenque (who, by the way, knocked me out of 4th place on GC with that performance of his).

After days of being in the top five on GC the inevitable happened, and I will start the day solidly in 72nd place, 25:32 behind Thomas Voeckler. Of course, I knew all along that was gonna happen sooner or later. As much as I might enjoy it, let's just say that I have no illusions of being on the podium in Paris. I do have goals, and there are a couple of flat days left. I am going to do my best to win a stage on one of those days.

The team is doing well. Our two GC came in well today. Pietro finished 10th, alongside Voeckler and Armstrong and those guys. He's going really well and he was climbing with all of the top guys and felt comfortable and strong.

It's a good bunch we have on this team. Even though the team is sort of divided along the Scandinavian part and the Italian part, everyone gets along quite well and we all speak a bit of each others' languages.

Martin's departure from the race hit us all, but it hasn't really changed anyone's role on the team. The primary job now is to protect Caucchioli and Noe'. But like I said, when it comes to the mountains, I get the freedom to do whatever I want. My only goal is to finish the stage as fresh as I can and not to go through too much pain. The other guys are there to look after the team leaders, and they've done a good job all around. The boss seems pretty happy with the whole crew.

My big goal is to take things day by day and go with the flow. We'll see how tomorrow goes, okay? ■

the next break, but Bruyneel sent more chasers and put a quick end to that as well. Only when the nonthreatening riders Richard Virenque and Axel Merckx (Lotto-Domo) slipped away at 32 kilometers did Bruyneel relax.

"Even though Rubiera was the best in the classification, it was better to work than to let it go," explained Bruyneel, one of the finer tacticians in the game. "A big group you cannot control and a course like this—they can take 20 to 25 minutes. We decided to chase it back. When it was Chavanel and the three guys, we decided to chase it back because it would have meant that we would have had to chase all day because the leader had one rider in the front. Once Virenque and Merckx were in the front, we knew that the leader Brioches would take control of the stage."

Eyes rolled in the pressroom when Virenque tore away. It was a vintage move by the 34-year-old, flamboyant Frenchman, one of the most controversial figures in the peloton. Virenque was a member of the Festina team that was ejected from the 1998 Tour after customs officers found more than 400 doses of banned drugs in a team car. Virenque is remembered for breaking down in tears when race director Jean-Marie Leblanc told him in a roadside café the team wouldn't be allowed to carry on. "Long live cycling! Long live the Tour!" were Virenque's woeful parting words.

While other Festina team members quickly confessed to doping, Virenque denied the allegations vehemently and continued racing in 1999 and 2000. It wasn't until late 2000 that he finally was brought into court to face a judge, whereupon he quickly folded. Yes, he admitted, he had taken the drugs, along with his teammates; of that there was no question. He was handed a seven-month racing ban that kept him out of the 2001 Tour. "My career is over," he said tearfully. But at the end of his suspension, Virenque signed a new contract and bounced back. In the 2002 Tour, he won a long breakaway up Mont Ventoux, denying Armstrong a victory in the process. In 2003, he attacked into Morzine to win the stage and capture the yellow jersey for one day.

At 34, Virenque was fast approaching the end of his career and he wanted to leave in a blaze of glory. He started the 2004 Tour tied with Spanish rider Federico Bahamontes and Belgian Lucien Van Impe with six mountain titles. Claiming a record seventh King of the Mountains polka-dot jersey—and winning a Tour stage, too—would put him in the history books and perhaps overshadow the missteps in his career.

The French (and especially French housewives) absolutely love the Morocco-born climber and his soap-opera good looks, and the hundreds of thousands of fans lining the course put wind into his sails as the duo chugged over the six moderate climbs leading toward the main obstacle up the Col du Pas de Peyrol, at 173 kilometers. "I didn't attack because it's Bastille Day, but I wanted to have more points for the best climber's jersey," Virenque said later. "It was wonderful because there were so many people on the road. The sun is back and so am I."

For his part, Merckx, the son of cycling great Eddy Merckx, was making no effort to challenge Virenque over the early climbs. It was obvious the pair had worked out an arrangement—Virenque to gather the points and Merckx to gain the stage win. But, true to his character, it was an agreement that Virenque would quickly break. The twosome held a lead of 10:50 nearing the base of the Col du Pas de Peyrol, also called Le Puy Mary, the steepest climb the Tour had faced so far. The final 1.5 kilometers held an average grade of 12 percent—enough to catch some of the favorites by surprise. "The climb was a lot harder than the book said," observed Levi Leipheimer, who rode tucked in with the top guns. "I was riding a 33x23; I wished I had a 25 on there."

With two kilometers to go on the grinding ridge, Virenque steadily chugged up the green, treeless summit of the dormant volcano and dropped Merckx. Virenque rode a steady tempo that Merckx couldn't match and the Frenchman topped out 41 seconds ahead of the blond Belgian. Once past the crest, though, Virenque made no effort to wait for Merckx and cleared the Cat. 3 Col d'Entremont at 189 kilometers with a 1:05 gap that widened to 6:50 as Merckx gave up the chase over the Cat. 2 Col de Prat-de-Bouc with 32 kilometers to go.

Merckx was gobbled up by the peloton with 30 kilometers to go and didn't hide his feelings when he crossed the line. "I'm disappointed and bitter," Merckx said. "When we went away, we made an immediate agreement—he'd take points in the mountains, and if we get to the finish, we'd have an honest battle for the victory. On the Puy Mary, I was going up my tempo and I thought he would wait because we had an agreement. But no, he went, he didn't respect his word. If I had known that, I would have taken points from him on the climbs. I suppose the national holiday is too strong of an influence for him. I have respect for the rider, but my respect for the person has strongly diminished."

Virenque poured it on coming up the final 1-kilometer climb along the ramparts leading to the medieval walled city at Saint-Flour. Thousands of Sanflorians cheered Virenque as he powered across the line, fingers pointed to the heavens. France had its fourteenth Bastille Day winner since World War II and Virenque had his polka-dot jersey and his seventh career stage win at the Tour. In tears again, Virenque dedicated his win to a friend who died two days earlier and to his grandmother who died in June. He said he thought of them as drove through the pain of riding alone at the end. "Last year, I had the yellow jersey on Bastille Day, now I won this stage," Virenque said. "I was at the end of my strength. I had cramps everywhere."

While Virenque was making his run for glory, the main contenders were finally getting a good look at each other on a challenging course. Expectations were for a major showdown up the Le Puy Mary, but the favorites were like heavyweight champs sizing each other before a bout. Everyone was holding back on that first punch.

The peloton had thinned to about forty riders through a forested section before clearing into the treeless summit, packed with thousands of zealous fans. Wilting under the pace were McEwen, Pradera (who crashed the previous day into the barrier), Bäckstedt, and Hushovd. The "Cricket," Paolo Bettini, had also lost his snap—and the polka-dot jersey.

Missing the action was Iban Mayo, who seemed to be intent on winning the bad-timing award in the 2004 Tour. The Basque climber had little chance to show off his climbing legs because he was stuck at the back of the peloton, a victim of a mechanical failure. Just as the main bunch was nearing the steepest section, Mayo's rear derailleur slipped, causing him to smash his right knee into his handlebars. With the team car languishing near the back of the line of support vehicles, Mayo switched bikes with teammate Unai Etxebarria. But the bike was too small, and Mayo pushed on awkwardly until the team car worked its way up the narrow roads to deliver his own bike, now repaired.

It was becoming clear that this first major climb of the 2004 Tour wasn't going to be decisive. In fact, there appeared to be an unannounced cease-fire among the big guns. As the lead group swung right up the final hairpin, out of the trees and onto the sunbaked flanks of the extinct volcano, Ullrich was being led by revived lieutenant Andreas Klöden and Armstrong had his flank protected by José Azevedo. Neither the Kaiser nor the Boss seemed to be in any particular hurry, and the lead bunch was shoulder to shoulder across the road as they crested the climb, with Klöden, Ullrich, Armstrong, Azevedo, and Michael Rasmussen (Rabobank) taking the front line.

There were two horrible crashes coming down the twisting descent. The tires of T-Mobile's Mattias Kessler slipped and he careened off course into a roadside ditch, somersaulting over his handlebars. He flipped on his back and his head smashed against a fence post, his helmet surely saving him from serious injury. Incredibly, the tough German remounted his bike and finished the stage, but he would not start the next day, leaving Ullrich with one less helper. Sébastian Hinault, a French rider on Crédit Agricole, was even less fortunate. He fell in a ditch on a diving left turn and was carted away in an ambulance.

In the end, everyone agreed the Le Puy Mary was a dud. "Lance looked good, he sounded good on the radio," Bruyneel said. "It was a hard climb, still very far from the finish, because we cannot really know who is good, who is bad because there were no real attacks." Postal's assistant director Dirk Demol agreed. "They are just looking at each other," he said. "Today was a very long, tough day, but I think everybody is waiting for the real mountain stages. These stages here, it's hard to make any real damage. We think that the race will be decided in the last nine days of the Tour. Lance wants to be at the best in the end, we're almost there. He's okay. So far, so good."

STAGE 10, LIMOGES TO SAINT-FLOUR: 1. Richard Virenque (F), Quick Step, 237km in 6:00:24; **2.** Andreas Klöden (G), T-Mobile, 5:19; **3.** Erik Zabel (G), T-Mobile; **4.** Francisco Mancebo (Sp), Illes Balears; **5.** Thomas Voeckler (F), La Boulangère—all same time
OVERALL: 1. Voeckler, 42:42:14; **2.** Stuart O'Grady (Aus), Cofidis, at 3:00; **3.** Sandy Casar (F), fdjeux.com, at 4:13

TYLER HAMILTON—PHONAK

Tribute to Tugboat

Back in 1995, my parents owned a dog named Bosun. They bred him with a female named Baby. Tugboat was the pick of their litter. I chose him because he was the most animated of all the puppies. Quite often, Baby's owner would find Tugboat out of the puppy kennel and perched on its roof. He was an entertainer, even at a few weeks old.

When Tugs was born back in Massachusetts, I was living in Colorado. When he was old enough to be separated from Baby and his eight siblings, he spent a brief hiatus at my parents' home in Marblehead. Then he was loaded onto a plane headed for Denver, all by himself. It would turn out to be the first of his many trips across the country.

Bike racers generally don't have dogs. Especially bachelor bike racers, which I was back then. But I had just bought my first house and wasn't so sure at that time where the bike-racing thing was heading. In my mind, it was almost a fluke that I had morphed from collegiate cycling to the pro ranks. I thought my lucky breaks had probably run their course and that I'd be settling down in Colorado before too long.

As the months passed and the racing calendar heated up, Tugboat and I started living out of our suitcases fairly consistently. I would head off to the races and Tugs would shack up at a friend's house. I was lucky because Boulder has always been a dog-friendly town. And I had lots of friends who were willing to take him in while I was away. It was a pretty good system.

Then a few big changes impacted our lives. First, the team I was riding for, Montgomery Bell, got a new sponsor—the U.S. Postal Service. There were big plans for this organization to go to Europe and ride in the Tour de France. That meant the better part of 1996 was going to be spent on the road in the U.S. and going back and forth to Europe so we could prove ourselves as a developing team. Tugs and I were spending more time apart than together.

A girl named Haven came on the scene just before Tugboat's first birthday. She had grown up with a cat and a goldfish and had been chased by a neighbor's dog when she was a kid, so the odds of Haven and Tugboat hitting it off were a little slim at first. But together, Tugs and I eased her into the dog-loving life. Our first challenge was convincing her that golden retrievers aren't vicious. Our second was getting her to pet Tugboat with more than just her fingertips for a millisecond. It was slow going, but she came around. Tugboat could charm the socks off of just about anyone.

My first full season in Europe was 1997. Haven was working in Boston, Tugboat was staying with my family in Marblehead, I was living in Girona, Spain, and friends were renting my house in Colorado. Our lives stayed this way until 2000, when Haven moved over to Europe. We hesitated about bringing Tugs over at first because we worried that the 15 hours of crated travel to Europe would be inhumane. So he remained in Marblehead in-season and then came to live with us in the off-season. He never seemed to mind all the transitioning; he just rolled with the venue changes as if he understood that my career required him to do so.

Finally, in 2002, we decided the in-season separation was too much. His place was with us on the road, wherever that led. So we loaded him up in the all-too-familiar crate that had shuttled him between Colorado and Massachusetts so many times and brought him with us to Spain.

The airline we chose made him fly in cargo instead of baggage, which meant we had to pick him up in a different terminal. The flight arrived just before 6 p.m. We made a mad dash to the cargo terminal and arrived there at 6:35—only to find out that the cargo office closed at 6:30. They wouldn't let us pick up Tugs until 10 a.m. the next morning when the processing office reopened. We were horrified.

We protested and pleaded. Haven even cried. But they didn't care. They did agree to let us see him and take him out for a walk around the cargo warehouse, which looked like the inside of a Home Depot. Tugs was pretty happy to be released and immediately relieved himself at the end of an aisle of shelves holding boxes of pricey imports. We would have cheered if we hadn't been laughing so hard. Tugs was a trouper. He had to spend his first night in Europe in a cargo warehouse, and he accepted the challenge like a champ.

Tugboat was one of the largest dogs in Girona. Reactions to him were always mixed. Sometimes people would scream and run from him like they had just seen a two-headed monster. But there were just as many others who warmed to him instantly, like the lady across the street from our house, who owns a café. She always had a slice of queso ready for Tugs. In fact, it was hard to get him back in the house if he didn't get his customary treat.

I think Tugboat liked his vagabond life. Unlike dogs who live in one house and walk around the same block three times a day for their entire lives, he enjoyed a variety of experiences in his nine years. He traveled extensively in the U.S. and Europe. He covered a lot of ground in New England and out West. And overseas he visited Spain, France, Belgium, Italy, and Monaco. He traveled through the Dolomite Mountains with us while I previewed stages for the 2002 Giro d'Italia. He drove nearly the entire route of the 2003 Tour de France. He ran through fields in the Pyrénées and Alps. He swam in the Atlantic Ocean and the Mediterranean Sea.

Aside from his travels, Tugboat also got to do a few other fun things. He appeared in a documentary aired on Danish television, and he'll be featured in the IMAX film "Brain Power," which

continued ›

premieres worldwide in 2005. He also posed for countless photo shoots for magazines and newspapers. Haven thought it was funny when Tugboat would be invited to media interviews and she wouldn't. He even received fan mail and care packages from his admirers. But he never let his fame go to his big boxy head. At the end of every day, he was still good old Tugs.

There were a few things that never changed about Tugboat. He loved tennis balls. He could sit with a tennis ball at the end of his mouth for hours. He even invented his own game where he'd sit at the top of a staircase and wait for you to throw the ball to him. After he caught it and gave it a good chewing he'd drop his chin to the floor and push the ball out of his mouth with his tongue. It would roll down the steps back to whoever was in charge of tossing it back to him. We called this game "lazy-dog fetch."

Tugboat liked to eat. He never turned down food and often sought it out. He learned that kids in strollers equaled sticky treats, and pigeons crowded on the ground meant bread crumbs. He remembered where the cafés set up their tables during the day and did his best to help clean up after the patrons at night. The city of Girona could have hired him as a street cleaner.

Tugboat liked to sit in the front seat of the car and lean his head on your shoulder while you drove. He would lick the tears off your face if you cried. He would rest his head on your feet while you watched television. He would lie under the kitchen table while you ate dinner. He would bite your wrist gently to tell you he was happy to see you. He loved to roll on his back and punch the air with his paws. He yanked the stuffing and squeakers out of every one of his dog toys. He swallowed his dog food without chewing it. He loved helping with the dishes. He was a truly special dog, who supported me through thick and thin and was by my side all through the 2003 Tour. He knew I was hurting and he comforted and protected me in a way that was nearly human.

On July 12 Tugboat collapsed. He had been sick for about a month after a reaction to an anti-inflammatory arthritis drug that badly irritated his stomach. An endoscopy revealed multiple ulcers; it looked like he had road rash on his insides. The internal bleeding caused by the ulcers made him very weak. We can only assume he had been in the early stages of suffering from cancer when the drug reaction occurred. We think his system was so weakened from the blood loss that the cancer pounced.

After his collapse, the vet recommended emergency exploratory surgery. They found carcinoma and tumors throughout his body. One had ruptured on his liver and had caused the collapse. They recommended putting him down immediately while he was still sedated. They gave him no chance of survival.

My wife and I spoke that night, and we decided that Tugs had one last road trip in him. I needed to say good-bye and thank you to my trusty companion face-to-face. Haven brought Tugboat home Monday night and set out for Limoges, France, the next morning. Tugs made the final journey in good form. He was heavily sedated, so he never walked again, but he was alert enough to know he was with the two people who cherished him the most.

Tugs and I slept side by side that night. Ironically, one year after he had done so for me, I was comforting him at the Tour de France. Before the start of stage 10, I said my good-byes. Haven drove him back to Girona where the vet was waiting for her call. On the way into town, she stopped at a bakery and bought a whole bag of pastry. It had been weeks since Tugs had been well enough for a treat, but Haven's brother Derek, who traveled with her to France, suggested they take Tugs to a park for his final feast. They carried him out of the car and sat with him under a shady tree, feeding him his favorite chocolate- and sugar- and cheese-covered desserts until there wasn't a crumb left. He was still on earth, but I think, at that moment, he must have been in heaven. At the end, Haven tucked my jersey from stage 9 under one of Tugs's legs and his last Credit Lyonnais Lion under the other. He was a bike racer's dog from start to finish.

Haven's favorite memory of Tugs is walking down the Champs-Élysées with him last summer at the finish of the Tour, and asking, "Tugboat, do you know how far from Marblehead you are?" Somehow I think he knew. My favorite memory was ascending a 14,000-foot peak with Tugs when he was a puppy. We got caught in a snowstorm at the top, but that was just part of the fun. He was such a good friend. Such a good traveler. Such a good companion. Everyone who knew him felt a special bond with him. He loved unconditionally and will be missed by many. Especially me.

Tugboat, thanks for everything. ■

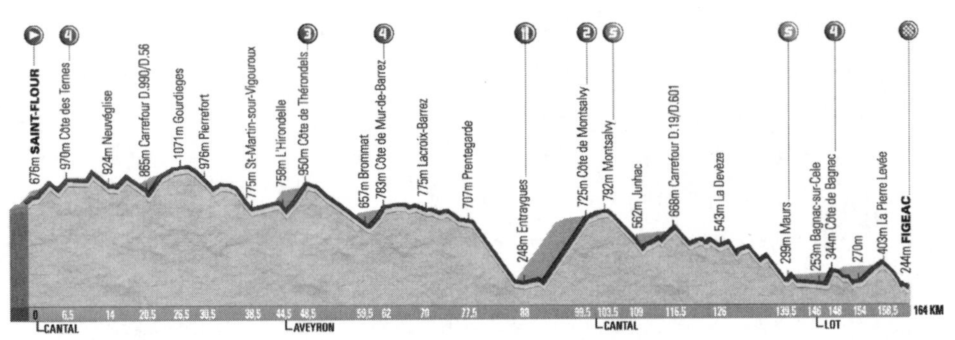

STAGE 11 | Saint-Flour to Figeac

The big attraction in the start village this morning was the brown cow that was going to be presented to the Bastille Day stage-winner, Richard Virenque. The Tour hands out 2.8 million euros in prize money, but a big, healthy cow could go a long way toward feeding a bike team.

After a late night celebrating Bastille Day, locals were waking up with hangovers, but the Tour was still waiting for something to happen. After the flop the previous day—unless you were French and a Virenque fan—many were already looking past the 164-kilometer 11th stage with eyes toward the Tour's first date with the Pyrénées. "The Pyrénées are going to be explosive," said Alvaro Pino, director of Hamilton's Phonak team. "The climbers have to take advantage every chance they get. No one can wait for l'Alpe d'Huez; by then it will be too late."

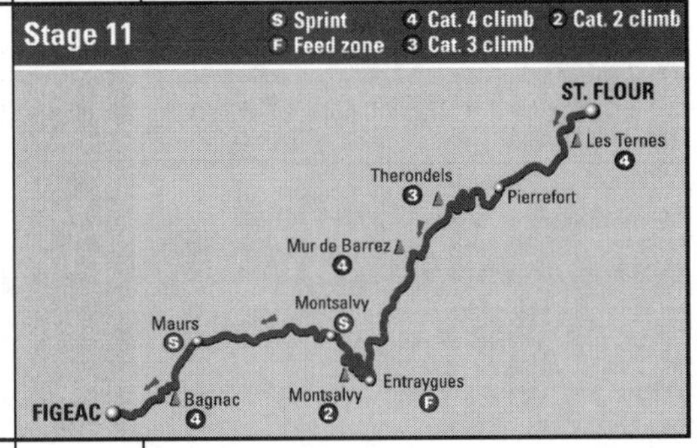

Most teams agreed with Pino's assessment, so it seemed likely that the "real" Tour would commence with the two-climb stage 12 on Friday to the ski resort at La Mongie, followed the next day by the grueling seven-climb, 127.4-mile stage 13 to Plateau de Beille. "They're tough, tough," Armstrong said of the back-to-back mountain stages. "The second day is epic. There's going to be 5,000 meters [16,500 feet] of climbing. There are not many days like that. Saturday suits me better. [Friday] is good for a small, explosive rider who can stay on the wheel."

Armstrong was especially chatty in the Saint-Flour start village as journalists crowded in around him. For the hacks covering the Tour, chasing Armstrong was a bit of a crapshoot. Some days he spoke at length, others he'd stay tucked away inside the U.S. Postal Service team bus. This particular morning, a reporter from Philadelphia ventured to ask him about antidoping tests. Armstrong's Postal

Service team was blood screened during the rest day and then Armstrong was called up for a random post-race doping test after stage 10. Was he feeling persecuted? "Perhaps. . . . Nothing against the French, but we know that here in France they're after us and they're after the sport of cycling. That's what we have to live with and deal with every day."

Armstrong had started the Tour under the spotlight following the publication in France of a book entitled *L.A. Confidential: The Secrets of Lance Armstrong,* which suggested that Armstrong used banned, performance-enhancing drugs. And this morning, the French daily *Le Monde* published an interview with three-time Tour winner Greg LeMond, who questioned Armstrong's cleanliness in doping matters. "What I'm saying is that I want to see the truth when I watch the Tour," LeMond told the newspaper. "Lance is ready to do anything to keep his secret but I don't know how long he can convince everybody of his innocence." LeMond said cycling had changed drastically since he won the Tour in 1986, 1989, and 1990. "Drugs are now so powerful that they can change a man physiologically," he said. "One could even convert a mule into a stallion."

Asked about Armstrong's comeback after he recovered from cancer, LeMond said, "There are no miracles in cycling, only explanations. After I suffered a hunting accident in 1987 it took me two years before I could race again and I never reached the same level." And the fact that Armstrong has never tested positive for banned substances does not necessarily prove he is not using drugs, LeMond insisted. "Everybody says that. But neither had David Millar tested positive and he now admits he took EPO. The problem with Lance is that [if you raise questions about doping] you're either a liar or you're out to destroy cycling," LeMond concluded.

It was an explosive and disturbing series of charges, and Armstrong later issued a statement in reply. "Greg LeMond was my idol as I grew up in cycling because he was a great champion and did great things on the bike," the statement read. "Many of his performances were so incredible, especially his remarkable return to form and win at the '89 Tour. I'm disappointed and dismayed that for the past four years Greg has continued to question my performances and character."

In his morning chat with the assembled journalists, however, Armstrong—who has never tested positive for banned substances and has always denied taking doping products—was more interested in describing the challenges he faces from the French press. He accused some French journalists of ferreting through his hotel room in the hope of finding proof the five-time Tour champion was doping.

"Just this morning, after we left, a TV crew from France 3 was going to the hotel, the reception, to the owner, asking for our room, trying to get in our room," Armstrong said. "They show up and they ask sporting questions to our face, but

MAGNUS BÄCKSTEDT, ALESSIO-BIANCHI

Homeward Bound

I'm disappointed.

It's not like I started today thinking about dropping out of the Tour de France. It just turned out that way. My back started really bothering me after the start. I could never get comfortable on the bike and it was even hard to grip my handlebars at times. I just couldn't get any power out—I would try and try and try and there was just nothing. I tried smaller gears, bigger gears, and still nothing. It was one of those days when I could neither spin nor turn gears.

The stage itself kicked off with the usual charge from the line and the attacks started right from the gun. There was a bit of a tailwind, too, so that boosted the speed even more. Even going up the climbs it seemed like a full-on sprint the whole first hour, and I was having a mess of trouble trying to stay on.

Unlike the other day, though, I couldn't keep fighting back. Over the next 20 kilometers my back kept getting worse and worse. I'd get dropped by the gruppetto on the uphills and reconnect on the downhills. Each time the gap would get a little bigger, and suddenly I found myself riding 70 kilometers on my own. That's not fun when your back is killing you and you don't have any power going to your legs. All in all, it was a pretty shitty day.

I'm really, really disappointed, but what can you do? So tomorrow I get on a plane and go home to Wales and my family. My wife and I are expecting our second child in September, so it will be good to be home for a bit. I will spend some time relaxing and trying to get my physical problems sorted out before focusing on the Olympics. ■

as soon as we leave they're digging in the rooms and looking for dirt. This particular guy from France 3 has been following us for months and it's scandalous," Armstrong continued. "The scary thing is, if they don't find anything and get frustrated after a couple of months, who's to say they won't put something there and say 'Look what we've found.'" The reporter in question later told the Associated Press that Armstrong's statements were ridiculous. But Armstrong may not have been convinced. For him, it was war on and off the bike.

Before the mountains, there was still today's hilly 164-kilometer stage across the Massif Central from Saint-Flour to Figeac to negotiate. With four rated climbs, including the Cat. 2 Côte de Montsalvy at 99.5 kilometers, the route served up ideal terrain for stage hunters. Team CSC was on the attack again, with the indefatigable Jens Voigt trying twice to escape in the opening 20 kilometers. Hamilton's teammate Oscar Pereiro, young Russian Vladimir Karpets (Illes Balears), and David Moncoutié (Cofidis) also tried as the course dipped and swerved. Virenque slipped out to grab the points at the Cat. 3 Côte de Therondels when Moncoutié tried again. Egoi Martinez (Euskaltel) shot out with him and the duo wound down the snaking descent to quickly open a gap.

Sensing that this move might stick, Juan Antonio Flecha (Fassa Bortolo), the Spanish rider who won a stage last year into Toulouse, bridged out in the next 7 kilometers. At 62 kilometers, the threesome had a gap north of two minutes. Boulangère was moderating the pace at the front and the lead widened to 7:40 by 90 kilometers. Struggling off the back was Alessio's Magnus Bäckstedt, the big Swede who won Paris-Roubaix in April, raced the Giro d'Italia, and came to the Tour with hopes of winning a stage. He was so knackered he couldn't stay on during a descent, and at 120 kilometers he pulled off.

Meanwhile, Moncoutié's ride just kept getting better. The son of a postman, the 28-year-old Frenchman grew up in the region and knew the roads well, giving him a distinct advantage over his two Spanish rivals. On a false rise 9 kilometers from the finish, Moncoutié made a blistering acceleration to open a gap. He glanced back once and then drove solo all the way to Figeac to capture France's third stage victory in the 2004 Tour.

Like O'Grady, Moncoutié spoke of the stress of the Cofidis Affair and the uncertainty of not knowing whether he'd be racing in the Tour. Moncoutié, who is reputedly so antidrug that he's earned the nickname "Mr. Clean," was unblemished by the doping allegations surrounding teammates David Millar, Philippe Gaumont, and Cedric Vasseur. "The last few weeks before the Tour were very hard, but I knew I had nothing to worry about so I was able to concentrate on the sporting side," he said.

While he might be clean, Moncoutié is also known for his decidedly lower expectations, something that seems to ail other top French stars. Big things were expected from Moncoutié after he finished 13th in 2002 and was the top Frenchman in that Tour, but as Cofidis team director Francis von Londersele summed it up, "He's a great rider but he never really delivered. Today, he produced the kind of great performance we would like him to come up with more often."

"I never had the character of a leader," admitted Moncoutié. "Even less so in the Tour, which is the biggest race on earth. Winning this stage is one of the highs in my career. Failing to win a Tour de France stage, there would have been something missing. One of my main goals has been achieved, now I must see if I can achieve more. But this win won't change anything. I know myself. I'm unable to set my goals too high."

For their part, the bakery boys had been driving home the bunch to keep Voeckler in the yellow jersey for another day. Meanwhile, the Posties were in the lead on the steep descent into Figeac and the two sweeping right turns bridging the river Célé. The sharp rise to the finish line revealed why; Armstrong was hammering the pedals as the bunch sprint arrived in an attempt to cause a split and sow confusion among the contenders. All week long, Armstrong had been buttering up his rivals—taking body punches, short jabs, getting them ready for the main event. Now, with the mountains approaching, he was preparing his first strike. Armstrong finished 9th in the stage and never was able to split the bunch, as he had hoped. But the Texan was ready for battle.

STAGE 11, SAINT-FLOUR TO FIGEAC: 1. David Moncoutié (F), Cofidis, 164km in 3:54:58 (41.878kph); **2.** Juan Antonio Flecha (Sp), Fassa Bortolo, at 2:15; **3.** Egoi Martinez (Sp), Euskaltel-Euskadi, at 2:17; **4.** Thor Hushovd (Nor), Crédit Agricole, at 5:58; **5.** Erik Zabel (G), T-Mobile—same time

OVERALL: 1. Thomas Voeckler (F), La Boulangère, 46:43:10; **2.** Stuart O'Grady (Aus), Cofidis, at 3:00; **3.** Sandy Casar (F), fdjeux.com, at 4:13

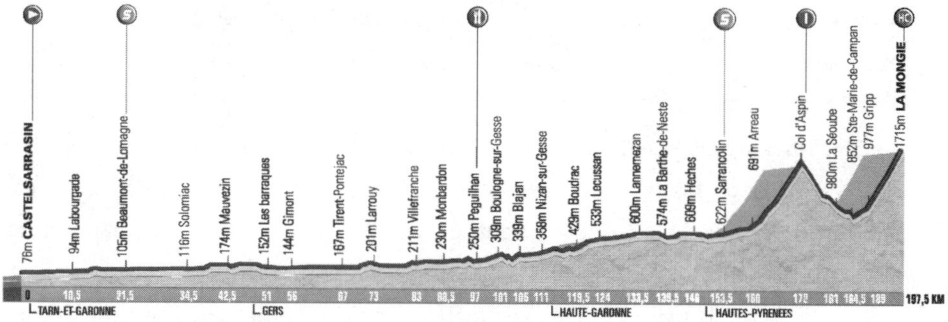

STAGE 12 | Castelsarrasin to La Mongie

After 13 days, 11 stages, 2,010.6 kilometers of racing, and nearly 47 hours on the bike, the "real" Tour de France was about to begin. The riders were finally moving out of terrain where the race could be lost and into the Pyrénées, where the race could be won.

But before the stage could begin in sunny Castelsarrasin, there was the messy business of Pavel Padrnos, Armstrong's Czech teammate who was caught up in a power struggle between cycling's governing body, the UCI, and the Société du Tour de France. Tour officials wanted Padrnos and Quick Step rider Stefano Zanini thrown out of the race.

"We have asked for the exclusion of these two riders for the same reasons that we invoked last Monday," said Patrice Clerc, president of Amaury Sport Organization (ASO), the parent company of the Tour. Earlier in the week, Tour organizers had booted out two riders, Stefano Casagranda and Martin Hvastija, because they were under investigation in a doping probe in Italy and thus in violation of the Tour's newly adopted zero-tolerance policy.

When Tour organizers learned that Padrnos and Zanini were to appear in an Italian court in October in a case involving alleged doping in the 2001 Giro, that was enough, in their view, to give the pair the heave-ho as well. But the UCI stepped in and blocked their dismissal. Zanini, said the UCI, had already been sanctioned for possessing an insulin injection, while Padrnos wasn't in possession of a banned substance at all.

ASO officials fumed and even threatened to pull the Tour and other top races they produce, such as Liège-Bastogne-Liège and Paris-Tours, out of the UCI's pet project called the Pro Tour, a new racing series set to debut in 2005. Ultimately, Clerc said, "There is a real conflict in the positions of the UCI and Tour organizers." Then he laid down the law. "It has to be clarified in the next few weeks," he said, "or ASO will not take part in the reorganization of cycling." With cycling politics in a temporary stalemate, the Tour and the UCI could exchange plenty of grave, sober statements. Padrnos and Zanini could ride unhindered. And the Tour would roll on to Paris. As it always does.

The opening 160 clicks of the 197.5-kilometer stage to La Mongie were about as flat as roads can be in France. Temperatures nudged into the high 80s as the 167 remaining riders rolled out of the neutral start. But with the mountains looming, some simply couldn't hang around, and Frédéric Finot (RAGT) and Marcus Ljungqvist (Alessio-Bianchi) attacked at the first kilometer. Not wanting to miss the head start were two more—Kim Kirchen (Fassa Bortolo) and Wim Vansevenant (Lotto-Domo)—who bridged out at just 2 kilometers. The foursome worked together to build a lead of 4:20 at 71 kilometers.

Clouds were brewing on the horizon as the towering Pyrénées finally pushed into view. The mighty chain of mountains separates Spain from France and chokes off Europe from the Iberian Peninsula, stretching from the Atlantic Coast, to the west, all the way to the Mediterranean Sea, to the east. Historically, the Tour's first major climbs came in the Pyrénées, when Tour founder Henri Desgrange included the Peyresourde, Tourmalet, Aubisque, and Aspin passes—all over unpaved roads—in 1910. It was over the Aubisque that eventual winner Octave Lapize swore at race officials and called them "assassins" for taking the riders over such treacherous terrain.

The Alps were brought on the next year, and invariably their longer, steeper climbs overshadowed those in the Pyrénées. But the Pyrénées stages, over narrower and rougher roads and generally with shorter but steeper pitches, have often provided the decisive moments of a Tour.

Armstrong has pleasant, if somewhat painful, memories of the Pyrénées. In 1999 he cemented his first overall victory by withstanding an epic solo attack by Fernando Escartin to Piau-Engaly. In 2000, Armstrong disappeared into the fog and rain at Hautacam to demoralize his opponents in what would become his trademark, opening-climb knockout punch. A year later, Armstrong surged into the yellow jersey after erasing more than a 30-minute gap to François Simon with a victory at Saint-Lary Soulan, and in 2002 he won back-to-back stages at La Mongie and Plateau de Beille. Furthermore, two of Armstrong's five successive Tour victories swung through the Pyrénées before hitting the Alps (2000 and 2002), and four of his 16 career Tour-stage wins, before the start of the 2004 Tour, came in these mountains.

But the defining moment that marked Armstrong as a great champion came in 2003, in one of the most epic stages in recent Tour history. The mountain was Luz-Ardiden. Armstrong entered the stage with a slim, 15-second margin over Jan

Ullrich and had struggled a bit on the 2,114-meter Col du Tourmalet that preceded the 13.7-kilometer ascent of Luz-Ardiden. He managed to catch Ullrich on the Tourmalet, and the leaders were together as they began the climb of Luz-Ardiden, helmets off. Suddenly, Armstrong was thrown to the ground, his handlebars tangled with a fan's *musette*. The Texan quickly remounted his bike—later discovered to be cracked along the right chainstay—and made a ferocious solo acceleration to win the stage 40 seconds ahead of Ullrich and seal his entry into the Tour's "five-win club." The prospect of repeating the double whammy of La Mongie and Plateau de Beille had Armstrong's spirits high, prompting him to joke before the stage, "It's very nasty. I think they should take it out. It's a violation of our human rights. I love it."

The leading quartet was going nowhere as rain started to fall with about 25 kilometers to go to the Col d'Aspin. It was going to be a great battle. Quick Step put the hammer down on the lower ramps of the Col d'Aspin, a Category 1 climb that averages 6.5 percent over 12.3 kilometers. The Belgian team was working for Virenque, who started the day in 4th place and had a slim chance to vault into the yellow jersey if youngster Voeckler stumbled.

The prospect of repeating the double whammy of La Mongie and Plateau de Beille had Armstrong's spirits high, prompting him to joke before the stage, "It's very nasty. I think they should take it out. It's a violation of our human rights. I love it."

It was no surprise when sprinters McEwen, Hushovd, Baldato, and Arvesen were quickly spit out the back. Somewhat more surprising was the poor form of Santiago Botero, the Colombian climber who won the King of the Mountains jersey in 2000 and the world time trial title in 2002. Once hyped as an overall threat, Botero had been a bust since joining Telekom, T-Mobile's predecessor squad, for the 2003 season. As the climb up the Aspin began, the Colombian was already having difficulty, and he would eventually limp in with the *gruppetto* at 26:10 back.

A heavy rain was dousing the riders as the Posties pushed to the front of the lead bunch. They set a steady, grinding pace, with Tour rookie Benjamin Noval and veteran Manuel Beltran taking early pulls. Then, with 7 kilometers to go, it was the steady legs of George Hincapie and Floyd Landis that took over.

Pushing higher into the clouds, Filippo Simeoni—the Domina Vacanze rider who was caught just meters from the finish line in Gueret three days earlier—attacked off the lead group, which still numbered about fifty riders. Christophe Moreau, the French favorite on Crédit Agricole, took a stab as Virenque shot across to form a leading trio about midway up the climb.

There were some faces twisted with pain as Postal Service kept applying the screws on the 1,489-meter summit. Haimar Zubeldia, the Euskaltel-Euskadi rider who finished 5th overall in 2003, lost contact, and Tyler Hamilton was having trouble hanging onto the back of the lead bunch. It wouldn't be the last time.

Meanwhile, Rabobank's Michael Rasmussen, the former mountain bike world champion who was hungry for a stage win in his Tour debut, attacked off the front. Rasmussen won a stage and finished in the top ten in the 2003 Vuelta a España and came into the Tour boasting a stage win from the Dauphiné Libéré. "I want to win a stage in the mountains," Rasmussen said in the first week of the Tour. "I will attack every time the road goes vertical. I think I'm the best chance for Rabobank to win a stage this year, at least in the mountains."

The descent off the Aspin was treacherous, with rivers of water washing rocks and mud across the road. Ullrich was risking all and briefly opened a 7-second gap on Armstrong as the riders snaked down the perilous, slender descent. The leaders came back together as a group of about fifty riders hit the base of the Cat. 1 climb to La Mongie, a ski station nestled about midway up the towering Tourmalet. The road steepens as it rises and averages 6.8 percent over 12.8 kilometers, but it's the final 3.8 kilometers at 9.5 percent that make the climb so demanding.

It was up La Mongie in 2002 that Armstrong had to tell then-teammate Roberto Heras to slow down, as the Spaniard was setting too fast a pace ahead of eventual runner-up Joseba Beloki. This time, Heras was lining up against Armstrong along with former teammates Hamilton and Levi Leipheimer, now leader at Rabobank. Postal Service was clearly in control, and Hincapie and Landis set the tempo on the lower reaches of the climb.

Riders were taking off their helmets, a dispensation allowed under UCI rules on climbs longer than 5 kilometers that finish on a summit. Masters of the small details, all the Postal Service riders coasted to the right side of the road to pass off their helmets in unison to a waiting team staff member.

Rasmussen's adventure at the front was going to end poorly. He nursed a 30-second gap with 9 kilometers to go, but it was shrinking under the pressure set by Postal Service. "Christ, the Postals are strong," said Australian Michael Rogers (Quick Step), who finished 22nd. He was still with the Postal-led group as it caught Rasmussen, and said of the catch afterward, "When they hit the gas, there is nothing you can do. You can see it coming; they all fall into place before the climb." The shaved Dane would have to hunt his stage win another day.

Things were quickly turning black for Hamilton as well. He was visibly struggling to maintain contact with the lead bunch. The surprisingly strong Hincapie continued to drive hard at the front, and with about 8 kilometers to go to, 33-year-old Hamilton slowly slipped off the last wheel. He waved off Phonak teammates Oscar Pereiro and Santos Gonzalez, urging them to ride for themselves. Looking flushed, Hamilton spun his pedals but couldn't maintain the cadence to generate the power he needed to stay with the leaders.

To add insult to injury, his former CSC teammate Carlos Sastre shot off the front in an aggressive move with 7 kilometers to go, forcing the front group to chase harder. Hamilton slipped farther and farther back, eventually finishing in a group of six riders at 3:27 behind. It was a crushing blow to Hamilton, who started the Tour as one of Armstrong's top rivals. "I have no excuses today; I had no legs. Since my crash on stage 6 to Angers last Friday, I've had pain in my back and climbing makes it worse because I have to sit down. I felt empty," Hamilton explained. "I'm disappointed but I'm not surprised. I'm trying to be optimistic but it's not easy. What's most disappointing is that I let my team down," he said sadly.

Hamilton wasn't going to be alone among big name disappointments. At the front, Chechu Rubiera and José Azevedo took over for the Postal team to chase Sastre, and the intensity of the rhythm set by Azevedo was putting tremendous pressure on Ullrich. The 1997 Tour winner sounded more confident than ever in the week preceding the mountains, but this quiet German who grew up behind the Iron Curtain was now riding headfirst into a very different kind of reality. With his face drawn in pain and his hair matted from his helmet into three narrow furrows atop his closely cropped head, Ullrich realized that his Tour hopes were exploding like the Hindenburg.

With 5 kilometers to go, Ullrich settled in with seven riders, including former teammate Bobby Julich, now on CSC. Sadly, at least for Tour fans hoping for another nail-biting race like 2003, Ullrich's difficulties spelled the end of an Ullrich-Armstrong duel. "It was a bad day and I knew it from the first climb in Aspin," said Ullrich, who crossed the line 20th at 2:30 back. "I noticed at the first mountain I didn't have good legs and I was cold on the downhill. But I fought until the end. With good weather and good legs, maybe I can come back. I'm going to keep fighting because the Tour is not over. It was a very, very hard day for me."

The surprises didn't stop there. Heras, the rail-thin Spanish rider who drove Armstrong to victory atop La Mongie in 2002, was also spit out the back early, finishing a disappointing 29th at 2:57. Saeco's Gilberto Simoni was doing the best he could, but he faded late to finish 12th at 1:32. Mayo—who says he hates the Pyrénées—would give nothing to the estimated 80,000 Basque fans lining the road. "I never ride well in the Pyrénées," said Mayo, who finished 9th at 1:03 back, a result that was perhaps better than his riding. By his own account, he had nothing in the tank. "Armstrong has been the only one who didn't crack," he noted. "Everyone else cracked today and the Tour might be over for all of us. I thought about winning the stage, but I didn't have the strength. In the first mountain stage there are always surprises and Armstrong is very, very strong."

Mayo was wrong. There were others who didn't crack. With all the attention on who was getting dropped, the list of riders remaining at the front was dwindling by the kilometer, but there were still some gamers. Stuck right on Armstrong's wheel was Ivan Basso, the young Italian on Team CSC. In fact, there were three former winners of the best young rider's category still in the lead group, with Basso (2002), Denis Menchov (2003), and Francisco Mancebo (2000). Also showing resilience was Tour rookie Michele Scarponi, Voeckler, who was hanging tough in the yellow jersey a bit farther down the mountain, and Andreas Klöden, whom Ullrich had waved forward to chase his own glory.

With all the attention on who was getting dropped, the list of riders remaining at the front was dwindling by the kilometer.

Sastre unleashed a second attack with just under 5 kilometers to go, and Mancebo attempted a sortie about 4 kilometers from the finish on the steepest part of the road. All eyes, however, were on Armstrong. Would he crack? Armstrong's face looked taut and somewhat strained; at 32, he was starting to show the wear and tear of racing. While there were a few more lines on his face this year, they certainly weren't cracks. Azevedo pulled off and Armstrong quickly revealed this was no 2003. His narrow victory the previous year had only motivated Armstrong to work harder. Now, on the steepest part of the climb in the first mountains of the 2004 Tour, he was showing the fruits of that labor.

When Mancebo attacked, it was Basso who took up the chase. Team CSC was trying to yo-yo Armstrong, with Sastre up the road and Basso staying with Armstrong, but the Texan responded coolly to the double-team even though he admitted he didn't like La Mongie. "I don't have a great relationship with this mountain," Armstrong said. "I don't know why but I always suffer here. Two years ago, Joseba Beloki and even Roberto Heras, who was a teammate at the time, were killing me."

Armstrong picked his moment and accelerated, and first Sastre and then Mancebo faded, leaving Armstrong and the 26-year-old Basso riding together in the final 2 kilometers. The rain had stopped and bright sunny skies and tens of thousands of screaming fans greeted the unlikely pair as they chugged up the final turns. Before the Tour started, no one included Basso among the names of top-tier favorites. In fact, neither did Basso's sport director Bjarne Riis. The balding Dane said his latest protégé would probably win the Tour in two or three years, but now Basso was matching Armstrong pedal stroke for pedal stroke.

They raced side by side, a preview of the inevitable transition of power within cycling. Armstrong was clearly not going to concede his crown without a fight, and as he spun his pedals up the twisting road, he was making obvious headway toward the elusive sixth-Tour crown. But it was equally obvious the quiet Italian was going to make life difficult for him, even if no one else could. With 250 yards to go, Basso went into the lead position and slipped across the line a winner ahead of Armstrong.

"There always comes a day in a rider's life when something changes, a day when everything clicks into place nicely. Today was my day," said Basso, who was quick to tip his hat to Armstrong. "It was the first mountain stage and the weather conditions may have worked Lance's way as he likes the rain," Basso said. He went on to admit, "From what we've seen, Lance is obviously the strongest."

Armstrong swept across the line and was pushed up the steep road by his pair of bodyguards to the waiting U.S. Postal Service bus parked another 300 yards along the road. He toweled down and answered questions as journalists pressed in around him. Did Armstrong let Basso win? He insisted no when a television reporter asked in French, but suggested he did when asked in English. "It was a pleasure for me to let him win," Armstrong said. "Ivan deserved to win the stage. He's a hell of a good guy and was super strong on the final climb."

Armstrong revealed that Basso's mother was fighting cancer and that she had recently entered an Italian hospital for treatment. "He and I have been friends for a long time. Now off the bike we're working on his mom's situation to see if she can win the fight against cancer. It was special for me to be out there with him. In the last week we haven't talked about the race but talked about his mom.

"For me the biggest surprise was that Ullrich and Hamilton lost time. I didn't expect that," Armstrong continued. The German crossed the line 2:30 down and fell to 3:37 behind the Texan, while Hamilton slipped to 4:22 back. "The race isn't over—Ullrich's never good on the first mountain stage—but we'll see what happens tomorrow. I think they'll get better," Armstrong added. "Ullrich might have taken one on the chin today, but he always comes back and is strong in the last week."

And as for his blue train, Armstrong said, "We have the best team in the race. From the beginning of the race we dominated the team time trial, which proves we have the strongest team. We started with confidence with the intention of winning the race. The team was super today." After a few more questions, Armstrong ducked into a waiting U.S. Postal Service team car and sped over the backside of the Tourmalet, disappearing just moments after the last-placed rider, Frédéric Finot—the same rider who started the day in the early escape—crossed the line 29:18 behind.

Armstrong had done it again, delivering a near-fatal first-round blow that left his rivals dazed and groggy. With the epic, seven-climb stage finishing atop Plateau de Beille on tap, Armstrong was clearly in the driver's seat. "He stunned the favorites a bit today," said Virenque. "Tomorrow, I think he's going to strike a sword blow on this Tour."

STAGE 12, CASTELSARRASIN TO LA MONGIE: 1. Ivan Basso (I) CSC, 197.5km in 5:03:58 (38.985kph); **2. Lance Armstrong (USA), U.S. Postal**—same time; **3.** Andreas Klöden (G), T-Mobile, at 0:20; **4.** Franciso Mancebo (Sp), Illes Balears, at 0:24; **5.** Carlos Sastre (Sp), CSC, at 0:33
OVERALL: 1. Thomas Voeckler (F), La Boulangère, 51:51:07; **2. Armstrong, at 5:24; 3.** Sandy Casar (F), fdjeux.com, at 5:50

649m LANNEMEZAN — 489m Nestier — 465m Tibiran-Jaunac — 458m Barbazan — 443m Sauveterre-de-Comminges — 603m Antichan-de-Frontignes — 797m Col des Ares — 512m Cazaunous — 599m Col de Buret — 496m Carrefour D.618/D.85a — 537m Henne-Morte-Couledoux — 1069m Col du Portet-d'Aspet — 693m St-Lary — 665m Orgibet — 525m Argein — 550m Bordes-sur-Lez — 735m Bethmale — 1395m Col de Core — 523m Seix — 1111m Col de Latrape — 753m Aulus-les-Bains — 1395m Col des Agnès — 1302m Carrefour D.8/D.18 — 1517m Port-de-Lers — 772m Vicdessos — 580m Niaux — 509m Ornolac — 544m Aulus — 1780m PLATEAU DE BEILLE

0 9.5 16 24 29.5 38 42.5 48.5 52.5 55 59 64 69.5 74 79 85.3 89 99.5 112.5 125 131 136 146 151 155 165.5 176 182.5 188 205.5 KM

HAUTES PYRENEES — HAUTE-GARONNE — ARIEGE

STAGE 13 | Lannemezan to Plateau de Beille

The 205.5-kilometer "queen's stage" from Lannemezan to Plateau de Beille had epic written all over it. Seven rated climbs, a motivated, five-time champion chasing history, and huge crowds of rowdy Spanish fans that spilled over the border to watch the orange-clad Basque boys from Euskaltel take on Big Tex promised to make this an interesting day.

Plateau de Beille has a rich history in recent Tour lore. It was here that Marco Pantani seized control of the Tour from Jan Ullrich in 1998, winning the stage by 1:40 and leaping into 4th place overall. Pantani went on to win that drug-blackened Tour four stages later on a brutally hard climb through slashing rain to Les Deux Alpes. And four years later, Armstrong sealed his fourth Tour victory on Plateau de Beille, putting an additional 1:04 on a struggling Joseba Beloki to take a comfortable 2:28 lead overall. (Armstrong would eventually finish the 2002 Tour with a 7:17 margin of victory over Beloki.)

The final 18.4-kilometer haul to the 1,780-meter Plateau would be preceded by a tough, 14-kilometer ascent to the 1,395-meter Col de Core and a much meaner, 10-kilometer grind up the 8.4-percent gradient to the 1,395-meter Col de Agnes. The race would then pop over the 1,517-meter Port-de-Lers before dropping to the valley of Ornolac to begin the final ascent.

It was a warm, sunny day as the 165 remaining riders pushed southeast out of Lannemezan over soft, rolling foothills. The day's first attacks started almost immediately as Rasmussen tried to get away with Virenque at the 3-kilometer mark. U.S. Postal Service was all over the move and kept the pace high over the opening 25 kilometers before Sylvain Chavanel, the young French star on Boulangère, slipped off the front with Voigt, the effervescent German on Team CSC.

The duo nursed a 35-second gap at 33 kilometers when Rasmussen, unfortunately nicknamed "the Chicken" for his skinny legs, tried once more to get away and bridge out. Chavanel and Voigt worked together over the day's first obstacle, the Cat. 3 Col de Ares, and Rasmussen chased them alone in dogged pursuit until finally catching up 4 kilometers from the top of the Cat. 2 Col du Portet-d'Aspet at 64 kilometers. Temperatures were pushing higher, but with Rasmussen aboard the leading trio found its groove, opening a 3-minute gap on the main bunch.

For all his hard work, Rasmussen was about to be taught a very tough lesson in racing. He was a relative newcomer to the road scene, having won the 1999 world mountain bike title before turning to the pavement to chase his professional dreams. He raced on a small, amateur road team in 2000 then got picked up by Riis in 2001 to race on Team CSC. In 2002 he won a climbing stage at the Tour of Burgos in Spain and penned a deal to join Rabobank. A wrist injury sidelined him from the 2003 Tour (though he claimed it was the pressure on the team to include another Dutch rider that kept him off the roster), but Rasmussen went on to make the most of the Vuelta a España, winning a mountain stage in the Pyrénées and finishing in the top ten. The skinny Dane came to this Tour with hopes of winning a stage, and he wasn't letting any opportunity slip by.

But he should have thought twice about chasing down a break that included Voigt. The big German held a grudge and was not about to let Rasmussen go anywhere. Back in June at the Dauphiné Libéré race, Rasmussen found himself in a two-man break with Basso. The twosome was working together well; Rasmussen wanted a stage win, and Basso was primarily interested in testing his form in his final tune-up before the Tour. Coming up a steep climb near the finish, Basso was waylaid with mechanical problems. While Team CSC mechanics hurriedly worked to fix the problem, Rasmussen kept on driving. As he recounts it, had he waited, he might have risked getting caught. But to Team CSC, Rasmussen left Basso hanging. Now it was payback time.

For the 130 kilometers that the trio stayed away, Voigt never rode in front. Chavanel was eventually dropped, but even then, Voigt shadowed Rasmussen's wheel, refusing to share the work. "I told Jens to get into the move so we wouldn't have to do any work early," said Team CSC manager Bjarne Riis. "I also told Voigt not to take one pull. We don't forget these things."

Tyler Hamilton's 2004 Tour de France ended unceremoniously at 83 kilometers. Plagued with back pain since his crash in stage 6, Hamilton simply couldn't generate the power to remain in contention. It was the first major stage race he'd ever abandoned. "It wasn't so much the pain. If it was just the back pain, I could have gotten through that," Hamilton said. "It was just that I couldn't get any power

▲ Jakob Piil (CSC) tries his luck in another ill-fated breakaway in stage 8. The 31-year-old Dane held the dubious honor of being on the attack for 551 kilometers out of the 1,449 kilometers raced in the first eight stages.

▼ Thor Hushovd (Crédit Agricole) wins stage 8 into Quimper, later claiming the "Vikings have returned to Brittany," while the crash-weary peloton looked forward to its first rest day and a chance for better weather.

▲ Robbie McEwen (Lotto-Domo) wins by a nose ahead of compatriot Stuart O'Grady (Cofidis) into Gueret, where attacking riders Filippo Simeoni (Domina Vacanze) and Iñigo Landaluze (Euskaltel-Euskadi) were caught within sight of the finish line.

◄ Axel Merckx (Lotto-Domo) tried to follow Richard Virenque (Quick Step) in stage 10, but later felt betrayed when the controversial Frenchman soloed to victory and jumped into the best climber's polka-dot jersey.

► With his jaw clenched, Jan Ullrich (T-Mobile) plows alone through a sea of orange-clad Basques. The Basque fans adopted Euskaltel-Euskadi's team colors as their emblematic symbol throughout the climbs in the Pyrénées.

ONNAIS
Škoda
ag2r
Škoda

▲ U.S. Postal Service controlled the tempo in the grueling seven-climb summit finish to Plateau de Beille. Here, José Luis Rubiera (left) and Benjamin Noval protect Armstrong's flanks.

◄ Tour favorite Iban Mayo suffered through the Pyrénées after enduring a painful crash in the Tour's first week. He pulled out before stage 15 as the race entered the Alps.

► Rain and wind made the already treacherous roads in the Pryénées even more dangerous. The weather improved as the bunch rolled east toward the Alps.

challenger
2168 XQ 64
HU 4079 M

▲ Tyler Hamilton is clearly in agony as Santiago Perez tows him up an early climb on the route to Plateau de Beille. ▶ The back pain proved too much for the gritty New Englander and he abandoned the Tour for the first time in his career.

◀ Thomas Voeckler fought an emotional battle on the final climb to Plateau de Beille to defend the yellow jersey and carry the lead out of the Pyrénées.

▶ Ivan Basso (CSC) is ecstatic after beating Lance Armstrong atop the first summit finish of the 2004 Tour at La Mongie in stage 12. Armstrong showed, though, that he had left the troubles of the 2003 Tour behind.

CSC
cervelo

▲ Lance Armstrong sets a pace that puts the hurt on his struggling rivals, with Francisco Mancebo (Illes Balears) grimacing in pain on the lower flanks of the Plateau de Beille summit finish.

▼ U.S. Postal Service was clearly in charge in the decisive stage 13 as the peloton rolled past the monument for Fabio Casartelli on the Col du Portet d'Aspet early in the stage.

out of my pedal stroke. You saw me going up La Mongie, I just couldn't go any faster. It was very frustrating. I'd rather have two broken collarbones than hurt my back like that."

It was a major disappointment for Hamilton, who had risked everything by leaving Team CSC to join Phonak, the unproven Swiss squad that had never raced the Tour. The Phonaks had been in disarray since the team time trial, and Hamilton's early departure took the life out of the team. The others fought on, with Oscar Pereiro best placed in 11th at 4:29 back, but the Tour would be a very different race without their leader. "We knew about it all week, we just didn't want to let the other teams know it was so serious," said Phonak team manager Urs Freuler. "You could see Tyler, when he was struggling a little bit in the Massif Central, then up La Mongie. It's all too bad. He put so much into it, sacrificed everything to be ready for the Tour . . . baagh, what can you do?"

There were other giants falling on the road. Haimar Zubeldia abandoned just 19 kilometers into the stage. Fifth overall last year, the quiet Basque rider was hampered by knee problems due to overtraining early in the season. Another member of the Spanish Armada, Roberto Heras, took a spill coming down Col de Core. The Liberty Seguros captain quickly remounted, but he'd lost his punch and finished a miserable 49th at 21:35 back. Denis Menchov, the tough Russian on Illes Balears who won the Tour of the Basque Country, abandoned at 28 kilometers, also with knee problems.

Then it was Iban Mayo's turn. As the peloton hit a grueling 30-kilometer section that included the Cat. 2 Col de Latrape, the Cat. 1 Col d'Agnes, and the Cat. 3 Port-de-Lers, Mayo wavered. Struggling since his crash in stage 3, the once-mighty Basque coasted to the side of the road just one kilometer into the 10-kilometer climb up the Col d'Agnes and stepped out of his pedals. The Euskaltel-Euskadi team car quickly pulled up and there was a moment of confusion. Was Mayo abandoning or switching bicycles? Unai Etxebarria and Iker Flores gathered around their fallen captain and urged him to continue. Julian Gorospe, the team's sport manager, jumped out of the car and put Mayo back on his bike, admonishing him to at least finish the stage.

"I don't know what happened. I could have never dreamed I would be in this situation," said Mayo, who sat more than 45 minutes down on Voeckler by the end of the day. "I couldn't ride, I couldn't do anything, my legs were empty. I wanted to go home, but my teammates encouraged me to keep going."

Mayo had started the Tour with ambitions of knocking the crown off Armstrong's head. Following a dominant spring that saw him win five races in a nine-day run in May and humiliate Armstrong up Mont Ventoux in the

Dauphiné Libéré, Mayo entered the Grand Boucle with the hopes of all of Spain on his slender shoulders. Now he was a crushed man. "This was the hardest day of my life and I'm not exaggerating. I feel impotent," he confessed. "But in life, you learn more when you're down than when you're winning. So I am learning a lot. There are more Tours, there are more years left for me, life goes on."

The Tour almost ended for Julich, too. He crashed on a descent of the Col de la Core after getting tangled up with one of the team cars when he went back to fetch water bottles. The 32-year-old Coloradan landed hard on his right wrist, nearly breaking it. He rode the hardest half of the stage in intense pain and finished with the *gruppetto* at 42:20 back. "About five unfortunate things happened at the same time and my handlebars got caught on the rearview mirror," Julich said. "Stupid thing. I was on top of the world at La Mongie—we had won the stage—but then it came crashing down and four of us are limping home. It just goes to show that in this sport you're on top one day, you're on the bottom the next. We just have to hope it turns around again. My one and only motivation is to help Ivan. That's what CSC is all about—teamwork," he said at the finish.

Back on the mountain, the Posties were up to their old tricks, driving a menacing pace up the narrow, twisting roads. At one point on the Col d'Agnes, with 60 kilometers to go, the lead group was trimmed to about 20 riders. Five of them were *Les Postiers*, as the French daily *L'Equipe* called them. "I tried to attack but the Postal Service was like a giant train that you couldn't escape," said Francisco Mancebo (Illes Balears). "I was hoping some other riders would join me, but they were scared after they saw the effort I made for nothing. No one would risk it."

Tensions were rising when an estimated 85,000 Basque fans from nearby Spain choked the final 11-mile climb to Plateau de Beille. Following setbacks by star Basque riders Mayo and Zubeldia, some unruly fans were ready to vent their frustration. Once the lead bunch hit the base of the final 15.9-kilometer climb to Plateau de Beille, "Chechu" Rubiera and "Ace" Azevedo, so nicknamed by their very happy boss, took their familiar positions ahead of Armstrong, who was looking more relaxed than he did on La Mongie. With 14 kilometers to go, riders were getting spit out the back at an alarming rate. The casualty list read like a who's who of pre-race favorites: Sastre, Simoni, Karpets, Scarponi, Gonzalez, Heras, and Mercado were among the principal early victims.

At the 11-kilometer mark, Ullrich and Leipheimer were in obvious pain. The pair slowly drifted back under the pressure set by Azevedo. "I was doing fine but just ran out of energy," said Leipheimer, who finished 19th on the day at 6:39 back. "I came to the Tour hoping to finish in the top five, but now even the top ten could be difficult. I hope I can rebound in the final week. I always seem to ride better in the third week of a grand tour." Leipheimer's Rabobank teammate Rasmussen was still hanging off the front with Voigt stuck on his wheel, but he was soon to be swallowed by the blue train of Postal. The skinny Dane's attacks were all in vain. There are long memories in road racing—lesson learned for the former mountain biker.

Over the next 4 kilometers, Azevedo maintained a searing pace, eliminating Ullrich, Klöden, Mancebo, and Georg Totschnig, the quiet Austrian on the Gerolsteiner team. Voeckler was 2:24 back at 7.25 kilometers to go, and it appeared that Armstrong was destined for the yellow jersey. In a repeat performance from La Mongie, Basso was glued tight to Armstrong's wheel. Azevedo pulled off with just over 7 kilometers to go, leaving Armstrong and Basso to mount the final assault. The Texan rode with his jersey unzipped, his gold chain and crucifix swinging around his neck, and his shades planted on his forehead. The Italian rode with a Team CSC cap backward, his eyes hidden behind sunglasses. Both looked comfortable as they zipped past the frenzied crowds.

Things were getting ugly as the infuriated Basque fans poured their anger onto Armstrong. Fans had camped out overnight, some had been drinking all day, and after baking for hours in the hot summer sun, they had reached a simmering boil. Even in the uncontrolled, anything-goes atmosphere at the Tour, this was something different. Basque fans booed Armstrong, threw water on him, and flipped him the finger as he and Basso pushed through the throng. Several angry signs were painted on the road, including "Lance Pig" and "Lance Doped." One fan was seen spitting on the five-time Tour champion. "The Basque fans were expecting a lot with Mayo. I said to Basso it was unbelievable that we made it through there without being killed," Armstrong said later. "When we passed the Basque people, they were—how can I say this—excited. Very loud and aggressive."

Armstrong said the atmosphere reminded him of last year's Tour on Luz-Ardiden when, with Mayo on his wheel, he crashed after getting his handlebar tangled on a spectator's bag, sending both of them tumbling to the ground. But this was even worse—this was overt hostility. "I tried to stay as much in the middle as I could, but when they're waving flags, it's sometimes tough," said Armstrong. "The other problem was the guys who ran [alongside]. We were not able to ride as fast as we could because they were blocking us."

The packed crowds and the aggression from some of the fans was becoming an ongoing headache for the Tour officials. Philip Sudres, the Tour's press coordinator, tried to shrug it off, pointing out that 45 police motorcycles patrol the course while more than 30,000 members of France's military police guard the race and its 12- to 15-million fans during the 20-stage event. "Generally, the security is good at the Tour," he insisted. "On the Tour, if you see someone with a knife in one hand, they have a piece of sausage in the other," he shrugged. Behind the scenes, though, Tour officials and the teams alike were becoming wary. One million spectators were predicted to line the upcoming Alpe d'Huez time trial in four days, where many spectators were already camped out. Who could control that mob if things got out of hand?

For its part, the Postal Service team had assigned two bodyguards to protect Armstrong when he was negotiating the crowds before and after each stage. "We trust the Tour to make the course as safe as possible," said team spokesman Dan Osipow. "We make sure Lance is safe away from the race, but we don't think anything will happen. That's what makes cycling so great, that the fans can get close to the stars," he said evenly. Privately, though, the Postal officials were worried. Armstrong looked increasingly indomitable as the days wore on, but one crazy fan could change the outcome of the race. It had happened to the great Eddy Merckx in 1975, as he chased his sixth Tour win. A spectator struck Merckx as he climbed the Puy de Dôme, punching him so hard in the kidney that the Belgian was unsure whether he could continue. Merckx did indeed manage to finish, but he relinquished the lead and never again won the race. Sure, that was a once-in-the-Tour-history thing, but who could say that it wouldn't happen again?

"On the Tour, if you see someone with a knife in one hand, they have a piece of sausage in the other."

With less than 2 kilometers to go, Armstrong and Basso rode the final section inside the protection of the Tour's temporary fencing. A day after giving away a stage victory to Basso, Armstrong was not going to award any gifts. With 450 yards left, Armstrong zipped up his jersey and shot past Basso's left shoulder to win his 17th career Tour stage and earn a 20-second time bonus for the victory. "Today was a full-on sprint," Armstrong said. "I wanted to win because the time bonuses count—20 seconds is 20 seconds." And, he added, "It's always good to win a stage."

After the dust settled, Basso was sitting 1:17 behind Armstrong in the overall standings. Basso had matched Armstrong up two summit finishes, meaning that he had lost all of his time to Armstrong in the opening prologue (29 seconds) and the team time trial (50 seconds). Not a bad performance. Armstrong, meanwhile, had reason to be happy after Plateau de Beille. Although Klöden was hovering at 2:56 back and Mancebo at 3:06, the Texan opened important gaps on Ullrich

(6:35 in arrears), Simoni (9:28), and Heras (27:13), and he all but eliminated Mayo. Hamilton was on his way back to Girona for MRI scans on his bruised back. And Armstrong's U.S. Postal Service team was looking stronger than ever.

Two horrible days in the Pyrénées had sucked the life from Ullrich. Groans erupted when he slipped off the pace. No Ullrich in contention meant no repeat of the wild ride of 2003. Armstrong appeared to be back on cruise control, something the 30-year-old German was quick to recognize. "It seems as if Lance Armstrong is unbeatable again," said Ullrich, three times runner-up to Armstrong. "I am disappointed because I came here to win the Tour de France. Now I have no chance. I hope I will do better in the Alps. I felt better today than yesterday, but when it's going like this, it's difficult."

Ullrich's defeat now made Basso the main object under Armstrong's watchful eye. "We take him seriously," Armstrong said. "He's riding super strong and he's a rider we consider to be a threat and one of the brightest hopes for the future of the Tour de France." Armstrong had in fact picked Basso as an outside threat even before the Tour started, mentally scribbling him on a short list of riders that the team would track during the course of the Tour. Basso had made slow but steady progress since turning pro after winning the amateur world title in 1999. In 2002 he was the Tour's best young rider, and in 2003 he quietly finished 7th despite having only two teammates to help him. Like most climbers, but unlike Armstrong, Basso's Achilles' heel was his dismal time trialing skill. Last year, he forfeited more than 12 minutes to Armstrong in two flat time trials.

Now Basso was riding strongly and presenting a new kind of threat for Armstrong. In five successive Tour victories, Armstrong had mainly battled contenders like Ullrich—riders with bigger builds who shine in the time trials but lack the Texan's explosiveness in the climbs. Only Marco Pantani, the double winner of the 1998 Tour and the Giro d'Italia, had been able to match Armstrong's climbing accelerations, and it was in 2000 that the Pirate last rode the Tour. No one had come close since, and the deeply troubled Pantani had died of a cocaine overdose in February.

In an attempt to improve in the race against the clock and minimize potential losses to Armstrong, Basso and teammate Carlos Sastre had traveled in early May to the Massachusetts Institute of Technology in Cambridge for wind-tunnel testing. Riis and a team mechanic tagged along for the three-day trip (which cost Riis 20,000 euros) to make a computer model of l'Alpe d'Huez. Riis and the MIT team at the Center for Sports Innovation placed Basso and Sastre on their new, aerodynamic bikes and refined their positions, monitoring their power output along the way. The goal was clear: "I have to cut my losses in half in the time trials," Basso said. "The final time trial this year is 55 kilometers. I could still lose three or four minutes to Lance." That's just what Armstrong was counting on.

The biggest cheer went up for Voeckler when the 25-year-old Frenchman rolled under the finish-line clock with 22 seconds to spare. Dressed head to toe in the brilliant yellow of the Tour race leader, a wide grin broke out across his face as he pumped his fist when he realized he'd keep the jersey one more day. Voeckler's inspiring performances brought new hope to the beleaguered French fans who'd had little to cheer about since Bernard Hinault's last Tour victory in 1985. Armstrong was impressed as well. "It was our intention to get the yellow jersey, but when you have a guy like Voeckler who kept getting dropped but came back and fights all the way to the end, that's what's beautiful about this event," Armstrong said. "He gave his maximum on the last climb. He absolutely deserved it. I'm very, very impressed with him."

Voeckler had hit the bottom of the final slog with an overall margin of 5:24 on Armstrong. Quickly dropped by the favorites on the grueling climb, Voeckler still rode like he was gunning for the overall title. Fans ate it up as he gamely fought against the inevitability of conceding the jersey in the coming days. "When I climbed on the podium yesterday, I told myself it was my last day with the yellow jersey on my back," he said. "Today in the stage, I tried to hang in there as much as I could and climb at my own pace. But it's true that I impressed myself. I didn't think I was capable of losing less than five minutes today. That yellow jersey has made me aware of my real abilities."

Voeckler had won the French national championship only a week before the Tour start, and his tenaciousness, his quick smile, and his easy manner were causing his fan club to grow by the day. "Sportwise, I've discovered myself," he said. "This is not going to change my life, but on a sporting level, it is important. Now for me, it's mission accomplished and any other day with the yellow jersey will be a bonus. I'm not getting carried away and I know there are more mountain stages and a big time trial ahead." There was still a week to go, but Voeckler would take the yellow jersey out of the Pyrénées. And that was just fine with Armstrong.

STAGE 13, LANNEMEZAN TO PLATEAU DE BEILLE: 1. Lance Armstrong (USA), U.S. Postal, 205.5km in 6:04:38 (33.815kph); **2.** Ivan Basso (I), CSC—same time; **3.** Georg Totschnig (Aut), Gerolsteiner, at 1:05; **4.** Andreas Klöden (G), T-Mobile, at 1:27; **5.** Francisco Mancebo (Sp), Illes Balears—same time

OVERALL: 1. Thomas Voeckler (F), La Boulangère, 58:00:27; **2. Armstrong, at 0:22; 3.** Basso, at 1:39

Chapter 8: Week Three

No Quarter

It took Lance Armstrong all of 11 kilometers in the French Pyrénées to suck the life out of the 91st Tour de France. After months of hype and expectations of a down-to-the-wire battle culminating in a showdown on l'Alpe d'Huez, Armstrong's one-two punch at La Mongie and Plateau de Beille at the end of the Tour's second week left his rivals shattered and dispirited.

The favorites fell like a house of cards: Hamilton, Zubeldia, and Menchov, 4th, 5th, and 11th, respectively, in 2003, abandoned, and a struggling Mayo now looked to be the next victim. The Spanish riders were in turmoil, with only Mancebo rolling out of the Pyrénées relatively unscathed in the "virtual" 4th place behind Armstrong's 2nd. Heras, Armstrong's former teammate-turned-rival, stumbled in at 49th at 21:35, while Ullrich—who had never finished worse than 2nd in six Tour appearances—had surrendered another 2:42 and was entering the final week 6:39 in arrears.

The unlikely hero of the Tour's second week was Voeckler, who delivered an inspirational performance at Plateau de Beille to carry the maillot jaune out of the Pyrénées. His 22-second margin on Armstrong set a nation cheering behind him.

With the chances of many of the pre-Tour favorites already in ashes, a group of fresh faces were making their presence known. Basso was leading this charge, while Klöden was putting three years of injuries and bad luck behind him. Mancebo also now seemed to have a shot at the podium.

To be sure, the two-day battle in the Pyrénées made it clear that Armstrong had returned to dominant form, the same form that saw him sweep to relatively easy victories in 2001 and 2002. But the Tour is never without hope, and the design for the final week of this edition gave Armstrong's rivals strength. Three hard days in the Alps, capped by the climbing time trial at the Alpe d'Huez in stage 16, would provide fertile ground for attacks, especially if Armstrong showed any sign of weakness.

Of Armstrong's likely rivals, Basso remained most dangerous, entering the trio of Alpen giants just 1:17 behind the Texan. It wasn't the slender 34-second gap Armstrong nursed going into the Pyrénées in last year's dramatic Tour, but it was the second-narrowest Armstrong held this late in the Tour since 1999. The surprising Klöden was 2:40 further adrift while Mancebo, sitting 2:50 behind Armstrong, had taken up the banner for the crushed Spanish Armada.

Besting Armstrong in the final week was beginning to look like a long shot, of course. Protected behind the blue and red fortress of U.S. Postal Service, Armstrong seemed to be getting stronger as the Tour rolled on. While other teams were ravaged by injuries or broken spirits, the Posties' morale was high. More than ever, Armstrong's men seemed intent on delivering their leader into the history books.

Armstrong himself was quietly confident he could roll out of the Alps with an even wider lead. He had spent several days training on l'Alpe d'Huez in May to study the decisive climb. His Postal Service teammates were motivated and riding strong, particularly Hincapie, Landis, and Azevedo, who catapulted Armstrong to success in two stages in the Pyrénées.

And waiting at the end of the week was Armstrong's ace in the hole: a 55-kilometer rolling time trial that favored him. Armstrong had won every final time trial en route to four successive Tour victories and was toe-to-toe with Ullrich last year in Nantes before the German crashed, allowing Armstrong to finish the rainy, treacherous course at a safer, slower speed.

If any of Armstrong's challengers were able to keep him close in the Alps, they'd have to then mount an almost superhuman effort to best him in the time trial. As the third week opened, that prospect seemed unlikely.

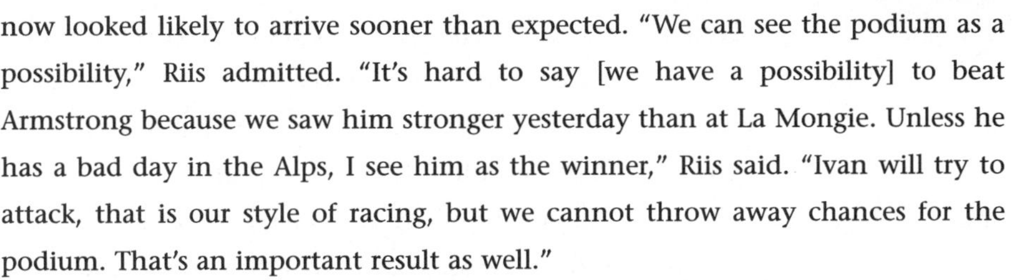

STAGE 14 | Carcassonne to Nîmes

Ivan Basso was all smiles at the start of the 14th stage in Carcassonne. For the past two days, the bright-eyed Italian had been the only rider able to follow Armstrong up the steep ramps high in the Pyrénées. Now sitting comfortably in 3rd, just 1:17 behind the Texan, Basso was suddenly the man of the hour. Dozens of journalists squeezed in against the Team CSC bus to toss questions at the Tour's new star, but Basso's interest lay elsewhere. He scooped up his baby daughter, Domitilla, and planted sweet kisses on her cheek. "I only want to think about it day by day. I can't think too far ahead," Basso said. "The Pyrénées were great for me, but I know it will be difficult to think about beating Lance. I will try to stay with him. I know the podium is a real possibility. I will keep fighting and not lose my focus," he vowed.

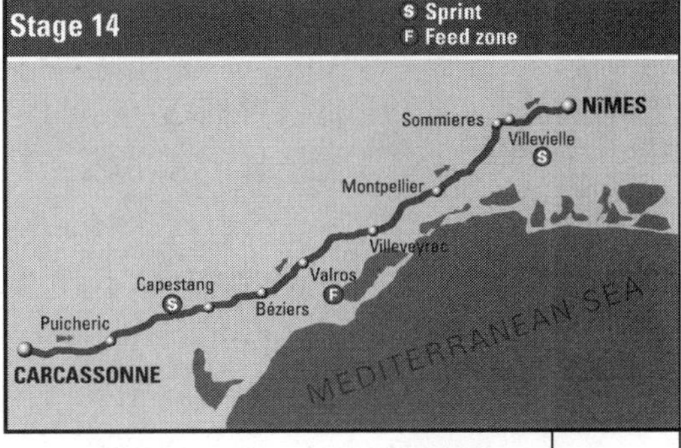

CSC manager Riis was also playing it outwardly cool, but inside the brainy Dane was brimming with pride and ambition. Stung by the departure of Hamilton to Phonak at the close of the 2003 season, Riis recruited Basso with a three-year contract and the goal of putting the talented Italian on the Tour podium within those three years. That goal now looked likely to arrive sooner than expected. "We can see the podium as a possibility," Riis admitted. "It's hard to say [we have a possibility] to beat Armstrong because we saw him stronger yesterday than at La Mongie. Unless he has a bad day in the Alps, I see him as the winner," Riis said. "Ivan will try to attack, that is our style of racing, but we cannot throw away chances for the podium. That's an important result as well."

Since retiring as a rider in 1999, Riis has built one of the most singular operations in modern cycling. Teamwork and sacrifice for the collective good come before personal gain under Riis's watch. This approach is embodied by his legendary training camps on the island of Lanzarote, which are more like an Army boot camp than leisurely, early season training. Working with BS Christensen, the Danish equivalent of a Navy SEAL, Riis builds teams based upon teamwork, sacrifice, and communication—all of which come ahead of individuality.

Riis's winter camps resemble an Outward Bound course. During a 32-hour period, his rider recruits must work together to overcome obstacles and challenges. One exercise for the 2004 team included dumping Basso into the ocean more than a mile offshore. The training drill was enlivened by the fact that Basso doesn't know how to swim. Eight teammates had to tow Basso to shore on a surfboard. "My first goal is to make this a different kind of team," Riis said in what could have been the sport's understatement of the year. "There are so many old ideas in cycling. I am trying to change the culture. Make it more professional, more honest."

As a racer, Riis won only one Tour, but it was a pretty good one. Riis did what Tony Rominger, Gianni Bugno, Claudio Chiappucci, and a host of others never could—he beat Miguel Induráin. After five straight Tour victories, the seemingly invincible Big Mig looked a lock to win a record sixth title in 1996. Standing in his tracks, however, were Riis and a loaded Telekom team. Riis said he spent hours studying film of Induráin, trying to detect a weakness. "The way that I saw that he could be beaten was to isolate him," Riis said. "I studied him very carefully and he could handle 25 to 30 minutes on the mountain climb with no problem. He always had a strong team to bring him to the final climb, then he could do that final climb and recover for the next day. But if he had to do that on the second-to-last climb, maybe he would be weak on the final climb."

According to Riis, Induráin's strongest weapon was his uncanny ability to hide his pain when he was truly suffering. "Induráin had many bad days, but he never showed it," Riis said. "To be able to show that you're not weak when you're weak, only a strong-minded person can do this." Switching to the problem at hand, Riis pondered, "This might be the key to Lance, to study him, to see what it looks like when he's weak."

Had Riis been studying Armstrong? Not really, he said. "Up until now, no one's been strong enough to beat Armstrong," Riis explained. "We will attack Armstrong only if he shows weakness. We are waiting for that. We will watch him carefully; if we see a weakness, we will attack. First, we will ride to protect Ivan. I believe he can finish on the podium—if he can follow Armstrong in the next few stages."

For others, however, the Pyrénées were not as glorious as they'd been for Basso. Aitor González, the Spanish rider on Fassa Bortolo, blew up on the road to Plateau de Beille, limping across the line 90th, 33:49 behind Armstrong. González is best known for two things: winning the 2002 Vuelta in a final-day time trial duel with

TYLER HAMILTON, PHONAK

Not Where I Thought I'd Be

Well, I certainly didn't expect to be filing a journal entry from Spain during the Tour de France this year. With eight starts, I have never had to abandon the Tour before. It has been a difficult couple of days for me but everyone around me keeps telling me to stay focused on the future. I think that's good advice, so, as I always say, upward and onward.

I guess my Tour de France really ended on July 9th in stage 6 when I went down in the massive pileup just a kilometer from the finish. I went over the handlebars and landed on my back. We had been going about 65 kilometers per hour when I was hit by another rider inside the domino effect (which ensues when a rider goes down inside a tightly packed peloton where there is limited space or time for reaction). I went down so fast there was no time to react. I never had the chance to try and break my fall with an arm or an elbow. When I hit the tarmac with my lower back, it was the full weight of my body multiplied by the speed. It was the equivalent of dropping from the sky and landing on top of a telephone pole.

After the race, I called my wife and told her what had happened. I knew then that I had not just injured my back, but that I had done some damage to it. I know enough about pain to understand the difference between the superficial and serious stuff, and I knew early on we were dealing with the second category.

Still trying to be optimistic, I tried to deny how bad things were at first.

continued ›

Roberto Heras and then spouting off during the following off-season about "crushing Lance Armstrong like a toad in the road." He had yet to make good on that promise. The fun-loving González—the son of a rabbit farmer from Alicante along Spain's sunny Mediterranean Coast—enjoyed a breakout 2002 season, when he won two stages in the Giro d'Italia and then stormed to the Vuelta title with three stage wins and smiling panache that earned him the nickname "TerminAitor."

Suddenly one of cycling's hottest prospects, González wormed out of a fresh contract with Domina Vacanze and penned a lucrative deal instead with Fassa Bortolo—two seasons at $750,000 per year. But things didn't go well under the stern eye of Fassa's Giancarlo Ferretti, a tough, old-school director who liked his riders resilient and hardworking; González was more of a party-boy joker. Believing his true destiny lay in the Tour, González hesitantly started the 2003 Giro but faded in the mountains to finish 19th overall, his race salvaged by victory in the time trial. He didn't do well in 2003's other grand tours, either, quitting both the Tour and the Vuelta.

When the chiropractor on our team couldn't adjust my spine because it was seized up, I thought we'd just give it a day, and it would be okay. When Kristopher our physiotherapist, trained by my old pal Ole, let out a long sigh after working tirelessly to "unblock" my muscles, I told myself to be patient.

Luckily stages 7 through 11 were relatively tame, which gave me a few more days to try and recover from the injuries before we got to the big mountains. Similar to the strategy I used in the 2002 Giro, we didn't want to speak publicly about my back because we didn't want the other teams to attack us, especially during the trickier stages 10 and 11. My team did an incredible job of protecting me and got me to the first mountain stage in the best possible shape under the circumstances.

Preliminary X-rays have not revealed any fractures. But an MRI scan scheduled for later today may show us what we suspect to be true. The doctors think the impact has either badly pulled or torn the ligaments and muscles in my lower back, which would explain why I couldn't climb. A lot of people may think I had to abandon the Tour due to pain, but this is not the case. Although the injury is painful, it was really a lack of power that forced me to pull over on Saturday. Your legs can only function with the full strength of the muscles in your stomach and lower back. With one side out of commission, I didn't have the power I needed to push the pedals. If you saw the coverage on television, there was no suffering on my face, because I was physically unable to push myself to that point.

In 2004 González finally got his wish to focus solely on the Tour, and he came to Liège as a dark horse with his eyes on victory. But his dreams of the ultimate upset evaporated in stage 13. "I know I was brought to the team to contend the three-week races. I can understand why the boss is disappointed in me," he said. "Maybe I haven't been up to their expectations. After yesterday's stage I knew that my general classification bid was over. That's why today I want to go out and win a stage and start a whole new Tour." González was ready for revenge. At last, here was a stage that would suit his skills. The windy, hot, 192.5-kilometer stage from Carcassonne to Nîmes was one of only two stages in this year's Tour without categorized climbs, and thus perfect for a time-trial specialist.

González was not alone in his ambitions for the stage. After two hard days in the mountains, the headbangers awoke from their slumber, and dozens of riders tried in vain to escape in the opening 100 kilometers. A group of 20 riders took off at 20 kilometers, including Mark Scanlon (ag2r), Karsten Kroon (Rabobank), Nicolas Jalabert (Phonak), José Garcia Acosta (Illes Balears), and Daniele Nardello

It was disappointing to lose three and half minutes in stage 12, but under the circumstances I don't know how I didn't lose more time. The next morning, Alvaro Pino made the call in our team meeting. He had given the situation a lot of thought during the night and knew what we were up against. If it was clear at any point in stage 13 that I couldn't climb with the leaders, I had to stop. I almost couldn't believe what I was hearing. But Alvaro is a logical man who cares an awful lot about his riders and would never put them in a situation that would compromise them or their future. He was firm with his direction. Little did I know, he had spoken with Kristopher, who had told him my back was, well, to put it politely, "bad."

After the second Col, I knew I was cooked. The peloton was riding at a strong tempo and I couldn't push the pedals hard enough to stay in contact. With a heart rate probably under 120, I was having trouble staying in contact with the peloton. I was like a battery-powered toy on its last leg. I was going as fast as I could with the power I had left in me, but it was barely half of my potential. So I drifted back to Alvaro, and without much of a word he gave me the signal to stop. On a flat section of the course I made my rounds through the bunch and wished my teammates the best. Leaving these guys in the heat of the battle is one of the hardest things I've ever had to do.

There is no way to explain how much this team means to me or what those eight guys had done for me leading up to the Tour and at the race itself. I know

continued ›

(T-Mobile)—several familiar faces from breaks in earlier stages. Flecha (Fassa Bortolo) led another move at 33 kilometers with three other riders, then O'Grady (Cofidis), Julian Dean (Crédit Agricole), and Axel Merckx (Lotto-Domo) took a shot at 77 kilometers. Each time, one team or another decided to bring the breaks back, resulting in a fast average speed of 44.6 kilometers per hour for the first hour.

Jalabert tried again at 98 kilometers, and nine others eventually caught him, including Santiago Botero, González, Igor González de Galdeano (Liberty Seguros), and Mark Lotz (Rabobank). This time, enough teams were represented up front and none of the break's members were major challengers, so the gap jumped to more than 10 minutes with 60 kilometers to go. This one wasn't coming back.

González de Galdeano—another big name who had fallen flat in the Pyrénées—attacked with 9 kilometers to go. The escape group worked to bring him back, and then Aitor González shot across the road with 6 kilometers to go. Using his superior time trialing skills, he simply powered away. Huge crowds of

we arrived in Liège with the strongest team in the race. What we overcame in the team time trial to finish 2nd proved that. Without five mechanicals, I think we would have been able to show the world just how ready we were to fight a good fight. But sometimes things happen that are out of your control and that keep your goals beyond reach. I feel like I arrived at the Tour de France last year and this year in the best shape possible and ready to take on the challenges ahead. But fate is a lousy negotiator, and sometimes you have to take the hand you are dealt.

This is a crazy injury—one that I cannot control or overcome just by willing myself to do so. I would take the pain of two broken collarbones over this any day, and keep riding if I could. But something has come unplugged, so it's time to rest and start thinking about the races up the road. I'm hoping to be well enough to still compete in Athens. And there's always the Vuelta to consider. But first things first. I'll focus on recovery for now.

Coming off of the emotional stress of losing Tugboat, the disappointment of abandoning the Tour is in perspective. I know there will be another Tour de France next year, and I'm already looking forward to it. But this year's race is not over, and team Phonak is going to be going hard straight through to Paris. I spoke to Nicolas Jalabert last night after his long day in the breakaway and his impressive 2nd place, and he said "Man, I tried so hard to win for you today." This kind of loyalty and friendship means the world to me. All things considered, I'm a very lucky guy. My wife and I will be heading to Paris this weekend to cheer the boys home. It's a moment I'm looking forward to.

I'll be back with more thoughts about the Tour in the coming days. And I will share some of my stories about my final days and experiences with Tugboat as well. ■

holiday-makers pressed in on the narrowing finish in Nîmes to watch the TerminAitor come flying toward the line. It was the third stage win of the Tour for Fassa Bortolo, despite the absence of star sprinter Alessandro Petacchi, who packed it in during the first week. And the win was the 100th by a Spanish rider in Tour history.

"I think the strongest guy won today," admitted Jalabert, who came through in 2nd. "It was impressive. He attacked with 6 kilometers to go and, well, he's just a good rider," said the younger brother of retired star Laurent Jalabert. "There was a slight climb at the 3-kilometer mark, which made it a bit harder to chase him down." When González shot across the line, the main bunch was still 14 minutes down the road.

Waiting at the team buses for his riders to come in was Patrick Lefévère, manager of Quick Step. The mighty Belgian squadron was still nurturing potential Tour contenders Michael Rogers of Australia and Juan Miguel Mercado of Spain, while banking on crowd favorites Richard Virenque, Paolo Bettini, and Tom Boonen. The team had scored two stage victories so far, as well as Virenque's King of the Mountains jersey, so Lefévère wouldn't leave the Tour dissatisfied.

But in Lefévère's estimation, the Tour was already over. "Lance won the battle of the Pyrénées," he said. "The only way he'll lose is if he has a bad day. He is human, we suppose." Lefévère is one of Armstrong's biggest boosters inside the sometimes cutthroat world of professional cycling and always staunchly defends the Texan against any hint of criticism. Part of that empathy may stem from Lefévère's own battle with cancer. He had dodged a bullet when a tumor was found on his pancreas in 2000.

"Cycling is war, it's fought from the start to the finish and it's not just on the bike, but in the mind as well."

"There are no miracles in cycling," Lefévère said. "You have to work very hard and there are a lot of jealous people in cycling right now. They are frustrated that Lance keeps winning. Lance is a winner. If he loses he comes back two times better. Even when he has a bad day, he has a strong character to keep fighting. Look at last year," he pointed out. "How many riders could have suffered like that and still won the Tour? Cycling is war, it's fought from the start to the finish, and it's not just on the bike, but in the mind as well."

If Lefévère is right, and cycling is indeed a war, then sometimes just finishing a stage of the Tour constitutes a victory. That was certainly the case for Bobby Julich, who gimped across the line trying to keep his right arm protected from the huge crowds. As Julich unclipped from his pedals, he was swamped by fans. "I can't sign autographs, my wrist is broken!" he said. His wrist was, in fact, not quite broken, but it was grotesquely swollen. "I got really lucky that today was by far the smoothest road I've ever seen in France," Julich said. "I couldn't brake, I just had to sit in the back and pray it didn't go too fast. I just took it easy and hoped to get through.

"I would have definitely quit if the road was bumpier," he admitted. "I couldn't get out of the saddle, I couldn't shift, and I was screwed if it was a really hard race. I had it taped and it actually felt worse. I had the race doctor cut [the tape] off. As you can see, it's not good right now," Julich offered as he held his two wrists together. The left had the slender cut of a professional bike racer, while his right wrist was approaching the size of a small watermelon. Thankfully for Julich and the other 159 haggard riders, the next day was a rest day—time to recover and regroup for the run back to Paris. There were only six days of racing left.

STAGE 14, CARCASSONNE TO NÎMES: 1. Aitor González (Sp), Fassa Bortolo, 192.5km in 4:18:32 (44.675kph); **2.** Nicolas Jalabert (F), Phonak; **3.** Christophe Mengin (F), fdjeux.com; **4.** Pierrick Fedrigo (F), Crédit Agricole; **5.** Peter Wrolich (Aut), Gerolsteiner—all same time

OVERALL: 1. Thomas Voeckler (F), La Boulangère, 62:33:11; **2. Lance Armstrong (USA), U.S. Postal–Berry Floor, at 0:22; 3.** Ivan Basso (I), CSC, at 1:39

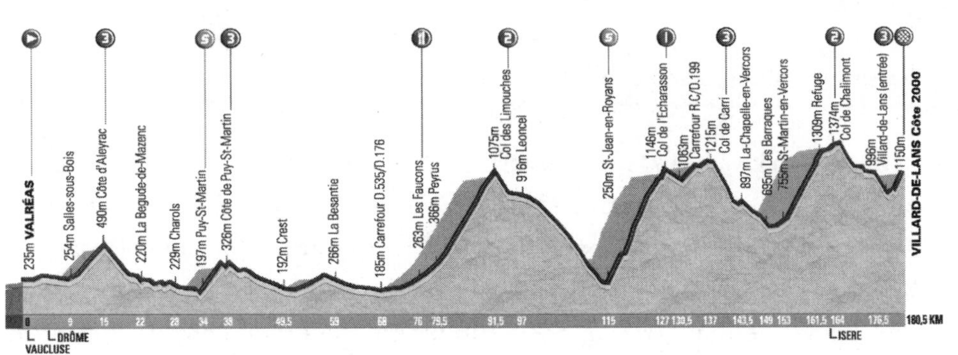

STAGE 15 | Valréas to Villard-de-Lans

The final rest day of the 2004 Tour allowed the 158 remaining riders to catch their breath before the assault into the Alps for three tough stages, including the much-hyped climbing time trial at l'Alpe d'Huez. In Valréas, there were reports that fans had already been camping for two days on the Alpe to secure the best viewing spots along the torturous road. Officials estimated up to 1 million fans would clog cycling's most famous climb.

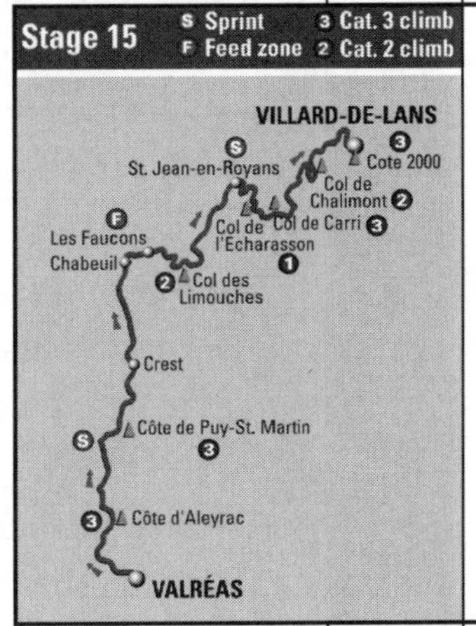

While Aitor González' victory into Nîmes saved face for the Spanish, teams were already doing a postmortem on the death of the Spanish Armada. Roberto Heras, Haimar Zubeldia, Igor Gonzalez de Galdeano, Juan Miguel Mercado, and Iban Mayo all took a tumble in the Pyrénées. The gloomy mood was only intensified by news that Mayo, the swaggering Basque who had promised to dethrone Armstrong, would not be starting in Valréas. For Spanish cycling, the 2004 Tour had been a major bust.

"Iban's problem was mental, not physical," admitted Euskaltel-Euskadi manager Miguel Madariaga. "He couldn't handle the pressure that he put on himself, and when he wasn't among the top five at La Mongie it scarred him. We can't analyze what happened now because we still have to keep going. We all know sometimes champions have crazy things in their heads."

Over at Liberty Seguros, things weren't any better. Team captain Heras simply couldn't stay with the favorites when the roads turned upward in the Pyrénées. "I'm not going to look for excuses," said Manolo Saiz, the veteran director at Liberty Seguros. "You have to be realistic and admit that what we are doing is very bad. For us to understand why things went bad wasn't because of one thing we didn't do, but the accumulation of small things." Spanish fans, journalists, and teams were all struggling to explain the disaster. Overtraining, not enough training, injuries; there were even whispers that strict new antidoping tests were taking their toll on the Spanish riders.

Over at the Postal Service team bus, Bruyneel had a less sinister explanation, at least when it came to Mayo. All spring Mayo had been tearing up the European race calendar, racking up five wins in nine days in May in Spain and giving Armstrong a Texas-size whupping at Mont Ventoux in the Dauphiné Libéré. For Bruyneel, who helps Armstrong build his strength to its maximum in July, Mayo's problem in the Tour was simple: He had peaked too early. "I always said, when everyone was talking about Mayo, these exhibitions he was making in May and June, you can't maintain that form until the Tour," he said. "The Mayo at the Dauphiné is much better than what we're seeing now. He was a rider all but assured for the podium. In my opinion, Mayo lost the Tour in June."

There were, however, two Spanish riders who were hanging tough: Francisco Mancebo (Illes Balears) and Carlos Sastre (CSC). Mancebo was following in the footsteps of Miguel Induráin, the legendary five-time Tour winner who hangs like an 800-pound albatross around the neck of Spanish cycling. Scores of careers were squashed—or at least overshadowed—because riders couldn't live up to the achievements of Big Mig, the most popular cyclist in Spanish history.

The Induráin effect had been widespread and enduring, but his last Tour victory came in 1995. The latest crop of Spanish contenders, coming to age in more recent years since, had been able to develop without immediately being tagged as the "next Induráin." Spanish fans had finally admitted that Induráin was a one of a kind.

Mancebo, a skinny, easygoing 26-year-old fresh from winning the Spanish national title came into the Tour in his finest form since taking the best young rider's category in 2000. Working with Induráin's old brain trust—team manager José Miguel Echavarri and Eusebio Unzue—Mancebo entered the Alps sitting 5th overall at 3:28 back. "His big strength is that he's always been very consistent," Unzue said approvingly of Mancebo. "When you look at the great Tour riders in history, their main asset was the same, consistency. He always rides at the front at his own pace and does not care what the others do."

Mancebo had made it through the treacherous first half of the Tour unscathed and had ridden well in the Pyrénées, staying close to Basso and Armstrong in both mountain stages. "My main ambition is to finish on the podium more than winning a stage. I have lots of ambition, I feel really well on this Tour," he said, as he looked toward the upcoming days in the Alps.

Over at Team CSC, Sastre was flowering under the watchful eye of Bjarne Riis. In 2003 Sastre rode to a solo victory atop Ax-3 Domaines, an achievement made indelible when he popped his baby's pacifier into his mouth at the finish line. "Every day I race with it in my jersey as a reminder of my daughter, my wife, a reminder to be a little careful and not take unnecessary risks because there is a life after cycling," he said. This year, Sastre had been superb at La Mongie, but faded at Plateau de Beille after back pain made it difficult for him to climb out of the saddle. Now sitting 12th at 10:03 back, Sastre was hoping for a rebound in the Alps.

Not all was well at CSC, though. Sastre's teammate Jakob Piil didn't start the stage. Piil had racked up the most kilometers of breakaways by a rider, but an aggravated knee injury sent the dashing Dane packing for home.

There was hardly a flat stretch of road on the 180.5-kilometer run to Villard-de-Lans, a cross-country ski station high above Grenoble. Temperatures in Valréas were already popping into the high 80s by the time riders spun out of town. The stage featured seven rated climbs with 48.8 kilometers of climbing—not quite the "queen's stage" of Plateau de Beille but no jaunt across Provence, either.

Polka-dot jersey Richard Virenque (Quick Step) was part of an early move that tried to shake the peloton, controlled by Postal Service. Virenque was gunning for a seventh climber's jersey and was keen to get into a move on this stage loaded with KOM points. "This year with the new rules, it's been harder than ever to fight for the jersey," said Virenque, referring to the Tour's revised regulations that doubled the amount of KOM points awarded at summit finishes. "I am not strong enough to fight for the overall classification, so I must get into breakaways to try to earn points. It's very stressful."

Axel Merckx, perhaps still steaming from his betrayal by Virenque at Saint-Flour, shot ahead to take the points over the day's first climb at the Cat. 3 Côte d'Aleyrac. Andreas Klöden (T-Mobile), the oldest new favorite in the bunch, crashed on the descent, but chased back on despite cuts to his hip and elbow. Yellow jersey Voeckler was caught in the second group as the peloton split at 38 kilometers coming over the day's second obstacle, the Cat. 3 Côte de Puy-Saint-Martin. Postal was chasing a nine-man break and Voeckler's Boulangère squad worked hard to make contact. It was going to be a torrid, difficult stage.

After more fits and starts, a group of seven riders was joined by another seven at the 50-kilometer mark. There were some familiar faces, including Jens Voigt (CSC), Virenque and his Quick Step teammate Laurent Dufaux, Michael Rasmussen (Rabobank), former world champion Laurent Brochard (ag2r), Stuart O'Grady (Cofidis), and American Christian Vande Velde (Liberty Seguros).

Virenque attacked the group to lead the charge up the Cat. 2 Col des Limouches at 91 kilometers, with Rasmussen, Santos Gonzalez (Phonak), Brochard, and Voigt following his wheel. With the day's third points sprint waiting in the valley,

CHRISTIAN VANDE VELDE, LIBERTY SEGUROS

A Day in the Break

It has been a few years since I've been racing in the Tour de France and most certainly a few years since I have been in a breakaway at the Tour. Today was a cool experience.

The Tour is unlike any other race in that there are spectators all the way along the course and cameramen on motorcycles capturing the expressions of all the riders. There are also at least four helicopters buzzing in the air at one time—a few covering the race with cameras and the others monitoring traffic. When I am racing I am not really aware of any of it, but sometimes I catch it all for a moment and realize all that is going on around the race.

When it's hot—and it was hot today—it is hard to drink enough and get enough food down. You realize that you haven't eaten enough when you start to feel a little dizzy and get goose bumps all over your body. In the last hour of the race today I started to feel like a goose out there, as I became dehydrated and tired from the efforts of the race and the challenges of the course.

I began to drift off, so I tried to ride with Ullrich as he came blasting by. After a while, though, I fell back, and soon Lance's group came charging up with Floyd setting a ripping tempo on the climb. He looked over at me and told me to get on his wheel if I didn't want to be dropped. I took his advice and hung on. The Postal team was impressive once again today, keeping Lance well protected in the front of the race and setting a tempo so strong nobody could attack. And if someone did try an attack, he didn't get far up the road.

O'Grady plunged down the col in an attempt to revive his campaign for the green points jersey.

The peloton hit the base of the 1,146-meter Cat. 1 Col de l'Echarasson at 115 kilometers to go, and T-Mobile's Giuseppe Guerini set a blistering pace that marked the beginning of the end for Voeckler. The fresh-faced Frenchman had surprised many by taking the maillot jaune out of the Pyrénées, and even he didn't expect to hold it for long. By the end of the stage, finishing 54th, the 25-year-old had slipped to 8th overall at 9:28 back. "I'm not disappointed, I knew it would happen," said Voeckler, who swapped the yellow jersey for the white jersey of the best young rider. "Even if I was getting used to wearing the yellow jersey after ten days, it was predicted that I would lose it even earlier than I did." Guerini's pace dropped Mancebo and Heras as well, as Spain's troubles continued.

Midway up the l'Echarasson climb, Ullrich took the initiative and surged ahead in a sharp acceleration to quickly put 50 meters on the lead bunch. It was

The roads and countryside around this area are incredible. Tonight we're in Grenoble and the valleys and mountains around are green and plush. It is great for cycling around here. But, damn, the racing is hard. Tomorrow we have an uphill TT up l'Alpe d'Huez; that will be interesting. I think a few of the sprinters will have a hard time making the time cut of 33 percent, as I know some of the climbers are going to fly up the mountain.

No doubt we'll see some surprises in the next couple of days of racing. Ullrich seems to be finding his form in the mountains and is sure to move up a few spots in the next days. It seems as though a lot of riders are really tired now, and the peloton is splitting up quickly. As predicted, this race will be between the guys who have saved their energy well in the first part of the race. Speaking of which, Lance is back in yellow. That won't really make much difference to the race as his team has been riding like he's been in yellow for the last week. They have kept the race in control, as Brioches la Boulangère couldn't really do too much in the high mountains.

Tonight I am looking forward to a good massage, a big dinner of nasty, white, French pasta, and a good sleep. At least we can sleep in a bit tomorrow as the time trial is in the afternoon. Time trial days are never really as restful as I try and lead myself to believe, though. They might be short in actual race time, but all the preparation, warm-up, and so on ends up making the day seem a whole lot longer than a road stage. At least the crowds will be insane and it'll feel like I am riding in the center of a stadium during a bowl game. ■

the first time since the Tour started that Ullrich had actually been ahead of Armstrong on a decisive climb. The Texan hardly seemed concerned. Standing out of his saddle, Armstrong only watched out of the corner of his eye as his most dangerous rival zipped away. There was no immediate reaction from Armstrong, who continued at a steady pace, but the fans loved it. Ullrich was finally taking a gamble and challenging Armstrong. His handlers at T-Mobile had quietly let it be known that the 1997 Tour winner had been taking antibiotics in the Pyrénées, but that he would be ready to attack in the Alps. With 4 kilometers to go on the climb, Ullrich opened up 41 seconds on the lead group, now down to eight riders: Floyd Landis and José Azevedo from Postal Service, Klöden, Basso, Sastre, Armstrong, Levi Leipheimer (Rabobank), and Marius Sabaliauskas (Saeco).

At the front, Virenque and Rasmussen were working together at 2:14 ahead of Ullrich and 2:53 ahead of the group of eight. But neither Virenque's lead nor Ullrich's attack was setting off any alarms in the Postal camp.

"We weren't very concerned," Armstrong said at the end of the stage. "We knew the course very well, we did it during the Dauphiné. After the summit, there's really no descent from that climb, it kind of stays flat to the next Cat. 3 climb. It was easy for two teams to work together, which is what happened with CSC. For us, it was not a problem. Now had I been alone, then it could have been bad."

But Armstrong wasn't alone. Doing great work for Postal was Landis, the quiet, hardworking former mountain biker who was back in top form. After breaking his hip during a training ride in January 2003, Landis fought back to start the 2003 Tour. This year he was injury free during his Tour buildup and was clearly one of Armstrong's strongest lieutenants in the mountains.

Ullrich, meanwhile, continued to drive on alone toward the Cat. 3 Col de Carri at 137 kilometers, picking up then dropping stragglers from the day's earlier move along the way. Voigt sat up, and it appeared the German was going to wait for his compatriot to help Ullrich gain time on Armstrong. Instead, he coasted nearly to stop to wait for Basso. "I feel sorry for Ullrich, but I had to work for the team," Voigt said. "We had the orders to protect Basso. I went into the break to keep the pressure off the team. In the end, many asked why I didn't stay with Ullrich, but the orders were clear."

Riis later defended his decision not to attack Armstrong. With Bobby Julich hampered by an injured wrist and Sastre showing signs of a back injury, Riis felt shackled at a key moment of the race. "I understand that not everyone understands my tactic. We have a very clear idea—to protect Basso. We have several riders who are not 100 percent, so we had to change our tactic a little bit and perhaps not ride as aggressive as we'd like. It would not have been worth it to go with Ullrich because there were two U.S. Postal Service riders with Lance."

With Voigt, Azevedo, and Landis driving the Armstrong group, Ullrich's adventure was suffering a quick death. Ullrich topped the Col de Carri with a 55-second gap but was swallowed up on the trough leading to the Cat. 2 Col de Chalimont. It was the last time Ullrich attacked during the 2004 Tour. "Some people will criticize my tactic today, but that's always the case no matter what I do," Ullrich said. "Some say I make foolish attacks, but it's better than to not try at all. I wanted to try something after my poor performances in the Pyrénées. I still want to be a factor in the final week."

Virenque and Rasmussen were still hanging 40 seconds off the front of the Armstrong-Ullrich group with 10 kilometers to go up the Chalimont. Postal's George Hincapie and Chechu Rubiera were close to catching on, but Armstrong decided to continue the hard pace being set by Landis and Azevedo to keep Ullrich from trying any more shenanigans. "George and Chechu almost came back. We were torn—do we wait for them and have two more guys or do we continue to ride with Voigt and Sastre from CSC to chase down Ullrich?" Armstrong said. "Player of the day was Floyd Landis, who was just incredible. There were 10 guys left on the climb and Floyd was one of them, which normally is not his cup of tea. His family was all there on the mountain, so maybe that helped him a little bit."

The lead group was down to three Postals (Armstrong, Landis, Azevedo), three CSCs (Basso, Sastre, and Voigt), two T-Mobiles (Ullrich and Klöden), solo fliers Leipheimer and Sabaliauskas, and stragglers from the early break: Vande Velde, Brochard, and Gonzalez.

Just as this group pulled within sight of Rasmussen and Virenque, Leipheimer shot away with less than 20 kilometers to go. If he could get over the col, it was a fast 12 kilometers downhill to the base of the rising finish into Villard-de-Lans. For a moment, it almost looked as if he could do it. But his timing was off. The scent of the finish line was in the air, and Leipheimer's chasers soon swallowed him up. With the leaders again consolidated, a group of ten came roaring down the twisting descent ready to charge up the final climb.

Just moments before the peloton was due to pass, spectators were frantically moving a large tree off the course. According to witnesses, some angry fans had chopped down a tree and pushed it across the road. Protests are nothing new in the Tour, with political groups often using the widely watched race as a platform to spread their message. But this seemed to be nothing more than sheer rowdiness from fans and another worry for Tour officials, long used to counting on the good conduct of its spectators.

Followers of the day's events, meanwhile, knew that there was no question whether Armstrong was going to bounce into the yellow jersey. Voeckler was languishing more than 6 minutes behind, and the Texan was now sitting near the rear of the group as the leaders came snaking down to the base of the final climb to the finish. At just over 2-kilometers, the Cat. 2 hump wasn't very long or steep, but after such an intense day of racing, it wasn't going to be easy. Azevedo, Voigt, Sastre, and Rasmussen fell off the pace to leave Leipheimer, Armstrong, Basso, Klöden, and Ullrich to fight for the spoils.

The Tour is often about measured efforts and keeping emotions in check, but surging to the finish line, Armstrong couldn't hold back. He wanted the win and he wanted the 20-second time bonus that went with it. Basso led the way, but Armstrong ducked under his left shoulder and powered forward. As he crossed the line to victory, Armstrong shot his fists in the air, claiming his 18th career Tour stage and the overall race lead.

"There's something special in winning in a sprint," said Armstrong of his second stage victory in four days. "To win alone on top of a mountain is fun, but to win a sprint is much more intense. Sure, I could sit up and finish 4th, but why sit up and give 20 seconds to your rivals? Johan was screaming in my ear that I had to win because of the time bonuses," said Armstrong. "It's still a question of a minute, 25, so every second counts—sorry, no pun intended," he added, a bit abashed by the inadvertent plug for his recent book of the same name.

Armstrong, it seemed, was back in the maillot jaune just in time to slam the door on the 2004 Tour. With but five days remaining, only Ivan Basso was thought to be strong enough to mount any kind of a challenge. Armstrong acknowledged Basso's presence, and was properly cautious about his chances. "I don't think the Tour's over," he said. "I think Ivan can ride a good race tomorrow." Behind the scenes, though, the Posties' confidence was sky high. With the 20-second time bonus that went with the stage victory, Armstrong had widened his lead over 2nd-place Basso by 8 seconds, to 1 minute, 25 seconds.

Moreover, Armstrong would enter the next day's climbing time trial up l'Alpe d'Huez cloaked in a mantle of almost impregnable confidence. He had won a stage atop the climb in 2001 and knew the course well, having trained extensively on the mountain in May. "We know every single meter of it. We know when the slope is steep or when it's gentler," said Postal Service director Johan Bruyneel. "It's a climb on which you must know what you're doing." Armstrong certainly did, and as race leader he would start the time trial last, gaining the advantage of knowing the time splits of his rivals as he pushed up the course.

"There's a part of me that wanted to ride a legendary mountain like Alpe d'Huez in the yellow jersey," Armstrong said as he surveyed the village of Villard-de-Lans, site of his latest triumph. "I cannot lie. It's exciting to take the yellow jersey, even if it's day number 61 or whatever. It's still a thrill."

And he was now perfectly poised to take his thrill ride right into Paris.

STAGE 15, VALRÉAS TO VILLARD-DE-LANS: 1. Lance Armstrong (USA), U.S. Postal–Berry Floor, 180.5km in 4:40:30; **2.** Ivan Basso (I), CSC–same time; **3.** Jan Ullrich (G), T-Mobile, at 0:03; **4.** Andreas Klöden (G), T-Mobile, at 0:06; **5. Levi Leipheimer (USA), Rabobank, at 0:13**
OVERALL: 1. Armstrong, 67:13:43; **2.** Basso, at 1:25; **3.** Klöden, at 3:22

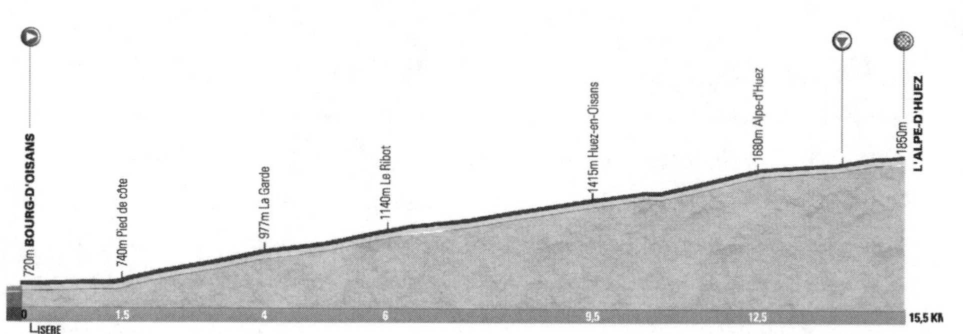

STAGE 16 | Bourg-d'Oisans to l'Alpe d'Huez

It was unclear whether the much-vaunted 15.5-kilometer time trial to the top of l'Alpe d'Huez was going to be the decisive moment Tour organizers hoped it would be, but fans were leaving nothing to chance. Journalists driving up the 21 hairpins the night before the major showdown on the Alpe found people everywhere. Fans were squeezed onto just about every flat pitch of real estate, sleeping in camper vans, buses, cars, tents, and simply on the road. Some fans just never went to sleep. The famous "Dutch corner" midway up the course was already a sea of orange as fans danced to techno music and drank Heineken until the sun came up.

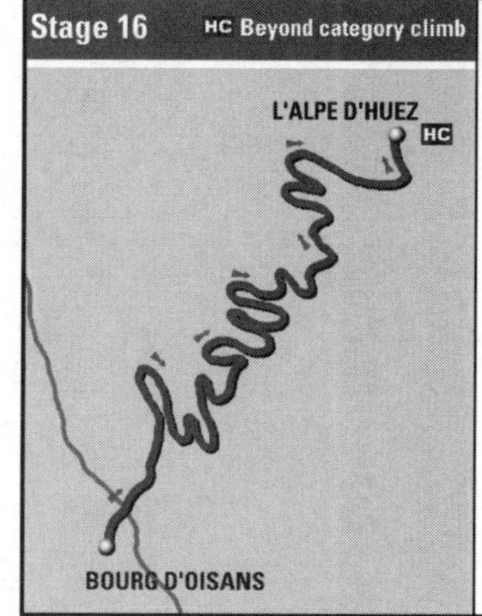

While officials were bracing themselves for up to 1 million spectators, later estimates put the number at about 600,000, still the largest crowd in Alpe history. With fencing restricting access to the course on the top 7 kilometers, coupled with the daunting prospect of walking all the way to the top, most fans elected to hover near the lower half of the mountain.

L'Alpe d'Huez, with an average grade of 7.8 percent over 13.8 kilometers, is not the hardest or longest climb in the Tour, but over the years it has captured the imagination of fans and media like no other climb. Some of the Tour's most memorable battles have been fought out on its 21 *lacets,* or switchbacks, which are numbered in reverse order with the names of winners brandished on each hairpin.

The mountain was introduced to the Tour in 1952 as the first summit finish in the race's history. At the time, l'Alpe d'Huez was a relatively new winter sports destination, and the trail to the top was little more than a goat track. Fausto Coppi became the first winner, taking the yellow jersey on the stage from his teammate Andrea Carrea and wearing it from there to Paris. It was a thrilling day, but because of the terrible road to the top, the Tour didn't return to the Alpe until

CHRISTIAN VANDE VELDE—LIBERTY SEGUROS

Switchbacks, Drunk Fans, and Road Art

L' Alpe d'Huez is probably the most famous climb of the Tour de France. Its 13 kilometers of climbing, 21 switch-back turns, and steep ramps have show-cased the epic battles of the Tour and typically draw the biggest crowds of any stage. This year was exceptional—we raced up it as a time trial, and Lance is on his way to his sixth Tour victory.

Prior to the start, Roberto had to change his rear wheel, as his bike was 100 grams under the legal weight. The climbers on the team have bikes with small wheels as well. Lance also had a weight problem before the start, and the Postal mechanics had to throw a couple of computers or something on his bike to bring it to 6.8 kilograms. I was pleasantly surprised that my stock race bike came in at 6.9.

The crowds were insane from the start of the climb all the way to the top. At times it was scary, as I didn't really know if I would make it through the crazy, screaming fans. By the time we started racing, the fans had eaten their lunches, finished their bottles of red, drained their cans of beer, and topped it all off with shots of grappa. When people are drunk, reaction times are slow and the noise is deafening, which is both good and bad when you're racing up a hill with sweat in your eyes.

It seems to me cycling isn't quite the fringe sport it was a few years ago in America. Stars-and-stripes flags were all over the slopes and there was at least a stadium's worth of Americans screaming. Up here the orange T-shirts are Dutch fans whereas in the Pyrénées they were Basques. The majority of the spectators seemed to be German and Dutch. I do have a few questions,

1976. In the Tours that followed, l'Alpe d'Huez quickly earned the nickname "Dutch Mountain" after Dutch riders won six of the next eight ascents.

Colombian Luis Herrera won in 1984, and five-time Tour winner Bernard Hinault won hand in hand with Greg LeMond in 1986 before passing the baton to allow the American to claim overall victory. In the 1990s Italians held court on the Alpe, claiming six victories in seven stops during the decade, and American Andy Hampsten won in 1992.

Now, more than 50 years after Coppi won the inaugural climb, the Tour was back for the 24th time. Instead of a bumpy dirt road, riders would ascend on newly laid asphalt that was already covered with names from bottom to top, painted there by the frenzied fans. The suffering for the riders was the same, however. From the base of the climb to the finish line at the ski station, the road pushes up 1,130 meters, about 50 meters per switchback, perhaps the best measure of its steepness.

though. I want to know who is painting the big penises on the climbs, and why? Anyway, I get a little chuckle every time I roll over one.

Jan is making his slow comeback, but I think it is too late. He might land himself a podium if he keeps improving the way he is, but Lance has made his mark as the dominant man of this year's Tour.

Tonight we are up on l'Alpe d'Huez, and it is quite a zoo up here. The ski resort is probably more packed with people now than it is in the heart of the ski season. Leah, my wife, came to our hotel for a visit after the stage. I am not sure who is more tired between the two of us, as she came to my room and crashed on the bed for a solid hour and a half. I was pretty excited to hear that she has a few NHL hockey players on tour with Trek Travel. I thought it was pretty cool that a bunch of Canuck hockey kids love every minute of this wussy biking sport.

A good percentage of the peloton is pretty worried about tomorrow's stage. Today the race claimed two riders to the time cut and tomorrow it could be a lot worse. Half of the guys going up the mountain today were just trying to conserve as much energy as possible for tomorrow. It's going to be another tough day. I am glad I took it somewhat easy today, as I am sure we'll be racing out of the gates tomorrow.

The race pretty much starts uphill, and I would not be at all surprised if the attacks come fast and hard from the get-go. I talked with my friend and fellow racer Michael Barry about a few of the climbs toward the end of the stage, as he lived in Annemasse for a few years. He tells me the Col de la Croix Fry is a tough climb with some pretty steep sections and it'll be a big battle between the hitters again. He claims these are the best roads for cycling he's ever ridden. We'll see. . . ■

The bottom two-thirds of the climb are its most grueling. As the road pushes left toward the first hairpin (or 21st, according to the numbering system), riders face a spirit-breaking wall with an average grade of 10.25 percent in the first 2 kilometers. Kilometer 6 is "easy" at 7.5 percent, but riders soon face ramps as steep as 14 percent before the entrance to Huez-en-Oisans, the major village between the valley floor and the ski resort. The final switchbacks are long and straight and more open to the wind, with the 10th kilometer at a gut-busting 11.5-percent gradient. The final 2 kilometers stream past cheering fans in l'Alpe d'Huez village, a collection of tacky gift shops and concrete-slab hotels. It's hardly the most picturesque setting for cycling's most famous mountain, but then the Tour doesn't come to the Alpe for the scenery. It comes to the Alpe for the Alpe.

The first start position belonged to last-place rider Sébastian Joly, the Frenchman on Crédit Agricole who was fighting with compatriot Jimmy Casper

(Cofidis) for the dubious honor of the *laterne rouge*, or red lantern, evoking the signal at the tail end of a train. Back in the Tour's heyday, the last rider could often score lucrative post-Tour criterium-appearance fees. Today, the red lantern gets little more than a smattering of cheers from the fans who arrive early.

Scheduled to start some 2 hours, 58 minutes later was Armstrong, decked out in the maillot jaune. History was on Armstrong's side at l'Alpe d'Huez. This was his fourth appearance on the mountain in the six Tours since his cancer comeback, and each time the grueling climb played a key role in his march toward making history.

In 1999 Italian Giuseppe Guerini brushed off a collision with a fan to win the stage, but Armstrong secured his first overall Tour title after finishing 5th in a group of six challengers at 25 seconds back. And it was here in 2001, in what he calls his favorite Tour stage victory, that Armstrong pulled off his greatest heist. Under pressure from the German Telekom team, Armstrong pretended he was struggling on earlier climbs to lull his rivals into wasting valuable energy. He then unleashed an attack at the bottom of the Alpe, giving his now famous "look" over his shoulder to check the condition of the suddenly powerless Ullrich.

Armstrong pretended he was struggling on earlier climbs . . . then unleashed an attack at the bottom of the Alpe, giving his now famous "look" over his shoulder to check the condition of the suddenly powerless Ullrich.

"It looked like the race was going against us," Armstrong later recalled. "Telekom was making the race and basically saying that they were going to dominate, but we came back as a team and I came back as an individual. It was quite a swing." Despite the victory, he wouldn't grab the yellow jersey until the race hit the Pyrénées a week later, but his win on the Alpe that day matched him with Coppi as the only rider to take the stage and the overall title in the same year.

In the Tour's centennial in 2003, his rivals got the first glimpse that Armstrong wasn't at his best when he finished third at 2:12 behind Spanish climber Iban Mayo on the Alpe. Armstrong couldn't shake his competitors as he'd done in previous years. Despite his lack of punch, however, he grabbed the yellow jersey and later overcame crashes, dehydration, and attacks to win a record-tying fifth title.

Although Armstrong was looking more and more like the inevitable winner of the 2004 Tour, there was plenty at stake on the Alpe, especially if he unexpectedly faltered. Basso (CSC) would be starting at just 1:25 back overall, and there was enough road still ahead to make it a good fight, especially for the final podium. German comeback-kid Andreas Klöden, 3rd at 3:22 back, was hoping to put pressure on Basso if the Italian couldn't match Armstrong's strength as he had in the Pyrénées.

Of the early riders on the course, Fabian Cancellara (Fassa Bortolo) ran best, putting his prologue-winning skills to work on the flat section at the bottom of the valley floor and covering the 1.5-kilometer distance in 2:01. Another fast time was set by Santos Gonzalez, the Spanish rider on Phonak, who blazed up the course in 41:52, the same as Guerini's winning time in 1999.

However, it soon became obvious that, as exciting as the race may have been, it was the temperature of the enormous crowds lining the course that was threatening to boil over. Fans pushing close to cheer their cycling heroes was nothing new, but on the Alpe the riders were just as often being heckled, booed, and jeered. There was a growing hooliganism in the Tour that hadn't been seen before. "It's an interesting mix of people there," Armstrong said later. "You don't just have French people, you have a lot of German people and they're very excited. You have a lot of American people and they're excited . . . a lot of French, Italians. . . . But what I don't understand," he emphasized, "you see some people, once their guy goes by they cheer and then everybody else, they give them a hard time. No class."

The German fans were particularly vicious. Armstrong said he was spat upon and jeered at as he pushed past Ullrich fans, while German Jens Voigt was booed and called a "traitor" after helping teammate Ivan Basso in the previous day's battle to Villard-de-Lans, rather than working with the attacking Ullrich.

"Today was anything but a nice stage for me—the thorn of disappointment is sitting deep," Voigt said. "I have nothing positive to say about the myth of Alpe d'Huez and the many enthusiastic spectators. The Jan Ullrich fans who don't understand that I was chasing him in the service of my team captain Ivan Basso on stage 15 were shouting insults of the worst kind at me. All the way up the mountain people were booing at me and showing Judas-posters the size of bed sheets with my name on it. The only good thing was that people didn't push me off the bike. Furious people were running next to me—at times you only go at 15 kilometers per hour. You can't defend yourself against something like that. Today I felt like I was in a witch hunt."

Tour de France director Jean-Marie Leblanc conceded that the crowd was out of control. "There were lots of aggressive fans," he said, calling the spitters "idiots." He later revealed that Tour officials had been tipped off by national security officials that Armstrong had been threatened. While Leblanc refused to say exactly what the threats were, the Tour quietly took extra measures to protect the Texan. Traveling inside the Postal Service car with sport director Johan Bruyneel, team mechanic Geoff Brown, and Armstrong's girlfriend Sheryl Crow, was a French security agent. Also, the motorcycles driving just before and after Armstrong weren't part of the regular Tour brigade but rather specially trained security guards.

Safely atop the Alpe at the end of the race, and surrounded by his protective entourage, Armstrong said the rowdy fans only fed his manic desire to win. "That motivates me more than anything," he said, clearly aggrieved. Calming down a bit, he said, "I don't want to make it worse than it was. This is big-time sport. If the Bulls play the Knicks and they go into Madison Square Garden, they're not blowing kisses to the Chicago Bulls, back in the old days. The people are excited and emotional and they have their guy but that doesn't take away from my love of the game, from my desire to win. In fact, as I said, I think it puts a little fuel on the fire."

Armstrong rode with a one-piece, aerodynamic bodysuit unzipped to the middle of his chest and a U.S. Postal Service cap turned backward. Fans choked the road to capture a photo, a glimpse, or even a touch of the American superhero. Spinning his pedals with a cadence of up to 110 revolutions per minute, Armstrong was using his months of preparation and training to perform with deadly efficiency. Armstrong's high-cadence spinning has been described by Australian journalist Rupert Guinness as a "dog digging for a bone," while TV commentator Phil Liggett tends to refer to Armstrong's rapidly pumping legs as "pistons." However it's portrayed, Armstrong's unusual style was delivering his best day in the 2004 Tour and quickly digging a hole for his rivals.

By the time he reached the first time check, at 9.5 kilometers at Huez-en-Oisans, Armstrong was already 40 seconds faster than Ullrich and 1:15 faster than Basso. The Italian, who started 2 minutes ahead of Armstrong, clearly didn't have the snap in his legs that had helped him follow the Texan in the Pyrénées. Ullrich was one of the few riding with aerobars and found his tempo in the middle section of the climb, holding the difference to Armstrong until the final upper reaches.

Once safely inside the protection of the crowd barriers with 7 kilometers to go, Armstrong was even more lethal. Back in May, he and a handful of select teammates had come to the Alpe to preview the climb. Although he'd ridden it three times in previous Tours, Armstrong wanted to leave nothing to chance. Now he was using the hairpins as a countdown to the finish line. "Training on the mountain and racing on it are totally different," he said, describing the way the thick clots of spectators had obscured the road. "The only reference I had were the numbers on the switchbacks. Every turn I was looking for the numbers, that's my reference. I broke up the climb into sections, from the villages, the sections of switchbacks."

With relentless drive, Armstrong was closing in on Basso, his "2-minute man." While Armstrong was focused and efficient, Basso was struggling, wagging his head from side to side and sitting heavily on the bike. Finally, at around the 3-kilometer mark, Armstrong pulled alongside his young challenger. Neither took their eyes off the road. Basso matched Armstrong's pace for about 100 meters, then finally stole a quick glance at his rival and slowly tapered off, his dreams of the ultimate upset victory disappearing with each stroke of Armstrong's pedals. "I normally ride the time trial better, but for some reason I didn't feel good today," said Basso, who finished 8th at 2:23 slower. "The Ivan Basso the world saw the past few days will be back tomorrow. If there's an opportunity, I will attack."

Chances to attack Armstrong, however, were running out faster than the asphalt on the way up the Alpe. Armstrong kept pouring it on, intent on leaving his mark on the Tour. Marco Pantani's record on the 13.8-kilometer climbing section was under threat, and when Armstrong charged across the line the winner with a time of 39:41, it was later calculated that he was all of 1 second slower than the Italian. Pantani could rest in peace.

Armstrong was intently studying the results sheet as he described his feelings to the world's press after winning his third stage in the last four days of racing. "I was very happy to win here today. L'Alpe d'Huez is the most important climb in the Tour," he said. "Today I was focused on just getting through the stage safe and getting the stage win and securing the lead overall. I'm real careful about counting to the number six. I'll do that on the final lap on the Champs-Élysées. Today was focused on today."

T-Mobile's Klöden rode beyond expectations, finishing third at 1:41 back and pulling within 1:15 of Basso. "I rode as if I was in a tunnel," Klöden said. "I concentrated on the rear wheel of the motorbike that was opening the road through the crowd and followed the white line in the middle of the road. I'm happy with my ride because I gained time on Basso. I'm still 1:15 behind him in the overall standings, but I've got the last mountain stage and then the final time trial on Saturday. I'm optimistic that I can move past him and finish 2nd."

Ullrich, meanwhile, was in unfamiliar territory for the first time since his remarkable debut in 1996. The 1997 champion had never finished worse than 2nd overall and now it was looking unlikely he'd even finish 3rd. Armstrong had beaten Ullrich by 1:01 on the Alpe—the same margin he held over the German when the Tour concluded in 2003. Despite a strong ride, Ullrich could only muster 4th place overall at 7:55 back. "I did everything I could and I was at my absolute limit," Ullrich said. "I didn't even listen to the intermediate times because I just wanted to go as hard as I could. At the beginning I could hear my name being called, but at the end I couldn't hear anything. There was so much screaming, my ears will still be ringing tomorrow."

Johan Bruyneel, director of Armstrong's U.S. Postal Service team, was breathing easier. Nothing had happened to his star rider and the noose had been pulled tighter around the collective necks of Armstrong's rivals. Only one more mountain stage stood between Armstrong and Paris. "Things are looking very good, but we have to keep thinking about the Tour de France and show respect for the three-week race," Bruyneel said. "It's the hardest race in the world and we've seen in the past there's danger around every bend. I think we have a very comfortable lead now. It will be up to the others to try to do something and we will try to respond to keep the advantage."

There were some riders even more disappointed than Basso and Ullrich. Francisco Mancebo saw his chances of making the final podium fade after finishing a disappointing 24th. He fell out of contention, dropping from 4th to 6th at 9:20 back. Levi Leipheimer, racing in just his second Tour, was also hoping for more. He finished 29th at 4:06 slower. "It's a day I have to write off," said Leipheimer, who slipped to 10th overall at 15:04 back. "I was real disappointed. It was the day I was looking to the most. Maybe that's why I was not so good, I was mentally blocked."

Armstrong said it was his hard work that made the difference on the Alpe. Later that night, as his team celebrated another stage victory and pushed closer to the Champs-Élysées, Armstrong talked again about his relentless approach to the Tour. "Our secret is that we work all year long," he said. "Everybody in cycling always wants to know a secret but I have to say—and I hate to disappoint skeptics—but the secret is 12 months a year. It's not a final exam you can cram for. This is the Tour and it requires a year-round commitment.

"If you guys come here in the month of May, it's literally a ghost town," Armstrong continued. "So you just stay here and you just ride up and down the mountain, alone or as a team, that's the stuff that we do. Although I didn't think that this would be the decisive day of the Tour, I still knew it would be important. But these are things we do, we've always done, and it's something I personally love more than anything. The people that are here then are the people that are repaving the roads, and the people that work in the one or two hotels that are open. For me, there are not a million people on the side of the road, it's me and a few people and that's what makes it beautiful. And to me, that's what makes the difference between winning and losing."

STAGE 16, BOURG-D'OISANS TO L'ALPE D'HUEZ: 1. Lance Armstrong (USA), U.S. Postal–Berry Floor, 15.5km in 39:41 (23.456kph); 2. Jan Ullrich (G), T-Mobile, at 1:01; **3.** Andreas Klöden (G), T-Mobile, at 1:41; **4.** José Azevedo (Por), U.S. Postal–Berry Floor, at 1:45; **5.** Santos Gonzalez (Sp), Phonak, at 2:11
OVERALL: 1. Armstrong, 67:53:24; 2. Ivan Basso (I), CSC, at 3:48; **3.** Klöden, at 5:03

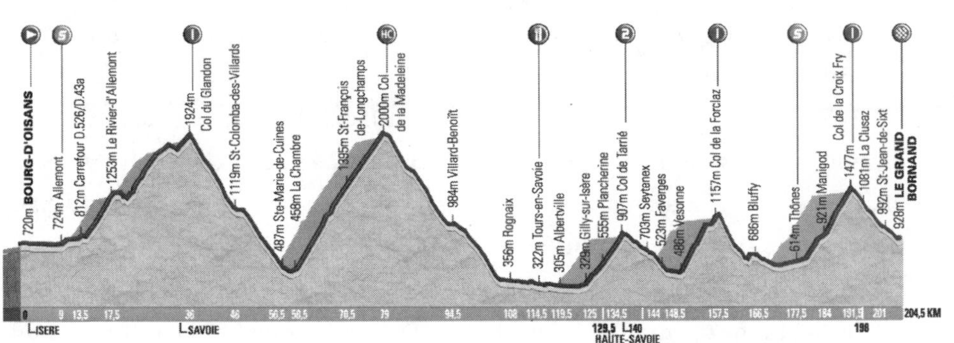

STAGE 17 | Bourg-d'Oisans to Le Grand-Bornand

The dust had barely settled on the Alpe d'Huez time trial when the peloton faced what might be its most grueling day of the Tour. On paper, the stage had the potential to be the hardest of the race: 205 kilometers, five mountain passes, and more than 5,000 meters of climbing, including a traverse over the Tour's highest point at the 2,000-meter Col de la Madeleine.

At the start in Bourg-d'Oisans, a bustling tourist village at the base of the Alpe, the peloton was three riders lighter as Laurent Lefèvre (La Boulangère), Alessandro Bertolini (Alessio), and Roberto Heras (Liberty Seguros) weren't taking the start. That third name on the DNS list was a shocker, at least to the pundits who had expected the slightly built Spanish mountain goat to challenge for the podium.

"We haven't been able to get him back to full fitness," Liberty Seguros team boss Manolo Saiz said before the start of the seventeenth stage. "We can't force it because later it can affect his knee and Roberto will defend his title at the Vuelta. We've had to take a decision that isn't to our liking, but we're professionals and life must go on. We're sure that he'll bring something to cheer about before the year is over."

Heras was one of the top guns in the Spanish Armada and one who had vowed to sink Armstrong in his run for a sixth title. With Armstrong sitting pretty in yellow, and just one mountain stage between him and Paris, it was the Spanish riders who were now running for cover.

Heras had defected from Armstrong's U.S. Postal Service team at the end of the 2003 season to try his luck at Liberty Seguros, the new incarnation of the mighty ONCE team. The 30-year-old Heras won the Vuelta a España in 2000 and 2003 but was never a threat in the 91st Tour. He had limped up l'Alpe d'Huez, complained of lingering knee pain, and now had abandoned while sitting in 45th place at 57 minutes down on Armstrong.

Blood was spilled early in the stage when Janek Tombak (Cofidis) suffered a horrible crash as he tried to fix the time sensor attached to the chainstay of his bike. He nearly lost a finger, which was sliced to the bone when his right hand slipped inside the spokes of his rear wheel.

With the 25-kilometer haul up the 1,924-meter Col du Glandon waiting right off the bat in the opening 36 kilometers, it didn't take long for the peloton to prepare for battle. Five riders—Michele Bartoli (CSC), Gilberto Simoni (Saeco), Filippo Simeoni (Domina Vacanze), Rolf Aldag (T-Mobile), and Ludovic Martin (RAGT)—tore away on the rollout from Bourg-d'Oisans and nursed a 5:30 head start over the Glandon.

Simoni was another rider who was sensing that his best was behind him, at least as far as the Tour de France was concerned. The two-time Giro d'Italia champion was thinking about one more stab at a stage win, but things weren't looking good. Armstrong was safely protected inside his blue and red Lycra cocoon of the U.S. Postal Service as the peloton worked its way up the first mountain.

"I never want to come back," Simoni told French journalist Philippe Brunel. "I've done four Tours without any success. The other day my director said I had to attack Armstrong, but how? In the lead group half of the riders were Postal Service. We were 20 and they were nine. The only solution is to take on Armstrong one on one, but even then, we've seen that Armstrong is very strong and very confident."

Simoni had bragged in 2003 about knocking the Tour crown off Armstrong's head, only to have to eat his words after being beaten down in the Alps. This time around, Simoni was keeping his mouth shut, and unfortunately for him, his legs weren't making much noise either. Up l'Alpe d'Huez, Simoni could only muster a middling 23rd at 3:40 slower, and he was starting today's stage in 12th at 15:41 back. "I envy Armstrong, like I envied Pantani for what he did," Simoni finally admitted. "Those two are bigger than me."

Simoni led the way over the Glandon with the chasing Mikel Astarloza (ag2r) clearing the summit 3 minutes behind him, and Quick Step's Richard Virenque leading the peloton at 5:30 back. Anxious to sew up a record seventh King of the Mountains jersey, Virenque and Christophe Moreau (Crédit Agricole) attacked on the descent of the Glandon, to the delight of the French fans.

Virenque's continuing popularity with his countrymen was something of a mystery to many riders in the peloton. After admitting to doping as a member of the ill-fated Festina team in 1998, the controversial French star had served a suspension and then returned to the Tour in 2002, whereupon he seemed to immediately win back the hearts of French housewives everywhere. His fortunes had only improved since. A post-stage TV interview would bring traffic to a standstill. French girls would nearly faint if they could get an autograph. In a country where the cynicism about athletic doping was higher than anywhere else in Europe, the exception granted to Virenque struck many observers as truly bizarre.

"They don't know what they want," said Armstrong of the fickle French fans. He had been alternately cheered and booed in this year's Tour. The cheers were expected; the boos were something new. "What kind of champion do they want? A champion who doesn't work hard and doesn't love his sport?" Armstrong asked rhetorically. "But don't boo me and cheer for someone who was involved in the biggest doping crisis in the history of the sport. That doesn't make sense."

Indeed it didn't, and yet despite his lurid past, Virenque was receiving the biggest cheers of any rider in the race—French or otherwise. Now he was out front again, and the TV cameras were riveted on him. Virenque and Moreau tore down the Glandon, reeling in and dropping Astarloza, but still remained 5:05 behind the leading quintet at the base of the Madeleine, the 21st time in Tour history that the monster col saw riders tackle its steep, stark approach.

"What kind of champion do they want? A champion who doesn't work hard and doesn't love his sport?"

Waiting atop the grueling, 19.5-kilometer climb was the Tour's 5,000-euro prize named in honor of Tour founder Henri Desgrange, which is awarded each year to the first rider over the top of the highest point of the race. The peloton was 7:20 behind Simoni and Co. as they started the long climb to the summit of the Madeleine. Postal Service was setting the pace of the main bunch, and scores of riders were having trouble staying on their wheels. Stefano Zanini and Tom Boonen (both Quick Step), Robbie McEwen (Lotto-Domo), Thor Hushovd (Crédit Agricole), and Filippo Pozzato (Fassa Bortolo) were among the dozens spit out the back as the Posties took command.

Virenque and Moreau, meanwhile, were making steady progress on the Simoni group, slicing the time gap to just 1:20 with 5 kilometers to go. Seeing the polka-dot jersey getting closer, Simoni accelerated and fractured the group. Bartoli, who would later be among the day's five abandons, drifted off the back. Simoni beat Virenque to the summit to grab the bonus and a little bit of pride. Virenque's Quick Step teammate Paolo Bettini led the peloton over the Madeleine at 6:50 behind. It was still a long way to Le Grand Bornand.

CHRISTIAN VANDE VELDE—LIBERTY SEGUROS

Hot, Hot, Hot, and Up, Up, Up

Okay, I am beat now. It was another hard day. They keep hitting us with these insane stages. Today was perhaps one of the hardest days on paper, with some serious climbing and the highest peak of the Tour, the Col de la Madeleine.

My watch tells me we did 5,000 meters of climbing in 71 kilometers. Kilimanjaro is 5,896 meters high so we didn't do too badly today. As a kid I used to do a loop back home with my Dad that was 70 kilometers around. I can remember thinking it was a pretty solid ride back then—today we climbed the same distance.

Today was hot. In the last three weeks we have had all sorts of weather thrown at us, and the extremes are taking their toll on the peloton. During the stage I went through about 15 water bottles and was still parched and dehydrated when I crossed the line. In hot weather it's hard to eat but easy to drink, and in cold weather it's hard to drink and easy to eat. I think most guys in the peloton are being reminded to eat and drink by their directors over the radios. Sometimes, you'll see the whole team on the front reach down for their bottles and take a long pull. You can bet that came right after their director just radioed, "Make sure you keep drinking."

Lance and the Postal crew hit the race with their wrecking ball again and left the field in rubble behind them. I looked up at the bottom of the Col de la Forclaz, and they had nine guys up there! We had two: Igor and me. Roberto went home this morning, as he hasn't really been feeling himself in the mountains. U.S. Postal's Pavel Padrnos, or "the Butcher" as Robbie Ventura nicknamed him, pulled the entire way up the Madeleine. It was quite impressive. He is a great climber as well as being a machine on the flats. He is probably the strongest guy in the peloton to win the fewest races. He looks intimidating, but he's actually a mellow and easygoing guy.

Tonight we're staying just down from the finish line in the Grand Bornand. The town is basically at the foot of another famous climb, the Col de la Colombière. Tomorrow we head down the valley toward Geneva for the start, and then we climb over another course that looks like a wolf's jaw on the profile. ■

Back in 1999 Le Grand Bornand became an interesting footnote to the Lance Armstrong story. In 2004 the picturesque mountain town was hosting its first Tour finish, but six years ago the hamlet lost deep in the French Savoie region saw Armstrong's first run in the yellow jersey begin in earnest. The previous day, Armstrong had recaptured the yellow jersey with a dramatic time trial victory at Metz. Many expected Armstrong, just back from his battle with cancer, to fold under the pressure of the grueling stage across the high Alps, which had started in Le Grand Bornand. But Armstrong responded to the challenge with panache, attacking and then dropping his rivals to win alone at the Italian ski area Sestriere, prompting his now famous retort, "How do you like them apples?"

Now Armstrong was the unquestioned king of the Tour and had only three more climbs before descending into Le Grand Bornand and all but certain victory in the 2004 Tour. How had things changed since that morning back in 1999? "Each victory brings more and more experience, which in this event is very critical," Armstrong said. "I can remember back in 1999, I was so nervous every day I was going to lose the jersey. I don't have those feelings anymore. I get nervous, I'll have bad days, but I have a lot of confidence in myself and in the team that we can control any situation, as long as I take care of myself physically and I do all the things I am supposed to do—eat right and show up at the start line ready to race every day. That comes with a lot of experience. When I was here in 1999, I hadn't started the mountains. I had won the time trial, but for all I knew I was going to get dropped in the mountains and lose the yellow jersey."

That didn't seem likely in 2004. After the long descent off the Madeleine, Team CSC gave Postal Service some help to trim the lead down to 4:50 heading to the base of the Cat. 2 Col de Tamié. Simeoni and then Martin dropped off the lead group, leaving Aldag, Simoni, Virenque, and Moreau to work over the top. The peloton maintained a steady pace, content to keep the leading quartet at a slight distance as Iker Flores (Euskaltel) went on a solo flier to try to bridge to the leaders.

Up next was the Cat. 1 Col de la Forclaz looming above the scenic Lake Annecy. There was no time for sightseeing, however, as T-Mobile now surged to the front. This was the last chance for anyone to try something against Armstrong, and the German squad seemed determined to make a move stick. T-Mobile's Sergueï Ivanov, one of six Russians starting the 2004 Tour, attacked the peloton on the lower flanks of the 9-kilometer climb, sending a shot of electricity through the main bunch. The grueling course, temperatures well into the 90s, and nearly 3,000 kilometers of racing to date were taking their toll, and the leaders were quickly reduced to about 25 riders.

Armstrong was counting on Hincapie, Landis, Rubiera, and Azevedo while T-Mobile's Ullrich, Klöden, Guerini, and Ivanov were stuck on their wheels. Basso was suddenly exposed with just the hobbled Sastre to help out. The resilient Oscar Pereiro and Santos Gonzalez (both Phonak), Rasmussen and Leipheimer (both Rabobank), Karpets and Mancebo (both Illes Balears), Totschnig (Gerolsteiner), and Voeckler (La Boulangère) were the other prominent names hanging tough in the lead group. The attrition was brutal up the Forclaz. Aldag couldn't match the pace and let Simoni, Moreau, and Virenque lead the way over the climb. The leading trio nursed a 2:35 lead with the Tour's last major climb still ahead.

Team CSC was determined to have one final go at Armstrong coming up the Cat. 1 Col de la Croix Fry. With 6 kilometers remaining of the narrow, twisting road clogged with delirious fans, Carlos Sastre unleashed an attack quickly followed by an effort by Basso. But their move would not stick. "I attacked twice and Basso tried to come out, but Armstrong and his team are too strong and they controlled the stage start to finish," Sastre said. "The last few kilometers of the final climb were like an eternity. Landis rode a climb that was incredible. Everyone was hurting."

Floyd Landis was setting a torrid pace that was simply shredding the race apart, and Simoni, Moreau, and then Virenque were swallowed up by the pack. Landis wasn't so much as attacking as he was simply grinding out a rhythm that was blowing up the peloton in his wake. Sastre was reeled in and the lead group shrunk to just Landis, Armstrong, Ullrich, Klöden, and Basso heading over the top of the Croix Fry. It was an impressive performance that earned Landis kudos from his boss.

"He was the man of the day, he was incredible. For him to ride tempo on the final climb to end up with five guys, that's hard to do," Armstrong said. "The people that were there were suffering to stay there."

At the top of the col, Landis pulled up alongside Armstrong, and the Texan gave his quiet, hardworking *domestique* the green light to attack. Armstrong recounted their conversation as they slipped over the lip of the summit:

"I asked him, 'How bad you want to win a stage in the Tour de France?'

"He said, 'Real bad.'

"How fast can you go downhill? He said, 'Real fast.'

"He said, 'Can I do it?' I said, sure you can do it. I told him, 'Run like you stole something, Floyd.'"

Landis tore ahead, using his best descending skills, but it was a long 13 kilometers to the finish. Klöden and Ullrich chased and caught Landis on the narrow descent. Landis tried to break away again at just less than 2 kilometers to go, but again the T-Mobile twins reeled him in. Klöden counterattacked with 800 meters to go and opened up what looked like a winning gap. Then something clicked inside Armstrong. If Landis couldn't win, he'd be damned if he'd let the T-Mobile riders take Floyd's glory. Armstrong shot one glance back and unleashed a surprising sprint with 200 meters to go. Astonishingly, Armstrong closed in, caught, and then passed the dying Klöden at the line for his fourth consecutive mountain-stage win—a first in Tour history.

Armstrong was looking downright Merckxian. With four straight wins in the mountains (Plateau de Beille, Villard-de-Lans, l'Alpe d'Huez, and Le Grand Bornand), he was gobbling up everything in sight as he clawed his way toward Paris. "Am I the new Cannibal?" said Armstrong, repeating the question put to him about whether he had adopted the great Eddy Merckx's winning tactics. "The answer is no," he said modestly. Others weren't so sure. The embittered Simoni admitted that "Armstrong is not a cannibal." But, said Simoni, "He's a piranha."

Armstrong was greeted on the podium by another five-time Tour winner, Bernard Hinault, who congratulated him on his lack of mercy. "When I stepped up to the podium, Hinault said, 'Perfect, no gifts.' I've given gifts in the Tour de France and very rarely has it come back to help me," Armstrong said. "This is the biggest bike race in the world, and it means more to me than any bike race in the world, and I want to win. No gifts."

In 2000, Armstrong had let Italian Marco Pantani win a stage at Mont Ventoux and later regretted it, as he has yet to triumph on the most famous climb in cycling. At La Mongie this year, he "gifted" a stage to Basso in the name of his mother who is fighting cancer. Now at Le Grand Bornand, it was clear that Armstrong would no longer be the Tour's magnanimous ruler.

Still, he admitted that he would have liked to have seen Landis take the win. "He was the man of the day. I hoped he could ride a fast descent and win the stage, but it did not happen," Armstrong lamented. "Today was his best day ever; that's why I really wanted him to win the stage. He deserved to win. I should dedicate this stage win to him. I think he wanted and needed it." Landis had crossed the line 5th for his best career Tour finish. But within the peloton, Armstrong had evened the score.

STAGE 17, BOURG-D'OISANS TO LE GRAND BORNAND: 1. Lance Armstrong (USA), U.S. Postal–Berry Floor, 204.5km in 6:11:52; 2. Andreas Klöden (G), T-Mobile—same time; **3.** Jan Ullrich (G), T-Mobile, at 0:01; **4.** Ivan Basso (I), CSC—same time; **5. Floyd Landis (USA), U.S. Postal–Berry Floor, at 0:13.**
OVERALL: 1. Armstrong, 74:04:56; 2. Basso, at 4:09; **3.** Klöden, at 5:11

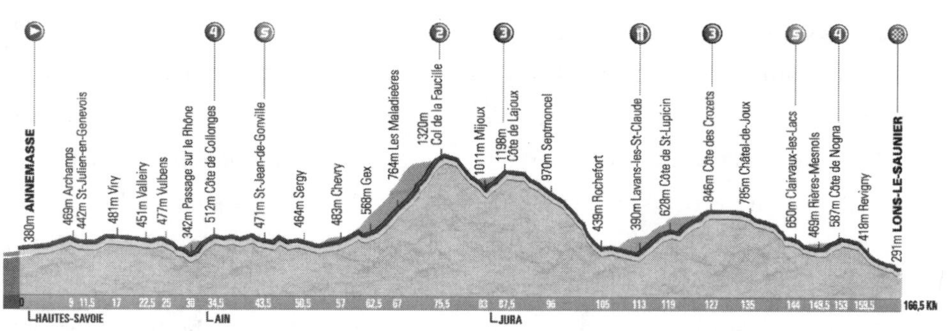

STAGE 18 | Annemasse to Lons-le-Saunier

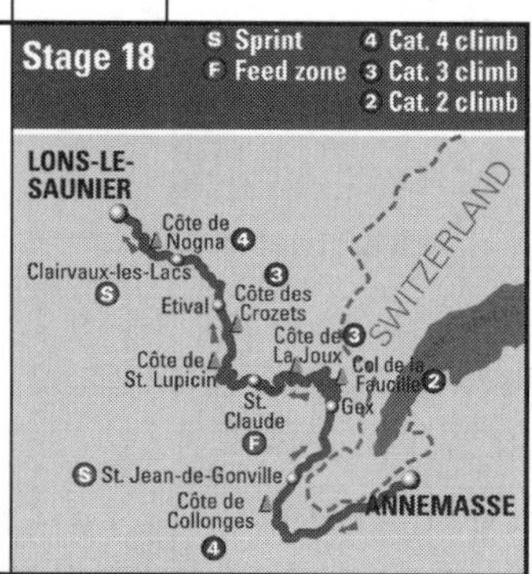

After three hard days in the Alps and the final time trial on tap the following day in Besançon, everyone was hoping for a quiet, uneventful ride in the 166.5-kilometer stage from Annemasse to Lons-le-Saunier that skirted France's Jura Mountains. While some were expecting the sprinters to have a chance to stretch their legs for the first time in a week, eight riders managed to extract themselves at 10 kilometers into the stage. Nicolas Jalabert (Phonak) and Ronny Scholz (Gerolsteiner) both flatted, leaving six to take the initiative.

But there was one more who wanted his chance. At 32 kilometers, Filippo Simeoni (Domina Vacanze)—the Italian who was gobbled up just 100 yards before the line in stage 9—shot out of the peloton to bridge to the group of six. Starting the day 114th at 2:42:55 back, the Italian was just the kind of nonthreatening rider the leaders don't usually worry about.

Suddenly, though, the maillot jaune came bolting out to quickly grab Simeoni's wheel. Thus began an ugly story that would overshadow the eventual heroics of stage-winner Juan Miguel Mercado (Quick Step). Armstrong towed Simeoni up to the break, which included Mercado, Vicente Garcia Acosta (Illes Balears), Marc Lotz (Rabobank), Juan Antonio Flecha (Fassa Bortolo), Dmitriy Fofonov (Cofidis), and Sébastian Joly (Crédit Agricole). The breakaway riders were flabbergasted to see the maillot jaune in their group. Moreover, they knew their chances of staying away were now zero, as T-Mobile reluctantly started to chase once the gap went north of 2 minutes.

According to several riders, Armstrong let it be known that he'd order his blue train to take up the chase if Simeoni were allowed to remain in the break. Garcia pleaded with Simeoni to sit up. Flecha was stronger, giving the Italian a mouthful about allowing the yellow jersey to join the break and ruin their chances to win a stage in the Tour's final days. Adding insult to injury, Armstrong even took pulls at the front to ensure that the peloton would chase in earnest, which indeed it had begun to do. The humiliation was complete. Simeoni agreed to pull out of the break and slowly drifted back until the peloton came speeding past.

"When I bridged out to the break, with Armstrong with me, the other riders got upset, which is normal because a breakaway with the maillot jaune won't stay away," Simeoni said. "Out of respect to the other riders, I decided to drop back. If I was there by myself, with just Armstrong and me, no way would I have stopped," he added.

What was Armstrong up to? It was wholly personal, bad blood dating back to Simeoni's appearance before an Italian court in 2002 when he testified he used doping products prescribed by controversial Italian doctor Michele Ferrari, who just happens to be one of Armstrong's current advisors. Later that year, Armstrong retaliated by publicly questioning Simeoni's integrity and, in a 2003 interview with the French newspaper *Le Monde*, calling Simeoni an "absolute liar." Simeoni, who served a four-month racing ban after admitting to taking EPO, then filed a defamation of character lawsuit in an Italian court against Armstrong. The hearing on Simeoni's case was still to come, but on the road in the Tour, the Texan was getting his pound of flesh.

"I was surprised by what Armstrong did today, but he showed in front of the whole world what kind of person he is," said a dejected Simeoni, who languished at the back of the bunch for the rest of the stage and finished third from last. "I am just a little rider but the yellow jersey stops my chance of having a little bit of glory at the Tour." As Simeoni drifted back to the peloton, Armstrong came alongside and put his right arm on the Italian's back. The pair exchanged words, but after the stage neither would recount what was said.

"He had very harsh, ugly words against me," Simeoni said. "I won't repeat what he said because it's just his word against mine, but they were ugly words." Simeoni later told *La Gazzetta dello Sport*, Italy's largest sports daily, that Armstrong said, "You made a mistake to speak against Ferrari, and you made a mistake to take legal action against me. I have money and time and lots of lawyers. I can destroy you."

As for Armstrong, he said it was part of his responsibility of "protecting the interests of the peloton." He was clearly enjoying his public embarrassment of Simeoni. After bringing back Simeoni and rejoining the peloton, he laughed with numerous riders and at one point made the motion of zipping his lips shut to French TV cameras.

"He's not a rider that the peloton wants to be in the front group," Armstrong said of Simeoni. "All he does is attack cycling and says bad things about the other riders and the group in general. All he wants to do is destroy cycling, to destroy the sport that pays him. . . . For me, that is not correct. When I went back to the group I can't say how many riders said 'Thank you very much.'" There was little doubt where Armstrong stood. After denying it for years, the Texan was indeed the peloton's *patron*.

Reaction, in fact, was muted among riders after the stage, none of whom was anxious to ruffle Armstrong's feathers. Other observers, though, were quick to criticize the blatant show of power. "Simeoni should have been allowed to do his job," said Laurent Jalabert, the former pro who's now a French television analyst. "He's a professional cyclist who should have had the right to join a breakaway without being swarmed upon by the yellow jersey."

With Armstrong back in the main bunch, the break drove uncontested over the four remaining rated climbs. Spanish mountain goat Mercado used his climbing legs to jump away from the break, heading up the Cat. 4 Côte de Nogna with 15 kilometers to go. Garcia Acosta, the Illes Balears rider who won a stage into Draguignan in 2000, marked his wheel and the pair charged in for the sprint. Mercado surprised Acosta, who couldn't change into his lowest gear, and snuck across the line for Quick Step's third stage victory of the 2004 Tour.

STAGE 18, ANNEMASSE TO LONS-LE-SAUNIER: 1. Juan Miguel Mercado (Sp), Quick Step, 166.5km in 4:04:03; **2.** Vicente Garcia Acosta (Sp), Illes Balears—same time; **3.** Dmitriy Fofonov (Kaz), Cofidis, at 0:11; **4.** Sébastian Joly (F), Crédit Agricole; **5.** Marc Lotz (Nl), Rabobank—all same time

OVERALL: 1. Lance Armstrong (USA), U.S. Postal–Berry Floor, 78:20:28; 2. Ivan Basso (I), CSC, at 4:09; **3.** Andreas Klöden (G), T-Mobile, at 5:11

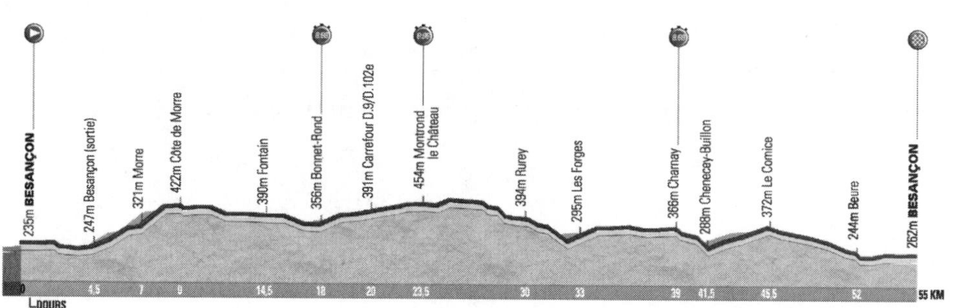

STAGE 19 | Besançon-Besançon

There was more than one American in the Tour, although the efforts of the others were often overshadowed by Armstrong's domination. But the Tour's final individual time trial—a deceptively hilly 55-kilometer course in France's Franche-Comté region—provided the perfect stage for the others to show their stuff. Five Americans figured in the top 12, with all six remaining Americans in the top 25.

The course started in downtown Besançon, an ancient city—and, appropriately enough, a clock-making capital—nestled in a loop in the Doubs River. The route climbed 175 meters out of the valley onto the heavily wooded hills south of town and then headed toward Châtillon-sur-Lison before pushing back toward Besançon with 22 kilometers to go.

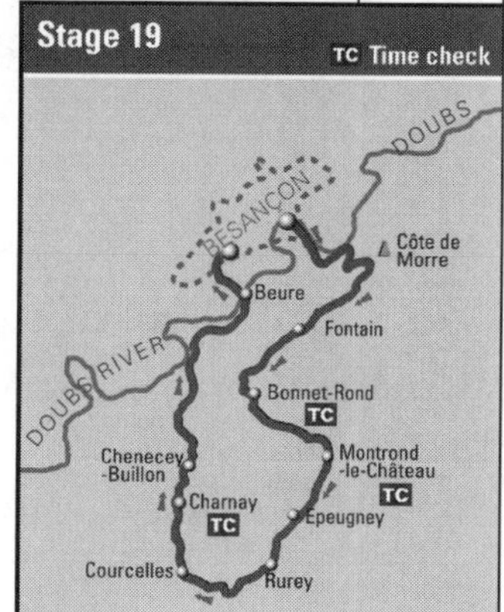

First out of the gate for the American contingent on the hot, muggy day was Christian Vande Velde, the former Postal Service rider who found his return ticket to the Tour via the Spanish Liberty Seguros team. Liberty was in tatters, with disappointing results for team leaders Roberto Heras and Igor González de Galdeano. "It was harder on them than I thought," Vande Velde said. "This team is a dynasty and they're used to kicking some booty in this race. It was hard for them to take it on the chin."

For Vande Velde, getting to the end of the Tour after crashing out in his last Tour appearance in 2001 was a personal victory. For the final time trial, Vande Velde said he "gave it a shove. My parents were in the team car. [Liberty team assistant] Marino [Lejarreta] was yelling at me, telling me to push a bigger gear, saying I was riding like a ballerina.

"I could have never done this at the beginning of the Tour," Vande Velde continued, who finished the day 24th at 5:42 slower. "I was scared I was going to go home, crash, get sick, so it worked out well and I'm fitter now than when I

CV

JULY 24

CHRISTIAN VANDE VELDE—LIBERTY SEGUROS

Venga! Venga! Venga!

Saturday night. The minibar is out of beer, I'm hungry, kinda buzzed, and ready to go home.

Lance smashed everyone today. Jeez, men and boys—well, a few big boys and then the rest of us prepubescent kids. Impressive. The dogs were all let out of their respective cages today and got to give it a go, which led to four Posties in the top ten! There was a lot of barking going on. Klöden jumped over Basso, which I expected, but it was close. Basso ended up doing a great ride and didn't let Ullrich come close; benne Basso. Anyway, who cares about the results? Lance smashed all and is riding down the Champs, in yellow, for the sixth time tomorrow afternoon. All those Americans (and there are a ton) can wave their flags and go nuts tomorrow.

My parents made the trip over today and got to ride in the team car with the famous Marino Lejaretta. He's our second director here and a badass, old-school bike rider. I'm sure they were a bit confused with all the "vengas" and "muy biens" going on, but they had a great time, nonetheless. My dad, famous for yelling at sporting events, grabbed the mic from Marino at one point and started yelling. In my state of suffering, it took me a little while to realize that it wasn't Marino sounding like a crazed dad from Chicago. Mom, for sure, was sitting in the backseat with her nails 3 inches into the seat in front of her holding her breath the whole time. It was fun to have them behind me and helped get me through another day.

I set off with the mind set of just riding the stage. Then, after 2 kilometers,

started. After this, now I'm confident I can get back to the form I know I can have. Last year, a lot of things went bad, so I'm happy to be here. It means a lot to me to be finishing."

Next down the course was Bobby Julich, the well-spoken Coloradan who finished 3rd in the 1998 Tour—at the time just the second American to reach the Tour podium. A lot had changed since those days, and Julich was glad to be back in the Tour after being overlooked by his former Telekom team in 2003. Under the guidance of Bjarne Riis at Team CSC, Julich was back at his best.

Julich posted the early fastest time at 1:09:37, nearly 2 minutes faster than Olympic time-trial champion Viatcheslav Ekimov (U.S. Postal). It would stick for 5th place on the day. "I can't believe it because I have 1:13 on my [computer]," said Julich, his right wrist still wrapped in bandages from his accident on stage 13. "I must not have reset my clock. So with 2 kilometers to go I said, 'I don't have the best time.' I said, 'Hey enjoy the last two Ks.' And I was almost smiling. Then

I decided that it was going to hurt one way or the other, so I gave it a shove. I didn't break any sound barriers, that's for sure, and didn't even come close to the top ten, but I was content with the ride and really just happy to be getting this thing over with.

Oh yeah. I almost forgot about the start. The "Cutters" whooped me into a frenzy at the start. You've probably seen those guys on OLN with the blow-up Shamu and the Postal paraphernalia. They are present every day and always seem to be having a good time. I yelled at them and alerted them to the fact that my dad was there (one of the Cinzano bad guys from the movie "Breaking Away") and they all started chanting, "Cinzano, Cinzano, Cinzano!" It was great; good versus evil again, but this time in Besançon, France and not Bloomington, Indiana. Then they turned their attention back to me and got me all jazzed. Actually, I got a little too excited for a 55-kilometer TT. I didn't touch the pedals for the first 500 meters then started to hurt a bit on the first hill when the adrenaline wore off. Thanks, guys! I got your hats for you.

Tomorrow is the Champs, and if somebody attacks from the start you can be assured he will have his name engraved in the hall of shame. And I will be holding the chisel. Anyway, the green jersey is still on the line, and the stage is *still* 100 miles, so you have to eat, not crash, and probably suffer a little or a lot on the cobbles going up to the Arc d'Triomphe. So I'm not saying anything until the fat lady sings. I am looking forward to seeing the Eiffel Tower, drinking champers on the Champs, and giving my wife a big sweaty kiss.

Until then. . . . ■

I came across the line and see that I had the best time by 2 minutes. I have a little luck with me after all."

Julich had ridden with abandon in support of team captain Ivan Basso in the mountains, and now he was rightly proud of his results for this Tour. "It beats the heck out of watching the Tour on TV," he quipped. "There's nothing like being here. I should have been out of the Tour two or three times because of my injuries but my team kept pulling me back. Bjarne is the perfect leader for me. Team CSC is just a dream. I hope we continue our relationship together."

Julich's time stood until 16 riders later, when Floyd Landis (U.S. Postal) stopped the clock at 1:09:14, capping a superb Tour for the former mountain biker. "Oh, it's not a bad time but 20 other guys are going to beat it," Landis said. He was wrong—only three did. "It was muggy and hot today but I had my wife Amber in the car today so that was extra motivation for me," said Landis, who laughed when asked what advice he would give to Armstrong. "Ha! Lance doesn't need any help. What course doesn't suit him? He's won every kind of stage in the last five days. I think he's all right."

George Hincapie—the only rider to be part of Armstrong's six winning efforts—posted an excellent ride as well, finishing 11th on the day. "I usually do pretty well in the final time trials, so I wanted to give it a go," Hincapie said. "The ambiance on the team is very good. Every year it gets harder, every year there's more pressure. We've been together for a long time; we know exactly what we need to do. It's great to see it work out so far. The first ten days were really stressful, for him, the team, for everybody. If we're not riding at the front, we're at the side of the group. Lance is not a sprinter so ten days for him are really hard."

With just one stage standing between Armstrong and history, Hincapie said he felt especially proud of his work. "It's a big honor—it's up there with any win I've ever had," he said. "I wouldn't change it for anything right now."

Levi Leipheimer, who started the Tour with an outside shot at the podium, needed to erase a 1:11 gap to Carlos Sastre to match his 2002 Tour debut of 8th. Despite a strong ride to finish 12th, Sastre finished 17th to keep his hold on 8th place by 21 seconds. "I was pretty happy with it. Carlos has been riding very strong in the third week, he's a good time trialist. While I hoped to pass him, I knew it would be very difficult," Leipheimer said. "To come within 20 seconds is okay. I felt a lot better than at l'Alpe d'Huez. I made sure that I was bit more ready at the start, my legs were opened up and I was able to go pretty deep."

With two top-ten finishes in two Tour appearances, Leipheimer would normally have been hailed as a grand tour contender. But his sometimes-rocky relationship with Rabobank management and the Dutch press didn't earn him kudos back in Holland. He wasn't expected to resign with Rabobank but there was also talk that he would rejoin U.S. Postal Service—soon to be named Discovery Channel under its new sponsorship—for the 2005 season. For Leipheimer, his future remained in the Tour.

"It's nice to confirm what I did in my first Tour," he admitted. "It's only my second Tour. There were days I performed better. Today was better than any of my time trials in the first Tour. I had two mountain stages that were better than in my first Tour, but unfortunately I made a big mistake on Plateau de Beille. I bonked, something that I should have been aware of," Leipheimer said. "All in all, I'm happy. I got more experience. Now I'm ready to go into next year's Tour with a lot more confidence."

There was one American left. Of the 147 riders remaining in the Tour, Armstrong was last off the ramp, and the 32-year-old soon set a blistering pace.

At the day's first split at 18 kilometers, Armstrong was already 43 seconds faster than Ullrich. He widened the gap on the German by 8 more seconds over the next 22 kilometers and cemented his fifth stage victory of the 2004 Tour in a blazing 1:06:49, 61 seconds ahead of second-place Ullrich.

The victory marked the fifth time in six years that Armstrong had won the final race against the clock en route to the overall title. "I'm really glad it's almost over," the Postal leader said, who truly sounded relieved. "I'm tired in the head, the legs, and all over. I can't wait for the Champs-Élysées. It's always a special feeling, not only for me but for the entire peloton."

Armstrong has always used the time trials to dominate the Tour, and this victory marked the 21st of his Tour career, with nearly half—10 to be exact—coming in prologues and individual time trials. After his nail-biter in 2003, Armstrong had returned to the wind tunnel in the off-season to hone his position for the 91st Tour. The efforts had paid off with three impressive performances, two on his own and one in the team time trial. "I've done a lot of work on my position and worked with engineers in wind tunnels. But there's also the equipment, the bike, the helmet," Armstrong said. "My team worked a lot last winter. We made a project last winter, in the wind tunnel, with all the suppliers like Trek, Shimano, Nike, Giro Helmets, all together, like a Formula One team, to get the fastest material. There were a lot of gurus of position."

Ullrich finished second at 1:01 slower, the same difference by which he had lost Wednesday's time trial up l'Alpe d'Huez, as well as the same time by which he had lost the Tour to Armstrong last year. Sixty-one was becoming Ullrich's unlucky number. And despite his 2nd-place finish in the time trial, Ullrich was unable to make up the time difference he needed to overtake 3rd place and finish on the final podium. For the first time of his career, Ullrich had neither won nor finished 2nd. The 30-year-old German would enter Paris for the final stage in 4th place. He would still get a chance to mount the podium, though; his T-Mobile team was poised to win the team's competition.

Three teams—Postal, CSC, and T-Mobile—hogged the top 11 finishing spots on the day, with only Vladimir Karpets, the long-haired Russian on Illes Balears, breaking up the sweep. Karpets easily surged into the best young rider's jersey at the expense of Thomas Voeckler, the newfound French hero. Voeckler finished the time trial more than 6 minutes behind Karpets to slip to 3rd in the white jersey classification, behind compatriot Sandy Casar.

Team CSC's Bjarne Riis was hoping the money he spent on that two-day trip to MIT for wind-tunnel testing was going to pay off. The 1996 Tour champion's protégé was holding a slim 1:02 margin over 3rd-placed Andreas Klöden. Some expected Basso to fold and lose the final podium spot to Ullrich, lurking at 3:59 back, but Riis wasn't among them. He was looking forward to a good ride from the 26-year-old Italian.

With the big guns on the course, all eyes were on the splits between Basso and Klöden. At 18 kilometers, the Italian was tied with the German, but then he slowly lost ground as Klöden's superior technique started to pay dividends. Over the next 22 kilometers, Klöden was 1:17 faster, and at the end he recorded a margin of 1:23 over Basso. It was enough to move Klöden one step higher on the podium.

"Basso did the time trial of his life . . . He's improved tremendously in that particular discipline and I believe we have a future Tour winner in him."

Despite losing time to Klöden, Basso had come through 6th at 2:50 slower than winner Armstrong, and just 2 seconds slower than Julich. Riis could now say the trip to the United States was money well spent. "Basso did the time trial of his life and his place on the podium is fully deserved," Riis said. "He's improved tremendously in that particular discipline and I believe we have a future Tour winner in him."

After overcoming his initial disappointment at falling to third place in the overall, Basso reflected on his performance over the past three weeks. The ambitious Italian was the only rider strong enough to follow the Texan in the Pyrénées and had even won a stage for his efforts. "I'm disappointed for my team and for myself but I'm still happy to finish on the Tour podium," Basso said. "Being able to climb on the podium in Paris is the most important thing. I tried to do the time trial at 100 percent, without making any calculations and thinking about how well Klöden was doing. It turned out that I lost 2nd place but there was nothing I could do about it. Klöden is a time trial specialist."

In fact, Klöden had ridden a remarkably consistent Tour. Once heralded as the next great hope in German cycling, after winning Paris-Nice and the Tour of the Basque Country in 2000 and then sweeping the Olympic road medals in Sydney with teammates Ullrich and Alexandre Vinokourov, Klöden had been hampered by injuries and poor form in recent years, which had left him winless for three successive seasons. On the eve of the ceremonial ride into Paris, Klöden wasn't sure how to evaluate his 2004 Tour. "It's still difficult to say how I feel because it still hasn't sunk in," he said. "I'll probably need a couple of days before I manage to understand what it means, but tonight I'm going to switch off my mobile phone and savor the moment."

He had come to the Tour with the ambition of helping Ullrich take on Armstrong, but when Ullrich faded out of contention in the Pyrénées, the door had opened for Klöden to step up with the best Tour performance of his career.

"I wanted to help Jan Ullrich win the Tour and my job was to ride for him in the last 10 kilometers of the key mountain stages," he said. "When he struggled on the first mountain stage to La Mongie I actually felt pretty good and so the team gave me the green light to ride my own race. It was a big surprise to perform so well but I don't know if it'll affect my position in the team. Jan Ullrich is still the captain of the T-Mobile team and I'm happy with that. Jan was the first to congratulate me on taking 2nd place. That was nice and shows we get on."

Klöden's superb Tour had come at just the right time: his contract with T-Mobile was up at the end of the season.

STAGE 19, BESANÇON-BESANÇON: 1. Lance Armstrong (USA), U.S. Postal–Berry Floor, 55km in 1:06:49 (49.389kph); 2. Jan Ullrich (G), T-Mobile, at 1:10; **3.** Andreas Klöden (G), T-Mobile, at 1:27; **4. Floyd Landis (USA), U.S. Postal–Berry Floor, at 2:25; 5. Bobby Julich (USA), CSC, at 2:48**
OVERALL: 1. Armstrong, 79:27:17; 2. Klöden, at 6:38; **3.** Ivan Basso (I), Team CSC, at 6:59

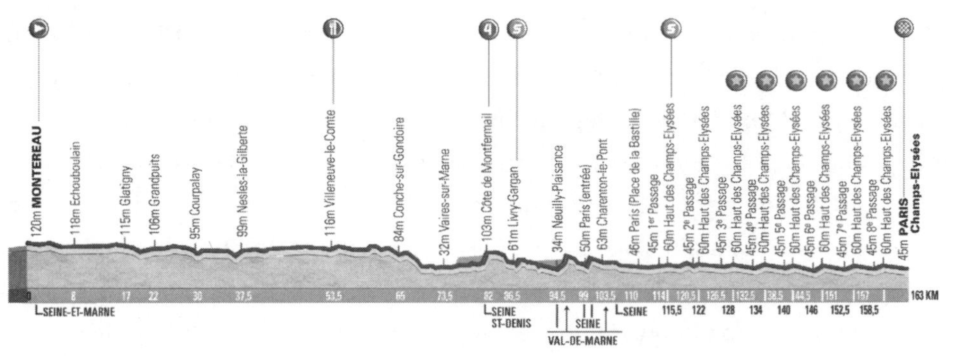

STAGE 20 | Montereau to Paris

No one told Filippo Simeoni that the Tour's 163-kilometer final stage would not become a race until it reached the final ten laps on the Champs-Élysées. The veteran Italian was still fuming from his humiliation in stage 18. So while Armstrong and the other Tour jerseys rode slowly side by side, posing for photographers in the traditional procession into Paris, Simeoni ruined the party with an attack at the 1-kilometer mark, quickly causing a reaction in the peloton.

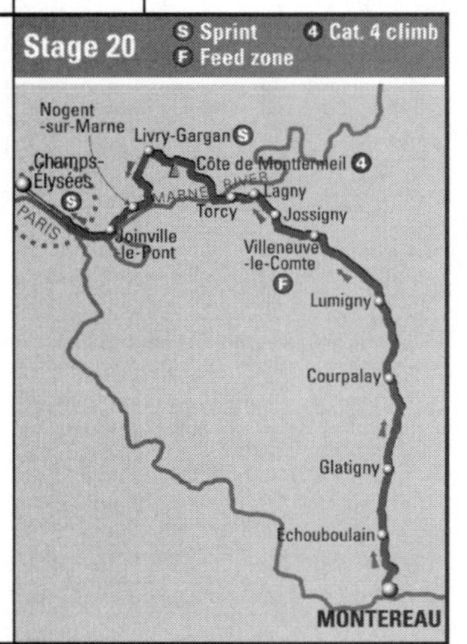

Retrieved but not contrite, Simeoni attacked twice more to try to beat Postal Service to the Champs-Élysées, but each time Armstrong's faithful teammates did their work to bring him back. Despite the Postal team's reluctance to let Simeoni shine, he was awarded the day's most combative rider award by Bernard Hinault, one of seven members of a panel that select each day's winner.

An estimated 600,000 fans awaited the riders as Postal led the charge onto the most famous boulevard in the world. American flags nearly outnumbered the tricolor of France as thousands of Armstrong fans took their front-row seats for history.

Ten riders attacked after two laps and built a lead of 40 seconds, but early moves on the Champs' finishing laps rarely work; there are too many teams interested in having a mass gallop to the line. Cofidis, Crédit Agricole, and T-Mobile helped lead the charge to reel in the attackers with 8 kilometers to go.

In the final stretch to the finish, Stefano Zanini chased down an early sprint by Danilo Hondo (Gerolsteiner), opening the door for Tom Boonen to shoot through for his second stage win of the 2004 Tour. Boonen's victory gave Quick Step four stage wins (two with Boonen, one with Juan Miguel Mercado, and another with Richard Virenque, who also grabbed his record seventh best climber's

TYLER HAMILTON—PHONAK

To Paris, Back Home, and That News Story

Being home during the month of July for the first time in nine years felt a little strange, to say the least. Watching the Tour on television was something I had hoped would be reserved for retirement. But life throws you a curveball every so often. The trick is making the catch and hucking the ball back where it came from. I'm getting ready to do just that. Give me another week or so to mend.

My wife and I traveled north to Paris to see the finish of the Tour. I stopped in my tracks when Haven informed me that I would need a "pass" to get near the finish line. I had never been a spectator on the Champs-Élysées before, so I had some learning to do as her sidekick. But it was good to be there and cheer the guys onto the cobblestones. We sat in the grandstand for the first couple of laps and then I motioned to Haven that we needed to hit the road. We headed over to the area where the team cars await the riders after the finish. This spot also serves as the pickup and drop-off point for VIPs who want to take a trip around the Champs in a team car.

I jumped in with Alvaro Pino, our head director. We had two guys in the breakaway that lasted until the final lap or so. I spent most of the ride shouting over the radio in my broken Spanish and French. In an instant I had become that crazy man in the earpiece who drives every rider nuts during the races. It was half in jest and all in good fun, although I doubt my Tour-tired teammates thought it was nearly as entertaining as I did.

We celebrated the team's first Tour de France with a big dinner that night. More than 150 Phonak employees from all over the world came to see the finish, so it was good to be able to thank them in person for all their support of the team. We do, after all, "race for better hearing." There's a special motivation behind this team, and it's great to be a part of that. Reducing the stigma associated with hearing loss is a big

continued ›

jersey), second only to Postal Service's haul of five stage wins by Armstrong and the team time trial victory.

Aussie fighter Robbie McEwen crossed the line 4th, good enough to win his second green points jersey in three years. A year after losing it on the line to compatriot Baden Cooke (fdjeux.com), the scrappy McEwen had held on until the end. "I wanted to come and win a stage because last year I came to Paris in green and I left absolutely empty-handed," McEwen said. "With two stage wins, the stress was off a bit. But also I decided I was wearing [the green jersey] for such a long time that I wanted to keep it."

TH
continued

challenge. And increasing the quality of life of those who suffer from hearing loss is a mission I'm honored to be a part of.

Recently my cousin Charlie, who has been hearing impaired his whole life, was outfitted with the latest Phonak equipment. He sent me an e-mail telling me how great it was to be able to be out in a noisy restaurant and hear his wife speaking clearly. Hearing his story made me realize how important this equipment is and what a difference it can make in people's lives.

I think in light of all the challenges we faced at the Tour de France this year, the Phonak team has a lot to reflect on and be proud of. Oscar Pereiro finished 10th overall, which was a huge accomplishment considering he lost more than 3 minutes in the team time trial due to a mechanical, and he did an unbelievable amount of work for me in the first ten days of the race. The team finished 6th out of 21 teams, which was also impressive. And watching Nicolas Jalabert duke it out for 2nd place in stage 14 was a highlight as well. We still consider ourselves a growing and developing team, so I hope everyone can use the 2004 Tour as a springboard for the future.

My back is on the mend. I've started riding again, which feels good. The heat has been cranked up to high here in Spain, which is just what the doctor ordered. I'm seeing a number of specialists to design a good recovery program. So far the MRIs and X-rays have been negative for fractures and tears. Damage can be a little difficult to detect when there is as much

As he had done last year, Armstrong coasted across the line rather than risk a messy sprint. His languorous finish cost him 19 seconds, but his winning margin of 6:19 over Klöden was close to Armstrong's average margin of victory of 6:55 in his first Tours. In fact, the Tour seemed stuck on repeat. Armstrong was once again King of Paris, at least for a day, and President Bush called once again to congratulate his fellow Texan. "You're awesome," Bush told Armstrong. Not to be left out, Democratic presidential contender John Kerry also reached Armstrong by phone.

Armstrong's children weren't there to share the moment this year, but with his mother and rocker girlfriend Sheryl Crow looking on, Armstrong took his familiar position atop the cycling heap. For six straight years, the 32-year-old cancer survivor had beaten whatever was thrown at him.

Joining Armstrong on the podium were Andreas Klöden and Ivan Basso, two riders who weren't at the top of many pundits' lists of podium contenders. When T-Mobile captain Jan Ullrich faded in the Pyrénées, Klöden rode steady through La Mongie and Plateau de Beille to be poised in 4th less than 3 minutes behind

swelling as I have, so we are keeping a close eye on things and will do followup scans next week to confirm what we hope is true.

Many thanks to everyone who has written, called, e-mailed, and stopped us to extend condolences regarding Tugboat. Being home in Girona has forced reality to set in a little sooner than it would have. We sure do miss him around the house. But every day we get a little less sad and a little more grateful for the time we shared with him. He was a great dog.

And finally, as if July wasn't a tough enough month for me personally, I arrived home from Paris on Monday afternoon to read the story on the Internet some of you have referenced in the guest book on my Web site. A former part-time team physician has made derogatory public statements about my former U.S. Postal teammates and me. This is not the first time this man has done this.

It has always been my policy to try to take the high road and keep some thoughts to myself. But I also realize there are a lot of young cyclists who follow my career, so it is on their behalf that I will finally respond. The claim that I, along with another teammate, approached a team doctor and asked him questions about doping products back in 1996 is absolutely false. I swear on my wife's life and the grave of my dog that I never asked that man about anything of the sort. If you know anything about me, you know this is as emphatic as I can be. I'm truly saddened to have to respond publicly to such an accusation.

Thanks for reading. ■

Armstrong. The 29-year-old Klöden strengthened as the Tour pushed into the Alps, finishing a very strong 3rd up l'Alpe d'Huez, just 1:41 behind Armstrong. More importantly, he took 42 seconds on Basso to nudge closer to 2nd. While Basso took time bonuses at La Mongie (20 seconds), Plateau de Beille (12 seconds), and Villard-de-Lans (12 seconds), Klöden earned some back, taking 3rd at La Mongie (8 seconds) and 2nd at Le Grand Bornand (12 seconds). Klöden's superb time trialing skills paid off at Besançon when he bounced ahead of Basso into 2nd place, becoming just the second German to finish on the Tour podium.

Basso created excitement in the Pyrénées when he made his trademark accelerations on the Tour's summit finishes as the only rider strong enough to follow Armstrong. The 26-year-old Italian zipped ahead of the Texan to win at La Mongie and the pair swapped positions atop Plateau de Beille. Basso finished 2nd again to Armstrong at Villard-de-Lans but suffered at l'Alpe d'Huez, where he forfeited 2:23 to Armstrong, and with it any hopes of an upset. At Le Grand Bornand, Armstrong and his U.S. Postal Service teammate Floyd Landis easily

CHRISTIAN VANDE VELDE—LIBERTY SEGUROS

Dude, Where's My Car?

Mondays. No, I don't have to go to work—quite the opposite. But it still hurts. Mondays have to be much worse for NFL players, but I'm feeling like I put the pads on for a few quarters. This Tour was tough.

Flying home right now, I'm thinking of my bed and what kind of state my apartment was in when I left. And where is my car? I know that I parked it somewhere in Girona. . . . Do I have coffee in the house? Ah man it's another holiday in Spain, so nothing will be open. No milk for the coffee even if I do have beans. I've grown pretty used to being taken care of for the last month, but it's time for a change and this is a change I'm looking forward to. Well, okay . . . I'm not really looking forward to doing laundry.

Yesterday was a long day. We woke up a little earlier than usual and jumped on the TGV from Besançon to a suburb of Paris. So we sat on the train for almost three hours and then tried to get up for the last race of the Tour. My legs felt like wood in the neutral and I was thinking of how nice it was that I didn't have to be worried about an attack from the start. Then I looked up the road and saw Filippo Simeoni flying up the road. Next thing we know the pack is broken into a few pieces and some of us are really suffering and pissed off.

Lance unleashed the dogs on him and he was soon brought back in and put in his cage. What an ass. "Grande juevos," Igor said after this happened, but still an ass. It's one thing if he and Lance want to have a little war, but when it starts affecting everyone else, it kinda sucks. It killed the moment, and it seems like there aren't too many more moments like that these days,

held off Team CSC's attempt to send Carlos Sastre and Basso away on the final climb. While he lost his grip on 2nd place overall to Klöden by just 21 seconds, Basso had every reason to be optimistic. With steady improvement in the time trial to go along with his already proven climbing skills, Basso was looking worthy of the widespread expectation that he could be the next Tour winner. Ambitious and coolheaded, Basso became the first Italian to finish on the Tour podium since Marco Pantani won in 1998.

Also joining Armstrong on the podium were the other jersey winners: Robbie McEwen, the puckish Australian sprinter in the green jersey; Richard Virenque, in the polka-dot best climber's jersey; and Vladimir Karpets, the enigmatic Russian discovery who quietly powered his way into the best young rider's white jersey.

It was later revealed that McEwen rode the latter weeks of the Tour with two fractured discs in his back, which he suffered in the crash at stage 6 in Angers. The

with all the directors yelling at their riders to attack from the gun.

Anyway, once it all settled in, we rode easy and were able to catch up with the guys that we have been sharing the road with for the last three weeks but haven't necessarily said one word to. Maybe "hey" and a "get out of the way" and not many "how are the wife and kids?" Speaking of that, I'm getting old. All my friends are having kids or have already had kids. Wasn't it just last week that we were all riding our first Tour and talking about cars and girls? Now the "girls" we're talking about are daughters, and the cars? Guys are now comparing features on their new minivans. I guess we'll just live through Tom Boonen for now, with his Miss Belgium girlfriends and bragging about how he went through a tank of gas in 120 miles in his new Audi.

Sorry, got distracted. Where was I? Oh yeah . . . riding to Paris. Halfway through the race I thought that I was going to get dropped on the Champs. Then, upon hitting the bricks, I started to come around and stopped hurting and just had fun. I helped Allen out, and the race was over before I knew it. Then I cleaned up, gave Leah a big kiss, hugged the parents, did a lap of the Champs, and had a good dinner with the family. And finis!

I don't know if it was the longest month of my life or the fastest. Liège sure seems like it was ages ago, and the Vuelta still seems years away, but I know that I'll find myself on the starting ramp again before I know it. In fact, I'm doing Hamburg this Sunday and then the Tour of Holland after that. But I can't even think of that yet. I'm looking forward to some sleep, home-cooked meals, and my own car . . . that is, if I can remember where I parked it. ■

sometimes roughhouse Aussie stormed his way to two stage victories and took the green jersey for good in stage 8, when he finished 4th behind winner Thor Hushovd, but four places ahead of Stuart O'Grady, who held a slim 1-point lead going into the stage. The 32-year-old from Brisbane entered the final stage into Paris with a comfortable 11-point lead, needing only to finish ahead of Hushovd to win his second jersey in three years. McEwen finished 4th, 12 places ahead of Hushovd, to win comfortably by 272 points to Hushovd's 247.

Virenque made history by becoming the first rider to win the climber's jersey seven times, surpassing the achievements of Federico Bahamontes and Lucien Van Impe, each of whom had won six. New rules that doubled the points awarded at summit finishes made chasing the jersey somewhat more complicated for Virenque, but he managed to secure his reign as King of the Mountains after winning into Saint-Flour in stage 10. From there, the 34-year-old Frenchman wore the jersey all the way to Paris, though Armstrong was threatening to snatch it away after his win at Plateau de Beille. Virenque won with 226 points to Armstrong's 172.

While all of France was cheering newfound hero Thomas Voeckler, the long-haired Karpets was quietly erasing his 14:13 deficit in the run for the under-25 best young rider category. Voeckler heroically defended the yellow jersey through the Pyrénées, but Karpets started to chip away in the Alps. Karpets got back 6 minutes at Villard de Lans, the day Voeckler gave up the maillot jaune for the white jersey. At l'Alpe d'Huez, the 23-year-old Karpets was 7th at 2:15 behind Armstrong as Voeckler gave up another 4 minutes and was barely hanging onto the white jersey by 45 seconds going into the final time trial. Karpets, a fourth-year pro who won the Tour de la Rioja in Spain in April, posted another solid ride in the 55-kilometer race against the clock to finish 8th at 3:33 behind Armstrong, and the Russian finished more than 6 minutes faster than Voeckler, who slipped to 3rd behind compatriot Sandy Casar in the best young rider's category. Karpets, meanwhile, finished 13th overall at 25:11 back, giving Illes Balears its second consecutive white-jersey winner to go along with Denis Menchov, the 2003 winner.

Finishing 4th overall, Jan Ullrich managed to find his place on the podium nonetheless. T-Mobile easily won the team's competition, 2:42 ahead of U.S. Postal Service and 10:33 ahead of Team CSC.

ARMSTRONG MADE MAKING HISTORY LOOK EASY. Nothing could stop the 32-year-old Texan in his three-week march to his sixth Tour title. Not overly optimistic rivals, not skeptic journalists who believe he's doped, and certainly not the formidable climbs of the Pyrénées and Alps. "Winning in 1999 was a complete shock and surprise for me," Armstrong said. "Not that I've gotten used to winning the Tour, but I do know what it means and I know what it feels like to ride on the Champs-Élysées in yellow."

For the sixth straight July, Armstrong gave the cycling world another drubbing. He won four consecutive mountain stages—something never done in the Tour—and then put the Tour on ice following victory in the final time trial. Some had suggested he was ripe for plucking after his 2003 cliffhanger, but Armstrong focused on returning to his dominant form of 2001 and 2002. "This is probably the funnest year I've had racing bikes," Armstrong said. "I was enjoying the competition more than ever—not to make history, not to make money, but just for the thrill of being on the bike and racing 200 other guys."

What was fun for Armstrong was misery for his rivals. Big-name challengers buckled under the Texan's assault and the dominance of his U.S. Postal Service team. Iban Mayo, Haimar Zubeldia, Tyler Hamilton, and Roberto Heras had all abandoned before the Tour rolled into the Alps. "The little guys, the pure climbers—Mayo,

The French public found a new hero in Thomas Voeckler, the French national champion who bravely defended the yellow jersey with distinction all the way into the Alps.

⊕ Former Vuelta a España winner Aitor González (Fassa Bortolo) helped erase disappointment by winning stage 14 into Nimes, ⊕ while Jan Ullrich (T-Mobile) went on the attack in stage 15 only to be reeled in by Armstrong's teammates.

⊕ American Bobby Julich (CSC) gets his injured wrist attended to on the road to Nimes. Third overall in 2003, Julich bravely finished the Tour and doctors later discovered that he rode the final week with a broken wrist.

It wasn't quite time for the passing of the guard as Lance Armstrong affirms his place atop cycling's hierarchy with a dramatic victory in the Alpe d'Huez time trial. Here, he's passing second-place rider Ivan Basso (CSC).

▲ Floyd Landis enjoys a light moment with Armstrong as the pair descends during stage 17.

◄ Andreas Klöden overtook Basso in the final time trial to bounce into second overall.

► Fans clog the road as the peloton chugs up the Col du Glandon in stage 17.

Illes Balears
lotto
domo
T-Mobile

▲ Ivan Basso (CSC) forfeited second place, but still rode a fine final time trial to become the first Italian on the Tour podium since Marco Pantani won in 1998. ▶ Armstrong, meanwhile, was unstoppable and stormed to his fifth stage victory. ▼ Things turned ugly, however, in stage 19 (below) when Armstrong played the enforcer and chased down a breakaway by Filippo Simeoni (Domina Vacanze).

The peloton roars into Paris anxious to wrap up the race and cap the 2004 Tour de France.

▲ For the sixth July in a row, Armstrong and Bruyneel had reason to celebrate, capping the record sixth Tour victory with a champagne toast on the road into Paris.

▼ Fans cheer Armstrong as he holds up No. 6. Will there be a seventh Tour for the Texan?

Tyler—the first week is very hard on them, always fighting for position, the wind. This becomes a problem for them after 10 days," Armstrong said. "That's the beauty of the Tour. If the race was 10 or 12 days long, they'd be much better." But, he noted, "You have to do it all."

"Many people ask the question, how is that possible? It's a great question and it's easy to derive sensational answers from there," Armstrong said. His reply, he said, was always the same: hard work. "What do you do on a Christmas Day? January first? Are you riding a bike? It's a full-year commitment, that's our secret."

Despite the controversy, Armstrong confirmed once again that he loves the Tour. And despite rumors he wouldn't be back for a run at No. 7, he insisted he hadn't made up his mind. "I don't know what I'll do next summer. I suspect I'll be here. It's too big of a race. My only hesitance is I think the people and the event perhaps need a change, new faces, a new winner," he said. "If I'm here, I race to win."

Back on the podium for the sixth straight year, Armstrong was shining in the yellow jersey. His actor buddy Robin Williams, wearing a cap that boasted of the six wins, sat with Armstrong's mother, who was elegantly turned out in a yellow dress. Actor Will Smith, promoting a new movie, edged near the side of the podium. With the loudspeakers blaring out first the "Star Spangled Banner" and then Crow's hit "All I Want I Do," the celebration was more Hollywood than *haute monde*.

It was time for Armstrong's victory lap. The tens of thousands of American fans on the Champs-Élysées cheered their superhero on wheels. The French might not understand him, but Americans do. Yells came out from the crowd and well-wishers called greetings from back home in Austin. There were whoops, hollers, and cowboys yelps. Armstrong held out his hand and counted off six—once even, teasingly, seven. Sure, he'd be back.

In the reflected light of Armstrong's seeming impregnability, Tour de France officials were still keen to remind everyone that the race was bigger than the Texan. "It's the race that makes the champion, not the opposite," insisted Tour director Jean-Marie Leblanc. "The Tour's strength is to give riders an incomparable echo in the media. His reign has not harmed the Tour but developed the interest for the race in the United States. For instance, the time trial at l'Alpe d'Huez was shown live on giant screens in New York, and the Tour will continue to grow without him."

The Tour without Armstrong wouldn't be the same—at least not for American fans. The French, however, might not mind.

STAGE 20, MONTEREAU TO PARIS: 1. Tom Boonen (B), Quick Step, 163km in 4:08:26 (39.367kph); **2.** Jean-Patrick Nazon (F), ag2r; **3.** Danilo Hondo (G), Gerolsteiner; **4.** Robbie McEwen (Aus), Lotto-Domo; **5.** Erik Zabel (G), T-Mobile—all same time
OVERALL: 1. Lance Armstrong (USA), U.S. Postal–Berry Floor, 3,391km in 83:36:02; 2. Andreas Klöden (G), T-Mobile, at 6:19; **3.** Ivan Basso (I), CSC, at 6:40

2004 Tour de France
Final Results

GENERAL CLASSIFICATION

1. Lance Armstrong (USA), U.S. Postal–Berry Floor, 3,391.1 km in 83:36:02 (40.56kph); 2. Andreas Klöden (G), T-Mobile, at 6:19; 3. Ivan Basso (I), CSC, at 6:40; 4. Jan Ullrich (G), T-Mobile, at 8:50; 5. José Azevedo (Por), U.S. Postal–Berry Floor, at 14:30; 6. Francisco Mancebo (Sp), Illes Balears-Banesto, at 18:01; 7. Georg Totschnig (Aut), Gerolsteiner, at 18:27; 8. Carlos Sastre (Sp), CSC, at 19:51; **9. Levi Leipheimer (USA), Rabobank, at 20:12;** 10. Oscar Pereiro (Sp), Phonak, at 22:54;

11. Pietro Caucchioli (I), Alessio-Bianchi, at 24:21; 12. Christophe Moreau (F), Crédit Agricole, at 24:36; 13. Vladimir Karpets (Rus), Illes Balears-Banesto, at 25:11; 14. Michael Rasmussen (Den), Rabobank, at 27:16; 15. Richard Virenque (F), Quick Step–Davitamon, at 28:11; 16. Sandy Casar (F), fdjeux.com, at 28:53; 17. Gilberto Simoni (I), Saeco, at 29:00; 18. Thomas Voeckler (F), Brioches La Boulangère, at 31:12; 19. José Luis Rubiera (Sp), U.S. Postal–Berry Floor, at 32:50; 20. Stéphane Goubert (F), ag2r Prévoyance, at 37:11;

21. Axel Merckx (B), Lotto-Domo, at 39:54; 22. Michael Rogers (Aus), Quick Step-Davitamon, at 41:39; **23. Floyd Landis (USA), U.S. Postal–Berry Floor, at 42:55;** 24. Oscar Sevilla (Sp), Phonak, at 45:19; 25. Giuseppe Guerini (I), T-Mobile, at 47:07; 26. Iker Camano (Sp), Euskaltel-Euskadi, at 47:14; 27. Jérôme Pineau (F), Brioches La Boulangère, at 47:43; 28. José Enrique Gutierrez (Sp), Phonak, at 50:39; 29. Laurent Brochard (F), ag2r Prévoyance, at 51:35; 30. Sylvain Chavanel (F), Brioches La Boulangère, at 54:43;

31. Santos Gonzalez (Sp), Phonak, at 1:01:01; 32. Michele Scarponi (I), Domina Vacanze, at 1:03:01; **33. George Hincapie (USA), U.S. Postal–Berry Floor, at 1:04:09;** 34. David Moncoutié (F), Cofidis, at 1:04:37; 35. Jens Voigt (G), CSC, at 1:07:07; 36. Alexandre Botcharov (Rus), Crédit Agricole, at 1:10:54; 37. Juan Miguel Mercado (Sp), Quick Step–Davitamon, at 1:11:31; 38. Evgueni Petrov (Rus), Saeco, at 1:12:24; 39. Patrice Halgand (F), Crédit Agricole, at 1:12:24; **40. Bobby Julich (USA), CSC, at 1:12:42;**

41. Egoi Martinez (Sp), Euskaltel-Euskadi, at 1:15:10; 42. Marius Sabaliauskas (Lit), Saeco, at 1:15:15; 43. Rik Verbrugghe (B), Lotto-Domo, at 1:16:42; 44. Igor González de Galdeano (Sp), Liberty Seguros, at 1:16:45; 45. Aitor González (Sp), Fassa Bortolo, at 1:17:23; 46. Manuel Beltran (Sp), U.S. Postal–Berry Floor, at 1:26:28; 47. Jean-Cyril Robin (F), fdjeux.com, at 1:32:06; 48. Daniele Nardello (I), T-Mobile, at 1:35:26; 49. Santiago Perez (Sp), Phonak, at 1:35:54; 50. Aïtor Osa (Sp), Illes Balears–Banesto, at 1:38:38;

51. José Ivan Gutierrez (Sp), Illes Balears–Banesto, at 1:39:16; 52. Iñigo Landaluze (Sp), Euskaltel-Euskadi, at 1:39:52; 53. Ronny Scholz (G), Gerolsteiner, at 1:42:44; 54. Marcos Serrano (Sp), Liberty Seguros, at 1:42:53; 55. Jörg Ludewig (G), Saeco, at 1:44:57; **56. Christian Vande Velde (USA), Liberty Seguros, at 1:48:11;** 57. Sergueï Ivanov (Rus), T-Mobile, at 1:49:51; 58. Paolo Bettini (I), Quick Step–Davitamon, at 1:50:10; 59. Erik Zabel (G), T-Mobile, at 1:50:21; 60. Iker Flores (Sp), Euskaltel-Euskadi, at 1:50:49;

61. Stuart O'Grady (Aus), Cofidis, at 1:51:41; 62. Mikel Astarloza (Sp), ag2r Prévoyance, at 1:55:04; 63. Kim Kirchen (Lux), Fassa Bortolo, at 1:55:52; 64. Andrea Peron (I), CSC, at 1:56:29; 65. Grischa Niermann (G), Rabobank, at 1:57:25; 66. Benjamin Noval (Sp), U.S. Postal–Berry Floor, at 1:57:41; 67. Laurent Dufaux (Swi), Quick Step–Davitamon, at 1:58:22; 68. Marzio Bruseghin (I), Fassa Bortolo, at 1:59:21; 69. Rolf Aldag (G), T-Mobile, at 2:02:55; 70. Claus Michael Moller (Den), Alessio-Bianchi, at 2:04:01;

71. Sylvain Calzati (F), RAGT Semences–MG Rover, at 2:09:34; 72. Nicolas Portal (F), ag2r Prévoyance, at 2:09:45; 73. Isidro Nozal (Sp), Liberty Seguros, at 2:10:33; 74. Michael Boogerd (Nl), Rabobank, at 2:10:39; 75. Santiago Botero (Col), T-Mobile, at 2:12:32; 76. Pierrick Fédrigo (F), Crédit Agricole, 2:13:14; 77. David Etxebarria (Sp), Euskaltel-Euskadi, at 2:14:42; 78. Sebastian Lang (G), Gerolsteiner, at 2:15:31; 79. Pavel Padrnos (Cze), U.S. Postal–Berry Floor, at 2:16:19; 80. Viatcheslav Ekimov (Rus), U.S. Postal–Berry Floor, at 2:16:44;

81. Bert Grabsch (G), Phonak, at 2:17:14; 82. Nicolas Jalabert (F), Phonak, at 2:18:42; 83. Benoît Salmon (F), Crédit Agricole, at 2:24:49; 84. Christophe Mengin (F), fdjeux.com, at 2:25:08; 85. Carlos Da Cruz (F), fdjeux.com, at 2:25:43; 86. Vicente Garcia Acosta (Sp), Illes Balears–Banesto, at 2:26:14; 87. Dmitriy Fofonov (Kaz), Cofidis, at 2:26:22; 88. Nicki Sörensen (Den), CSC, at 2:27:39; 89. Mark Scanlon (Ire), ag2r Prévoyance, at 2:27:49; 90. Marc Lotz (Nl), Rabobank, at 2:29:48;

91. Unai Etxebarria (Vz), Euskaltel-Euskadi, at 2:30:37; 92. Christophe Rinero (F), RAGT Semences–MG Rover, at 2:31:34; 93. Juan Antonio Flecha (Sp), Fassa Bortolo, at 2:33:38; 94. Dariusz Baranowski (Pol), Liberty Seguros, at 2:33:54; 95. Yuriy Krivtsov (Ukr), ag2r Prévoyance, at 2:34:16; 96. Scott Sunderland (Aus), Alessio–Bianchi, at 2:35:20; 97. Xabier Zandio (Sp), Illes Balears–Banesto, at 2:35:48; 98. Allan Davis (Aus), Liberty Seguros, at 2:36:16; 99. Andrea Noè (I), Alessio–Bianchi, at 2:36:36; 100. Koos Moerenhout (Nl), Lotto-Domo, at 2:36:48;

101. Thierry Marichal (B), Lotto-Domo, at 2:37:58; 102. Walter Beneteau (F), Brioches La Boulangère, at 2:38:36; 103. Anthony Charteau (F), Brioches La Boulangère, at 2:41:31; 104. Thor Hushovd (Nor), Crédit Agricole, at 2:42:45; 105. David Loosli (Swi), Saeco, at 2:44:24; 106. Danilo Hondo (G), Gerolsteiner, at 2:46:54; 107. Peter Farazijn (B), Cofidis, at 2:46:56; 108. Martin Elmiger (Swi), Phonak, at 2:47:22; 109. Fabian Cancellara (Swi), Fassa Bortolo, at 2:48:42; 110. Matteo Tosatto (I), Fassa Bortolo, at 2:49:06;

111. Bram De Groot (Nl), Rabobank, at 2:49:33; 112. Marc Wauters (B), Rabobank, at 2:50:16; 113. Peter Wrolich (Aut), Gerolsteiner, at 2:51:06; 114. Franck Renier (F), Brioches La Boulangère, at 2:53:16; 115. Karsten Kroon (Nl), Rabobank, at 2:53:22; 116. Filippo Pozzato (I), Fassa Bortolo, at 2:54:55; 117. Jan Hruska (Cze), Liberty Seguros, at 2:56:01; 118. Filippo Simeoni (I), Domina Vacanze, at 2:56:30; 119. Ludovic Martin (F), RAGT Semences–MG Rover, at 2:59:00; 120. Tom Boonen (B), Quick Step–Davitamon, at 2:59:07;

121. Massimiliano Mori (I), Domina Vacanze, at 2:59:12; 122. Robbie McEwen (Aus), Lotto-Domo, at 2:59:18; 123. Kurt-Asle Arvesen (Nor), CSC, at 3:00:35; 124. Salvatore Commesso (I), Saeco, at 3:01:21; 125. Uwe Peschel (G), Gerolsteiner, at 3:01:36; 126. Stefano Zanini (I), Quick Step–Davitamon, at 3:01:39; 127. Julian Dean (Nzl), Crédit Agricole, at 3:02:09; 128. Gilles Bouvard (F), RAGT Semences–MG Rover, at 3:03:28; 129. Frédéric Guesdon (F), fdjeux.com, at 3:03:40; 130. Pierre Bourquenoud (Swi), RAGT Semences–MG Rover, at 3:04:47;

131. Bernhard Eisel (Aut), fdjeux.com, at 3:05:44; 132. Marcus Ljungqvist (Swe), Alessio–Bianchi, at 3:07:51; 133. Erik Dekker (Nl), Rabobank, at 3:07:54; 134. Christophe Laurent (F), RAGT Semences–MG Rover, at 3:09:38; 135. Fabio Baldato (I), Alessio–Bianchi, at 3:10:46; 136. Guillaume Auger (F), RAGT Semences–MG Rover, at 3:11:10; 137. Jean-Patrick Nazon (F), ag2r Prévoyance, at 3:13:10; 138. Jimmy Engoulvent (F), Cofidis, at 3:13:55; 139. Baden Cooke (Aus), fdjeux.com, at 3:15:45; 140. Wim Vansevenant (B), Lotto-Domo, 3:22:15;

141. Christophe Edaleine (F), Cofidis, at 3:22:39; 142. Servais Knaven (Nl), Quick Step–Davitamon, at 3:23:07; 143. Francesco Secchiari (I), Domina Vacanze, at 3:25:37; 144. Matthew Wilson (Aus), fdjeux.com, at 3:36:31; 145. Frédéric Finot (F), RAGT Semences–MG Rover, at 3:39:21; 146. Sébastien Joly (F), Crédit Agricole, at 3:43:18; 147. Jimmy Casper (F), Cofidis, at 3:55:49.

SPRINTER CLASSIFICATION

1. Robbie McEwen (Aus), Lotto-Domo, 272 points; 2. Thor Hushovd (Nor), Crédit Agricole, 247; 3. Erik Zabel (G), T-Mobile, 245; 4. Stuart O'Grady (Aus), Cofidis, 234; 5. Danilo Hondo (G), Gerolsteiner, 227; 6. Tom Boonen (B), Quick Step–Davitamon, 163; 7. Jean-Patrick Nazon (F), ag2r Prévoyance, 146; **8. Lance Armstrong (USA), U.S. Postal–Berry Floor, 143;** 9. Laurent Brochard (F), ag2r Prévoyance, 139; 10. Andreas Klöden (G), T-Mobile, 131.

CLIMBER CLASSIFICATION

1. Richard Virenque (F), Quick Step–Davitamon, 226 points; **2. Lance Armstrong (USA), U.S. Postal–Berry Floor, 172;** 3. Michael Rasmussen (Den), Rabobank, 119; 4. Ivan Basso (I), CSC, 119; 5. Christophe Moreau (F), Crédit Agricole, 115; 6. Jan Ullrich (G), T-Mobile, 115; 7. Andreas Klöden (G), T-Mobile, 112; 8. Francisco Mancebo (Sp), Illes Balears–Banesto, 77; 9. Jens Voigt (G), CSC, 71; 10. Axel Merckx (B), Lotto-Domo, 65.

YOUNG RIDER CLASSIFICATION

1. Vladimir Karpets (Rus), Illes Balears–Banesto, 84:01:13; 2. Sandy Casar (F), fdjeux.com, at 3:42; 3. Thomas Voeckler (F), Brioches La Boulangère, at 6:01; 4. Michael Rogers (Aus), Quick Step–Davitamon, at 16:28; 5. Iker Camano (Sp), Euskaltel-Euskadi, at 22:03; 6. Jérôme Pineau (F), Brioches La Boulangère, at 22:32; 7. Sylvain Chavanel (F), Brioches La Boulangère, at 29:32; 8. Michele Scarponi (I), Domina Vacanze, at 37:50; 9. Mikel Astarloza (Sp), ag2r Prévoyance, at 1:29:53; 10. Benjamin Noval (Sp), U.S. Postal–Berry Floor, at 1:32:30.

TEAM CLASSIFICATION

1. T-Mobile, 248:58:43; 2. U.S. Postal–Berry Floor, at 2:42; 3. CSC, at 10:33; 4. Illes Balears–Banesto, at 52:26; 5. Quick Step–Davitamon, at 57:33; 6. Phonak, at 57:42; 7. Rabobank, at 1:26:24; 8. Crédit Agricole, at 1:30:35; 9. Brioches La Boulangère, at 1:32:12; 10. Euskaltel-Euskadi, at 1:47:46; 11. Saeco, at 2:08:14; 12. ag2r Prévoyance, at 2:24:46; 13. Liberty Seguros, at 2:55:25; 14. Gerolsteiner, at 3:02:38; 15. Lotto-Domo, at 3:14:13; 16. fdjeux.com, 3:19:53; 17. Alessio-Bianchi, at 3:42:55; 18. Fassa Bortolo, at 4:09:14; 19. Cofidis, at 4:25:53; 20. Domina Vacanze, at 5:13:52; 21. RAGT Semences–MG Rover, at 6:21:09.

Epilogue

AN AMERICAN IN PARIS: HOW ARMSTRONG RULED THE TOUR

The photograph on the Champs-Élysées perfectly summed up the post-Tour euphoria: a smiling Armstrong holding up a piece of cardboard with the number six and dozens of cheering American fans in the background. "They're all special," Armstrong said of his six victories. "But in '99 I never thought that we'd win a second one or a third one, or however many."

Armstrong had achieved what Jacques Anquetil, Eddy Merckx, Bernard Hinault, and Miguel Induráin could never do. On the eve of the final stage into Paris, where 400,000 fans were awaiting his arrival, even Armstrong seemed in awe of what he was about to pull off.

"I'm humbled by the event," Armstrong said. "A lot of people just one month ago thought it wouldn't be possible for me to do it."

The race, Armstrong agreed, had gone well for him. "We didn't have any major problems like last year. We had one small crash in the beginning, but overall it was a smooth race," he said. "Some of that has to do with training. Some of it has to do with luck. Some of it just has to do with real strong health throughout the race. But comparing this race to last year was black and white."

Armstrong overcame enough hurdles during the 91st edition to make it exciting, but few of them came from his rivals. The Texan rolled out of the Pyrénées with the peloton in ruins and his lead all but secure after two decisive mountain stages. "I hardly ever, if ever, attacked in this Tour," Armstrong said. "In the hard moments, I usually found myself in groups and only had to sprint. I didn't intend to dominate the race."

Instead, Armstrong had to shake off doping allegations, hostile crowds, jeering fans, and even fears that a French television crew was rummaging through his team's hotel rooms looking for evidence of doping.

"If Anquetil were alive today, he'd say they booed him all the time," Armstrong observed. "Eddy Merckx was booed every day. If I'm in that company, I'm okay. We race in a country that sometimes likes the man who comes in second a lot more than the one who comes in first. I'll take the boos and hisses."

Despite a somewhat tenuous relationship with the host nation, though, Armstrong is adored by the American public. Record numbers of American fans cheered him during the three-week Tour. The plaudits came pouring in with calls from President George W. Bush and Democratic presidential contender John Kerry.

Even Europe's press hailed Armstrong as the king of cycling. *L'Équipe* called his performance "The Absolute Triumph," while *El País* in Spain wrote "Armstrong Reaches Mars."

His team was equally effusive. "He's a great champion, someone who's capable of being so many years at the highest level," said Johan Bruyneel, Armstrong's director and confidante at U.S. Postal Service. "Especially after last year, when it was more difficult to come back to the highest level, that shows he's a true champion. I'm not in the best position to say whether or not he should have become the first to win a sixth Tour, but I can say he did it because he deserved it, not because someone gave it to him."

Of the five-time winners that Armstrong surpassed in the history books, none had a bad word to say against the American. Induráin congratulated Armstrong, saying he "deserved to win because he was the strongest." Hinault, the last Frenchman to win the Tour, also complimented Armstrong's professionalism. "He leaves no detail neglected as he prepares for the Tour," Hinault said.

Indeed, it was Armstrong's now-legendary obsession with detail that carried him to all of his wins. Cycling is a sport steeped in tradition, but Armstrong has dragged it into the 21st century. From the way he trains to his focus on the Tour, the 32-year-old Texan has stamped his own signature on cycling's marquee race.

Key to Armstrong's Tour success is his close working relationship with Bruyneel, the former Belgian pro who took over the reins of the U.S. Postal Service team in 1998. Working closely together, the pair targeted the Tour as their overarching goal, a decision that gives them a distinct advantage over other European teams, that are forced to chase results all season long to keep their sponsors and the local press happy.

"I had this ideal strategy," recounted Bruyneel of one of his early discussions with Armstrong. "I was a rider of a lower level but I've always performed well in the Tour and I had my own idea about how to prepare for the Tour, without thinking about sponsor interests or anything else."

With Armstrong, Bruyneel had the perfect pupil. Armstrong had lost 15 pounds during his bout with cancer, which helped transform him from a burly one-day rider into a stage-race contender. Coupled with Armstrong's already preternatural body—including such oddities as longer-than-average femurs and a heart that's nearly one-third larger, not to mention a resting heart rate that can jump from 32 to nearly 200 beats per minute during intense efforts—Armstrong had the ambition and drive to fulfill Bruyneel's vision.

His already impressive physical prowess was buttressed, oddly enough, by his battle with cancer, which was an important element in shaping his character as a Tour winner, especially psychologically. Although he's been cancer free since 1996, the disease is something that stays with him and he uses it to his advantage. "Pain for Lance on the bike is nothing. He never forgets his cancer. He can suffer more than the other guys," said Bjarne Riis, the 1996 Tour winner and manager of Team CSC. "He gets a 30-percent advantage from his strength of character. There are another two or three riders who have his ability, but they can't suffer like him."

More than any racer, Armstrong is indeed willing to suffer to win the Tour de France. That resolve pays off in training and in racing. Even Ullrich admitted he could not match Armstrong's single-mindedness. "I could never have battled to win five Tours," Ullrich told *L'Équipe*. "It's not in my mentality. I can't imagine being permanently at the top."

Armstrong also employs psychological warfare against his challengers to take them out of the game, and Ullrich has often been the focus of Armstrong's ploys. In 2001, he pretended to be suffering to lull Ullrich's team into working harder before he launched to victory up the Alpe d'Huez.

"He plays with his rivals like little puppies," said two-time Giro d'Italia champion Gilberto Simoni. "Look what he did last year after Luz-Ardiden. He got inside Ullrich's head on whether he waited for him and put pressure on anyone who questioned him. No one in cycling played those mind games before. He's taken it to a whole other level."

Another key to Armstrong's six successive Tour victories is his meticulous preparation. Some of his techniques are now part of cycling lore: sleeping in an altitude tent, weighing his breakfast portions, scouting Tour stages months before the race, and being a stickler about his equipment. It's not for nothing that his mechanics call him "Mr. Millimeter"; Armstrong wants everything just right.

"He has the best preparation for the Tour," agreed French star Richard Virenque. "The adversaries haven't learned from watching him for five years arrive at the Tour in perfect condition. Some criticize him for riding just the Tour, but he's going to break the record, so what will people remember in the future?"

Armstrong not only arrives for the start in perfect condition, as Virenque says, but he never allows himself to fall very far out of condition. In contrast to the old cycling model of shutting down for a few months in the off-season, Armstrong is always on. "Everyone wants to know our secret. I hate to disappoint the skeptics [but] this is not a final exam you can cram for," Armstrong has said. "The Tour requires a year-round commitment."

Armstrong notes that he rides the bike nearly every day and starts to build his Tour form beginning at the team's annual training camp in January. The few races he does enter, apart from the Tour, and the intense midseason training camps he organizes are all part of the larger goal of arriving at the Tour in top shape. Armstrong's rivals, on the other hand, often wait until the season is well under way to work into condition for the Tour. In April, for example, Ullrich was forced to pull out of the Liège-Bastogne-Liège classic because he wasn't fit enough to race the demanding course.

And other riders dissipate the energy that Armstrong marshals for the Tour. Spanish climber Iban Mayo burned valuable reserves winning minor races in the spring rather than focusing solely on the demands of the Tour. "When Mayo was winning in May and June, I knew he peaked too early and there was no way he could maintain that fitness into the Tour," Bruyneel said. "For me, Mayo lost the Tour in June."

But even Armstrong is capable of mistakes. His brush with defeat in 2003 almost shattered his proven Tour template. "What happened last year was good in a lot of ways," Bruyneel said of the 2003 Tour. "I think he took a few things for granted last year and didn't have the same dedication like we did in the past. In 2003, for example, in a few training rides we did, we didn't do two times, three times the final climb and in the past we had done that. If it was last year, we wouldn't have come to La Mongie because we know the stage, but I insisted this year. I said we have to go to La Mongie because I think it's going to be the most important day of the Tour, we have to ride it. So we did it three times. He went back to the dedication."

Behind the scenes, Armstrong worked hard this year to get the most out of his training. With Chris Carmichael planning a comprehensive program, Armstrong compartmentalized his regimen so that it fit in with his hectic schedule of fulfilling sponsor needs as well as leaving time for his personal life. In a column Carmichael prepared for the Associated Press, he described how Armstrong makes the most of his efforts.

"Lance's preparation became more about what he wasn't doing than about what he was," Carmichael wrote. "While some of Lance's rivals gained a lot of weight during the winter, he didn't because the process of spending the entire spring losing weight takes away from an athlete's ability to train effectively." Carmichael, a former pro cyclist and former U.S. national coach, noted that Armstrong monitors his weight carefully, keeping his carbohydrate intake below 1,000 grams per day.

"Lance doesn't waste time on his bike," Carmichael added. "He knows the goals of the day's workout before he leaves the house, and once his power meter tells him he has ridden long enough to accomplish those goals, he goes home. Extra time on the bike isn't necessary and just leads to more fatigue and longer recovery periods. Increasing the efficiency of Lance's training and nutrition programs also simplified his Tour de France preparations, giving him more time to relax and concentrate on his life outside of training."

The work paid off and Armstrong was able to return to the dominant form he had deployed in previous Tours. The factors of the 2004 race that kept Armstrong from powering away to solo victories as he'd done in the past were not weaknesses of form, but rather circumstances of the race. Basso was strong enough to follow Armstrong in the Pyrénées, and in two road stages in the Alps, a group stayed together because neither stage ended in a summit finish. But Armstrong was still able to grab time when it counted, making the two individual time trials essential to his final margin of victory.

"I believe Lance was the best he's ever been," Armstrong's teammate Hincapie summed up after the final time trial. "Last year he almost got beat and it really motivated him, and he worked harder than he ever did in the past. We're very happy with how it went. I believe this is his strongest Tour ever."

IT DIDN'T HURT THAT Armstrong's Postal Service team was nearly as strong as he was this year. Led by excellent performances in the mountains by José Azevedo, Floyd Landis, George Hincapie, and José Luis Rubiera, the Posties were so strong that Armstrong seemed to be riding in an impregnable bubble. "I tried to attack but the Postal Service was like a giant train that you couldn't escape," said Francisco Mancebo, a Spanish climber who dared to launch a probe in the Pyrénées. "I was hoping some other riders would join me, but they were scared after they saw the effort I made for nothing. No one would risk it."

In the Tour's toughest stages, Armstrong's strategy makes another departure from cycling convention. Instead of attacking early in the stage, Armstrong patiently bides his time until his blue train carries him to the base of the decisive summit finishes. At that point, the Postal leader lights his afterburners with his trademark high-cadence pedaling style to deliver a knockout blow.

"Armstrong takes the wind out of your sails with his attacks on the final climb," said Spanish climber Oscar Sevilla. "You hope you can carry on, but it's demoralizing when you're already behind after the first mountain."

Armstrong has said he gets confidence from the depth of talent on his Postal Service squad. He's built a solid foundation since joining the team in 1998, barely a year after his final chemotherapy treatments. While some faces have changed, Armstrong is always careful to assemble a roster of diverse talents, so that he has support for each of the Tour's different challenges, from the time trials to the fast, flat stages to the rolling hills and the mountains. "The entire team has lots of experience," Bruyneel affirms. "When Lance won the Tour in 1999, the team was weaker and less experienced and didn't know how to win. Now the team is very solid and has the experience it needs to control the Tour."

So deeply does Armstrong depend on his squad that when the team's future was uncertain in early 2004, before the Discovery Channel stepped in with an agreement to sponsor the team for three more seasons, Armstrong said he was thinking about quitting racing. "I might have retired rather than change teams," Armstrong later confirmed. "The team we have built up here is important to my success at the Tour."

EVEN BEFORE THE TOUR TURNED TOWARD PARIS, there was already a heated debate about Armstrong's place among the pantheon of cycling gods. Did Armstrong's sixth successive Tour victory make him cycling's greatest ever? The answer depended on who was asked.

"He's the strongest, but only because he doesn't have any rivals," grumbled Lucien Van Impe, winner of the 1976 Tour and six best climber's jerseys. "He won six Tours because the other rivals weren't strong enough or weren't at his level. He's no Merckx," Van Impe said in reference to his fellow Belgian. "He won six Tours, but he'll never be considered the greatest racer in history. Merckx won everything, all the big races, the big tours, the classics. Merckx should have been the first to win six; it's too bad he wasn't."

Van Impe's criticism of Armstrong's unwavering focus on the Tour at the expense of other major cycling events, such as the Giro d'Italia and the world championships, is common among traditionalists and not fully unsubstantiated—Armstrong has never raced the Giro and last raced the worlds in 1998.

"You cannot compare what's not comparable," said Hinault. "If Eddy Merckx had competed only in the Tour de France, he would have won it 15 times. The problem with cyclists these days is that they do what they're told to do because the media pressure and the expectations are so huge that the only thing that matters is winning. If you don't wear yourself out by entering other races during the year and you concentrate on competing only two months a year, then you have a big advantage over everybody else. And that's what Armstrong does."

The greatest cyclist of all time agreed with Hinault's assessment. "I'm happy for Lance, but I don't think you can compare champions from different generations," Merckx told *L'Équipe*. "The Tour has become much more important than during my era, or that of Bernard Hinault. We had to race the classics, the criteriums, and the six-day races in the winter. We had to be present from Milan–San Remo to the Giro di Lombardia to make a living."

On the other hand, the hard reality of the cycling life in earlier eras did not keep those champions from performing at their best in the Tour. In fact, Armstrong's dominance in the Tour is surpassed by—no surprise—Merckx and Hinault. In 2004, Armstrong bested Induráin's 60 days in the yellow jersey with 66 and, with 21 stage victories, pulled closer to Hinault, who had 79 days in the yellow jersey and 27 stage victories. But Merckx, the second rider to achieve five Tour victories, still holds the records for Tour stage wins, at 35, and days in the yellow jersey, at a formidable 96. Of course, Merckx also won five Giros, one Vuelta, seven *hors categorie* stage races such as Paris-Nice and the Tour de Suisse, 22 one-day classics, and three world titles for a total of 445 pro career victories.

Armstrong, meanwhile, has won neither the Vuelta nor the Giro, but has captured one world title and two classics en route to 86 career victories. "He's not the best of all time, but he's the best at the Tour," said Roger Legeay, a French team manager who led Greg LeMond to his third Tour win in 1990. "All records are made to be broken; why not a seventh?"

While cheered in America, Armstrong remains a divisive figure in Europe. When Armstrong first barnstormed to his first Tour victories, he ruffled the feathers of the French by proclaiming the Tour was "a race, not a popularity contest" and he struggled with the French language. The presence of bodyguards and Armstrong's penchant to stay hidden inside the team bus until the last minute before each stage has created the perception that he wants nothing to do with France's passionate cycling fans.

In 2004, his bullying of Filippo Simeoni, the Italian rider who testified against Armstrong's personal coach Michele Ferrari, only further cemented the image of Armstrong the enforcer. "As a rider he's respected, but as a person he's viewed as cold and distant," said Jose Miguel Echavarri, the team manager who steered Induráin to five wins. "When you speak of Merckx, Hinault, Induráin, he's not on that level. He doesn't have that class."

What was most surprising about Armstrong's 2004 victory was how fast many of his major rivals folded once the race hit the critical mountain stages in the Pyrénées and Alps. Armstrong was expecting to take fire from all sides, especially from Ullrich, Hamilton, and Spain's determined mountain goats. By the end of the Tour, though, when Armstrong was riding into the history books, everyone else was left wondering what went wrong.

"We never had a sense of crisis, only the stress of the rain and the crashes in the first week," Armstrong said. "I was surprised that some of the rivals were not better. Some of them just completely disappeared."

An unfortunate crash in stage 6 that resulted in severe bruising on his back all but eliminated Hamilton's hopes and subsequently sent him packing for home on the roads to Plateau de Beille. Ullrich was also a mystery. After his performance last year and his victory at the Tour de Suisse in June, more was expected from the 1997 Tour champion. His T-Mobile team quietly pushed the story that he was taking antibiotics in the Pyrénées and suffering from a fever that kept him from being at his best. Despite an attack on the road to Villard-de-Lans, Ullrich never had a chance. He finished 4th and didn't win a stage.

Under the pressure of the U.S. Postal Service, the Spanish riders were knocked out of contention at a dizzying pace. Haimar Zubeldia didn't make it out of the Pyrénées while pre-race favorite Iban Mayo, a victim of a crash in stage 3, quit before the Alps. Roberto Heras abandoned in the Alps, and potential attackers Aitor González and Oscar Sevilla lost so much time they were nonfactors.

Three Spanish riders did ride well to finish in the top 10. Francisco Mancebo shone in the Pyrénées and fought on to finish 6th, but fell short of his goal of the podium. Mild-mannered Carlos Sastre couldn't win a stage this year, but he gutted through intense back pain to finish 8th. Oscar Pereiro saved face for Phonak to finish 10th.

In general, though, Spanish fans, journalists, and teams were struggling to explain the disaster. Overtraining, not enough training, injuries; there were even whispers that strict new antidoping tests were taking their toll on the Spanish riders. "I'm not going to look for excuses," said Manolo Saiz, the veteran director at Liberty Seguros. "You have to be realistic and admit that what we are doing is very bad. For us to understand why things went bad wasn't because of one thing we didn't do, but the accumulation of small things."

AFTER THE TOUR, Armstrong stayed in Europe for a week, riding in criteriums in Holland, Prague, and the LuK Challenge, a two-man team time trial he entered with George Hincapie. Speculation was rife on whether he'd be back for a run at a seventh Tour. He was under contract to ride for at least the 2005 season for his new sponsor, Discovery Channel, but in the weeks following the Tour Armstrong said he hadn't decided which races he'd attack in the upcoming season. A lot depended on proposed changes to cycling's race calendar with the Pro Tour.

"Right now there's no firm plan," Armstrong said before the Prague criterium. "My time is limited, but I suspect that I'll do one more [Tour] if things go well."

After deciding to skip the Olympics, Armstrong was scheduled to return to Austin in mid-August for what's become a summer tradition: the welcome home to a conquering hero. The festivities included a parade, music, video presentations, and special guests. In September, Armstrong would celebrate his 33rd birthday as Texas's most popular figure.

Armstrong's record sixth victory seemed to inject new life into a film project about his life. Actor Matt Damon was heading a list of actors likely to play Armstrong in a biopic under development with movie producer Frank Marshall.

Other players in the Tour de France moved on as well. Many of the top riders participated in lucrative post-Tour criteriums, where racers can make several thousand dollars for a one-day appearance. The races themselves are often formalities, secondary to the turnout of the stars, and although few admit to it, the outcomes of the races are often arranged in advance. In one such event in Holland, Armstrong "beat" sprinter Robbie McEwen.

Ullrich and his T-Mobile boss Walter Godefroot hashed out their differences after Godefroot publicly criticized Ullrich's lack of dedication and faulty preparation for the 2004 Tour. The two had a closed-door meeting to exchange words and emerged with a vow to fight on in 2005 with hopes of derailing Armstrong at least once before Ullrich retires. Ullrich immediately returned to racing to hone his form for the Olympics, a venue where he'd beaten Armstrong when he won the gold medal in 2000. Alas, Ullrich's woes continued, and he finished out of the medals in Athens.

Filippo Simeoni, meanwhile, underwent three hours of questioning with Italy's police about his confrontation with Armstrong in stage 18. Italian authorities were considering filing charges against the Texan for violence, intimidation of a witness, and sporting fraud.

Tyler Hamilton retreated to Girona, Spain, to prepare for the Olympic games, where he won a well-deserved gold medal in the time trial event. Despite the frustration of losing out on two Tours after first-week crashes thwarted his form, the hardworking New Englander vowed to come back to the 2005 Tour as strong as he was for the 91st edition. Hamilton returned to France for the Tour's final weekend to celebrate with his Phonak team. He took the chance to corner Tour director Jean-Marie Leblanc once again to raise the issue of making stage finishes safer.

American Bobby Julich, racing with his right wrist bandaged, won the LuK Challenge with Team CSC teammate Jens Voigt. Julich went on to race the Clasica San Sebastián and won a bronze medal in the time trial at the Olympics.

In fact, the international cycling calendar didn't leave much room for racers or teams to catch their breath. The World Cup kicked back into gear with the HEW Cyclassics in Hamburg, Germany, the weekend following the Tour, a race promptly won by Stuart O'Grady, who said the World Cup victory was more important than his Tour stage win two weeks earlier in Chartres.

Gilberto Simoni returned to Italy, vowing never to return to the Tour, while Basso was already counting down the days to the 2005 Tour. His 3rd-place performance in just his third Tour start gave him lots to be optimistic about.

Several riders who weren't at the Tour—Cadel Evans, Alejandro Valverde, Alexandre Vinokourov, Joseba Beloki, and Damiano Cunego, among others—were already laying the groundwork for the French race in 2005 with their eyes toward the podium.

While the cycling world rolled on, the Tour remained the sport's center of gravity. Course details wouldn't be known until October, but everyone was already looking forward to the 92nd edition. The race was planned to start in France's Vendée region near the Passage du Gois, the same narrow, cobblestone causeway that was central to Armstrong's first Tour victory in 1999.

The "grande boucle" was coming back around again.

The Races within the Race

…rseys and …y Mean

YELLOW JERSEY

The yellow jersey, or maillot jaune, is worn by the overall race leader—the rider who has covered the overall distance in the least amount of cumulative time. Time bonuses (12 seconds for winning a road stage, 6 seconds for winning an intermediate sprint) are deducted, and time penalties (for infractions like dangerous riding or accepting pushes from spectators on the climbs) are added to riders' stage times before calculating their G.C. (general classification) times.

A major change this year was the limit on time lost by any team (and consequently by each rider who arrives with the first man to finish in the team) in the team time trial. The riders on the winning team (except for those who are dropped by their team) will all have their actual finish time added to G.C., but there will be a maximum loss of 20 seconds for the second team, 30 seconds for the third, then 10-second gaps to 13th place (a 2:20 maximum loss), and 5-second gaps down to 2:50 for the 21st (and last) team.

In 2003, instead of the result being:

1. U.S. Postal
2. ONCE, at 0:30
3. Bianchi, at 0:43

It would have been:

1. U.S. Postal
2. ONCE, at 0:20
3. Bianchi, at 0:30

If the new system had been in place last year, 18th-placed Euskaltel-Euskadi, would have lost only 2:35 instead of 3:22; Iban Mayo would have taken over the yellow jersey at l'Alpe d'Huez, not Lance Armstrong; and Alex Vinokourov would have displaced Armstrong as the race leader at Loudenvielle on stage 14.

2004 WINNER: LANCE ARMSTRONG, U.S. POSTAL SERVICE

KING OF THE MOUNTAINS

The polka-dot King of the Mountains (KOM) jersey is awarded to the rider who most consistently reaches designated summits at the front of the peloton. KOM points are given not only on major mountain passes, but also on the smaller climbs.

A new system of scoring the King of the Mountains competition is being introduced this year. There will be fewer points available at the intermediate climbs and double points on the final climb of every stage—assuming that it has a Cat. 2 or Cat. 1 designation. The aim is to put more excitement into the competition by placing the emphasis on the critical climbs.

Tour climbs are classified in five, somewhat arbitrary categories:

CAT. 4: Usually less than 3km in length, an easy pitch that amounts to no more than a sustained rise in the road

CAT. 3: Slightly harder, up to 5km in length

CAT. 2: Between 5km and 10km and steeper than a 4-percent grade

CAT. 1: Long and steep—between 10km and 20km and steeper than a 5-percent grade

HORS CATEGORIE (HC) OR ABOVE CATEGORY: Extremely difficult climbs, sometimes 15km to 20km, with grades often exceeding 10 percent

The new system should favor the pure climbers rather than less-gifted climbers who may break away in the early part of a stage and accumulate points on noncritical climbs. This system could work against six-time KOM winner Richard Virenque of Quick Step, who is shooting for a record seventh title this year.

2004 WINNER: RICHARD VIRENQUE, QUICK STEP-DAVITAMON

POINTS LEADER

The green points leader's jersey is awarded to the best all-around finisher on flat, rolling, and mountainous stages, as well as time trials and intermediate "hot spot" sprints. With the highest points being awarded on flat stage finishes, the points jersey is often thought of as the sprinters' jersey, but a consistent and strategic all-rounder can also be a contender.

2004 WINNER: ROBBIE MCEWEN, LOTTO-DOMO

How points are awarded

FLAT STAGES: 1st place 35pts

2nd 30pts; 3rd 26pts; 4th 24pts; 5th 22pts; 6th 20pts; and descending in 1-point increments to 25th place

ROLLING STAGES: 1st place 25pts

2nd 22pts; 3rd 20pts; 4th 18pts; 5th 16pts; 6th 15pts; and descending in 1-point increments to 20th place

MOUNTAIN STAGES: 1st place 20pts

2nd 17pts; 3rd 15pts; 4th 13pts; 5th 12pts; 6th 10pts; and descending in 1-point increments to 15th place

TIME TRIALS: 1st place 15 points

2nd 12pts; 3rd 10pts; 4th 8pts; 5th 6pts; 6th 5pts; and descending in 1-point increments to 10th place

INTERMEDIATE SPRINTS: 1st place 6pts

2nd 4pts; 3rd 2pts (three each day in stages 1–10, two each day in stages 11–20)

BEST YOUNG RIDER

The white jersey, or *maillot blanc*, is awarded to the best-placed G.C. rider aged 25 or under. In order to qualify for this competition at the 2004 Tour, riders must have been born after January 1, 1979.

2004 WINNER: VLADIMIR KARPETS, ILLES BALEARS

TEAM CLASSIFICATION

Established by the cumulative time of the top three individuals from each team on each stage.

2004 WINNER: T-MOBILE

MOST COMBATIVE

Signified by a red race number, the most combative award is a somewhat subjective points total given by race judges each day to the riders who demonstrate the most consistent efforts in attacks and breakaways. Each rider's points are cumulative every stage to give an overall classification.

2003 WINNER: ALEX VINOKOUROV (NOT RACING IN 2004)

Tour de France Winners

1903 Maurice Garin (F)
1904 Henri Cornet (F)
1905 Louis Trousselier (F)
1906 René Pottier (F)
1907 Lucien Petit-Breton (F)
1908 Lucien Petit-Breton (F)
1909 François Faber (Lux)
1910 Octave Lapize (F)
1911 Gustave Garrigou (F)
1912 Odile Defraye (B)
1913 Philippe Thys (B)
1914 Philippe Thys (B)

Stopped because of WWI

1919 Firmin Lambot (B)
1920 Philippe Thys (B)
1921 Leon Scieur (B)
1922 Firmin Lambot (B)
1923 Henri Pelissier (F)
1924 Ottavio Bottechia (I)
1925 Ottavio Bottechia (I)
1926 Lucien Buysse (B)
1927 Nicolas Frantz (Lux)
1928 Nicolas Frantz (Lux)
1929 Maurice De Waele (B)
1930 André Leducq (F)
1931 Antonin Magne (F)
1932 André Leducq (F)
1933 Georges Speicher (F)
1934 Antonin Magne (F)
1935 Romain Maes (B)
1936 Sylvere Maes (B)
1937 Roger Lapebie (F)
1938 Gino Bartali (I)
1939 Sylvere Maes (B)

Stopped because of WWII

1947 Jean Robic (F)
1948 Gino Bartali (I)
1949 Fausto Coppi (I)
1950 Ferdi Kubler (Swi)
1951 Hugo Koblet (Swi)
1952 Fausto Coppi (I)
1953 Louison Bobet (F)
1954 Louison Bobet (F)
1955 Louison Bobet (F)
1956 Roger Walkowiak (F)
1957 Jacques Anquetil (F)

1958	Charly Gaul (Lux)
1959	Federico Bahamontes (Sp)
1960	Gastone Nencini (I)
1961	Jacques Anquetil (F)
1962	Jacques Anquetil (F)
1963	Jacques Anquetil (F)
1964	Jacques Anquetil (F)
1965	Felice Gimondi (I)
1966	Lucien Aimar (F)
1967	Roger Pingeon (F)
1968	Jan Janssen (Nl)
1969	Eddy Merckx (B)
1970	Eddy Merckx (B)
1971	Eddy Merckx (B)
1972	Eddy Merckx (B)
1973	Luis Ocaña (Sp)
1974	Eddy Merckx (B)
1975	Bernard Thévenet (F)
1976	Lucien Van Impe (B)
1977	Bernard Thévenet (F)
1978	Bernard Hinault (F)
1979	Bernard Hinault (F)
1980	Joop Zoetemelk (Nl)
1981	Bernard Hinault (F)
1982	Bernard Hinault (F)
1983	Laurent Fignon (F)
1984	Laurent Fignon (F)
1985	Bernard Hinault (F)
1986	**Greg LeMond (USA)**
1987	Stephen Roche (Ire)
1988	Pedro Delgado (Sp)
1989	**Greg LeMond (USA)**
1990	**Greg LeMond (USA)**
1991	Miguel Induráin (Sp)
1992	Miguel Induráin (Sp)
1993	Miguel Induráin (Sp)
1994	Miguel Induráin (Sp)
1995	Miguel Induráin (Sp)
1996	Bjarne Riis (Den)
1997	Jan Ullrich (G)
1998	Marco Pantani (I)
1999	**Lance Armstrong (USA)**
2000	**Lance Armstrong (USA)**
2001	**Lance Armstrong (USA)**
2002	**Lance Armstrong (USA)**
2003	**Lance Armstrong (USA)**
2004	**Lance Armstrong (USA)**

About the Author

ANDREW HOOD is the European correspondent for *VeloNews* and has covered the Tour de France since 1996. A former newspaper reporter and editor, Hood never imagined covering European racing until the Internet boom in the mid-1990s opened new opportunities for would-be cycling journalists. Since then, he's worked for the *Dallas Morning News*, the *Denver Post*, *USA Today*, ESPN.com, and the Associated Press, as well as for cycling publications in the United States, Europe, and Australia. He's also appeared on ESPN radio, BBC, TXCN, and NPR. Hood lives in Spain with his wife. This is his first book.

Photo Credits

Page 1: A general view of the Tour du Languedoc, JOEL SAGET/AFP/Getty Images
Page 6: Armstrong in stage 5 of Dauphiné Libéré between Bollene and Sisteron, 11 June 2004, DAMIEN MEYER/AFP/Getty Images
Page 14: Hamilton, GRAHAM WATSON
Page 26: Ullrich, PETER WITEK, T. 07161/949713
Pages 28–34: Mayo; Zubeldia; Heras; Basso; Moreau; Simoni; Rogers; Scarpoini; Menchov; Mercado; GRAHAM WATSON
Page 36: Anquetil, AFP
Page 37, 39: Merkx; Hinault; COR VOS
Page 41: Induráin, GRAHAM WATSON
Page 43: Hincapie and Armstrong on the cobblestones, stage 3, CASEY B. GIBSON
Page 52: Hamilton diary mugshot, GRAHAM WATSON
Page 64: Bäckstedt diary mugshot, GRAHAM WATSON
Page 66: Vande Velde diary mugshot, GRAHAM WATSON
Page 111: Cancellara, prologue; Kirisipuu, stage 1; GRAHAM WATSON
Page 112: McEwen, stage 2; Hushovd, stage 2; GRAHAM WATSON
Page 113: Velo crash, stage 3, DOUG PENSINGER/Getty Images
Pages 114–15: Peloton, stage 3, LAURENT REBOURS/AP
Pages 116–17: Phonak, stage 4, GRAHAM WATSON
Page 118: U.S. Postal, stage 4, CASEY B. GIBSON; Bäckstedt, O'Grady, and Piil, stage 5, GRAHAM WATSON; Boonen, stage 6, DOUG PENSINGER/Getty Images
Page 159: Piil, Scholz, and Tosatto, stage 8; Hushovd, stage 8; GRAHAM WATSON
Page 160: McEwen and O'Grady, stage 9; Virenque and Merckx, stage 10; GRAHAM WATSON
Page 161: Ullrich, stage 10, GRAHAM WATSON
Page 162: Rubiera, Noval, Armstrong, stage 11; Mayo, stage 12; GRAHAM WATSON
Page 163: Peloton in the rain, stage 12, GRAHAM WATSON
Page 164: Hamilton and Perez, stage 12, Doug Pensinger/Getty Images; Hamilton, stage 13; Voekler, stage 13; GRAHAM WATSON
Page 165: Basso and Armstrong, stage 12, GRAHAM WATSON
Page 166: Armstrong, Basso, Mancebo, stage 13; U.S. Postal, stage 13; GRAHAM WATSON
Page 223: Voekler, GRAHAM WATSON
Page 224: González, stage 14, Getty Images; Ullrich, stage 15; Jullich, stage 14, GRAHAM WATSON
Page 225: Armstrong and Basso, stage 16, GRAHAM WATSON
Page 226: Armstrong and Landis, stage 17, Martin Bureau/AFP
Page 227: Col du Glandon, stage 17, GRAHAM WATSON
Page 228: Basso, stage 19; Armstrong, stage 19; Armstrong and Simeoni, stage 18; GRAHAM WATSON
Page 229: Peloton, stage 20, GRAHAM WATSON
Page 230: Bruyneel and Armstong, stage 20, GRAHAM WATSON; Armstrong and fans, stage 20, COR VOS